Holding to the Iron Rod
The Life Experiences of Shirley Ann Robideau

Shirley Ann Robideau
Sean E. Brotherson
2025

Holding to the Iron Rod:
The Life Experiences of
Shirley Ann Robideau

Copyright © 2025
by Shirley Robideau and Sean E. Brotherson
Published in the United States by Family Story Publishing.
All rights reserved.

No portion of this book may be reproduced in any form without written permission from the publisher or author, except as permitted by U.S. copyright law.

Identifier: ISBN 979-8-9986058-1-9 (Hardcover)

Clair Stockford, baby Shirley Ann Stockford, sister Jessie Mae Stockford, and mother Rosie Mae Stockford.

Shirley Ann Stockford as a polio patient in St. John's Hospital, Fargo, ND, 1949.

Shirley Robideau with the Holy Scriptures.

DEDICATION

This volume of life experiences and personal reflections
is dedicated to Charles David Robideau.
Together Forever.

FOREWORD

My first encounter with Shirley Robideau and her husband, Charles Robideau, came when my family moved to North Dakota in the late 1990s. We attended church services in the same building and I observed that she and her husband Charles were friendly, faithful and dedicated in their pursuit of living the ideals of the gospel.

Some years later, I had the opportunity to serve as a Latter-day Saint bishop and Shirley moved into our congregation. As we got to know each other, I came also to know the story of her life and her efforts to manage the multitude of challenges that had accompanied her across a lifetime. Raised in a loving and caring family, Shirley's diagnosis with polio at a young age shifted her life's pathway and left her with disabilities that were significant. However, supported by her hard-working parents and other family members, Shirley went forward with determination and hope.

In addition to the support of family members, friends, and other institutions, Shirley was able to forge ahead with hard work and a willingness to learn. While still in her young adult years, Shirley came into contact with Latter-day Saint missionaries and listened to their message about Jesus Christ and the Restored Gospel, and made a decision to make spiritual commitments to follow the Savior through life in The Church of Jesus Christ of Latter-day Saints. In that process, she came to learn of the story told in the Book of Mormon about holding to the iron rod, which appears in a prophetic dream as the word of God and leads a person to the love of God and His blessings of Eternal Life. Shirley made this her lifelong goal—to Hold to the Iron Rod.

One of my great interests has been learning the lives and stories of those around me through Family History. As Shirley and I became acquainted and she shared some of her life experiences with me, I suggested to her that perhaps it would be a good idea to record some of her story for others. Shirley was open to this possibility and also received similar suggestions from others who knew her as well.

How did this book then come about? Well, the outcome can be squarely placed on Shirley herself, who has persisted in doing the work needed to record her story for others. Though she was uncertain at first about her ability to write her own story, myself and others encouraged her and she began to write down elements of her life story one at a time. As the stories appeared in my email inbox or I listened to them in personal conversations, I found that Shirley has experienced a multitude of life challenges and responses to them that were quite extraordinary.

Polio, tornadoes, personal trauma, death of a child, car accidents, divorce—all of these challenges and many more have accompanied Shirley on her journey through life. And yet, there is much more—inspiring incidents of faith, sacred miracles, moments of love and service received, heavenly inspiration, and a rich network of family members and friends who have also been traveling companions on life's journey with Shirley. It is a most remarkable story, not the least of which is her 16 years of loving marital companionship with the love of her life, Charles David Robideau.

I have had the fortunate experience to accompany Shirley on this journey of telling her story, assisting with editing and organizing her material into a final format in this memoir about her life. I am grateful, for along the way I have learned about faith, forgiveness, hardship, resilience, sacrifice and love. And, most of all, I have learned that Shirley loves her Savior Jesus Christ, and expresses abundant gratitude for the gift of His divine love in her life.

Shirley has written the words of her story and I have edited them. As is common in a memoir, the names and certain details of some individuals have been changed to protect their privacy. For others, just a first name and last initial have been used. In her life, Shirley has now reached nearly eight decades of living, and she has had to adjust to sensory losses including blindness and hearing loss. Yet, her voice remains strong and kind, and full of faith—faith is the hallmark of her life.

It is Shirley's hope, and mine, that in reading her story you might laugh a little bit, learn much, and come away with the recognition that though life can be hard, we are not alone. God has a hand in our stories. He has certainly had a hand in her life story. May you read it or listen to it and be uplifted and blessed.

Sean Brotherson, Editor and Friend
March 2025

Holding to the Iron Rod: The Life Experiences of Shirley Ann Robideau

PREFACE

When you turn seventy-seven years old, your mind begins to reflect upon the things that meant the most to you as you have lived your days so far. At least, that is my feeling at this phase of my life. In some ways, there are many things I regret having done and I am not able to go back and change them. Yet, how grateful I am for the Gospel of Jesus Christ in my life, and for knowing that through its blessings I can be uplifted through the atonement of our Savior, Jesus Christ.

As I have gotten older, I have learned that no one really knows another person's heart. We do not know why someone does some of the things they do that causes hurt to another. I have become more understanding from my own limitations and have developed a more forgiving heart. Each of the periods of my life where abuse or difficulty had taken place gave me a strength and understanding that changed the path I was following.

Each one of us is on our own path, with choices every day that determine which path we want to follow. As for me, I prefer to look at the end of the road. My Dad taught me when I was learning to drive a car to always look far ahead to see where you are going and not to look right in front of the car. We need to look far ahead to see where we want to end up when we get to the end of the road of life. In sharing my personal story, I wish to share some of the experiences that have shaped my life and may be of help or interest to others who are walking the path of life.

I came into the world in Fargo, North Dakota in the spring of 1947, born as the second child to Clair Stockford and Rosie Mae Stockford. Our little family was close and I was raised during my first decade of life in Casselton, North Dakota. I enjoyed the guidance and support of my parents, my older sister Jessie Mae, and my younger brother John. During my second year of life I contracted polio and it left me with physical challenges that have been with me throughout my life.

Families can be together forever is an Eternal truth that I hold dear to my heart. I believe so strongly that I will see my parents again and Charles Robideau, my dear husband. I will hold my little girl Judith in my arms, as well as my little brother, and also see other family members and friends. With this knowledge to hold on to and treasure, life holds a whole new meaning. Knowing this truth gives me more reason and strength to hold fast to the plan of God. For me, the symbolism of grasping on and following a guiding rod of iron in my life, the word of God, has been a helpful and powerful metaphor to give me direction and purpose. As a result, I have given a title to this book which reflects that idea, *Holding to the Iron Rod: The Life Experiences of Shirley Ann Robideau*.

I hope as you read my stories that you will enjoy them and realize that I am writing according to my memory. I could have errors that you may know about but it was not my intent to make errors, but instead to share my life account according to my memory and my understanding of each event. This volume sets forth a collection of my life experiences and personal reflections, and reflects my small but grateful attempt to share how God has blessed my life, how I have learned to overcome life challenges and been supported by others, and experienced many of the trials and triumphs and true joys of life. It is my hope that it will bless the lives of those who are privileged to read its contents.

Shirley Ann Robideau
Fall 2024

Table of Contents

Foreword XX
Preface XX
Introduction 1

Section 1 – Family Beginnings and Early Life Experiences in Casselton

Chapter 1 – My Turn on Earth 11
Chapter 2 – Parental Beginnings 13
Chapter 3 – A World War II Romance 19
Chapter 4 – A Blizzard Baby 23
Chapter 5 – The Polio Epidemic of 1948 25
Chapter 6 – A Tapestry of Family Memories 31
Chapter 7 – Adventures with Family Relatives 39
Chapter 8 – Heavenly Protection 45
Chapter 9 – Casselton Connections 49
Chapter 10 – Special Holiday Memories 53
Chapter 11 – Public School Ups and Downs 57

Section 2 – Transitions to Adulthood and Living with Disabilities

Chapter 12 – New Adventures in Jamestown, ND 65
Chapter 13 – Life at the Crippled Children's School 71
Chapter 14 – Into Adulthood and Its Challenges 83

Section 3 - Finding Faith and Battling Hardships

Chapter 15 – My Search for Truth 97
Chapter 16 – Troubles in Texas 113
Chapter 17 – New Steps in Jamestown 119
Chapter 18 – A Season of Struggle 129

(Table of Contents - continued)

Section 4 - Life with the Man of My Dreams

- Chapter 19 – Square Dancing and a Surprise Proposal................143
- Chapter 20 – Temple Blessings and Being Sealed for Time and All Eternity 155
- Chapter 21 – Life Adventures and Making Things Work...............169
- Chapter 22 – Our Own Home in Casselton..........................185
- Chapter 23 – Health Troubles and Hard Times.....................193
- Chapter 24 – Change and Loss....................................203
- Chapter 25 – A Long Good-Bye....................................209

Section 5 - Sensory Losses and Moving Forward

- Chapter 26 – New Chapters.......................................221
- Chapter 27 – A New Marriage, A Mother's Loss....................227
- Chapter 28 – From Health to Hardship............................235
- Chapter 29 – A Season in St. George.............................243
- Chapter 30 – Lessons in Learning to Adapt.......................253
- Chapter 31 – Blindness Ahead and a Future in Minnesota..........267
- Chapter 32 – A Stunning Family Surprise.........................277

Section 6 - Reflections and Testimony

- Chapter 33 – A Tribute to My Family.............................289
- Chapter 34 – My Christmas Testimony.............................299
- Chapter 35 – In Conclusion......................................303

THE IRON ROD

(Hymn of The Church of Jesus Christ of Latter-day Saints, 1985)

To Nephi, seer of olden time, a vision came from God,
Wherein the holy word sublime was shown an iron rod.
Hold to the Rod, the iron rod; 'tis strong, and bright, and true.
The iron rod is the word of God; 'twill safely guide us through.

While on our journey here below, beneath temptation's pow'r,
Through mists of darkness we must go, in peril ev'ry hour.
Hold to the rod, the iron rod, 'tis strong, and bright, and true.
The Iron Rod is the word of God; 'twill safely guide us through.

And when temptation's pow'r is nigh, our pathway clouded 'er,
Upon the rod we can rely, and heaven's aid implore.
Hold to the rod, the iron rod; 'tis strong, and bright, and true.
The iron rod is the word of God; 'twill safely guide us through.

And, hand o'er hand, the rod along; through each succeeding day,
With earnest prayer and hopeful song; we'll still pursue our way.
Hold to the rod, the iron rod; 'tis strong, and bright, and true.
The iron rod is the word of God; 'twill safely guide us through.

Afar we see the golden rest, to which the rod will guide,
Where, with the angels bright and blest, forever we'll abide.
Hold to the rod, the iron rod; 'tis strong, and bright, and true.
The iron rod is the word of God; 'twill safely guide us through.

Introduction

When you turn seventy-seven years old, your mind begins to reflect upon the things that meant the most to you as you have lived your days so far. At least, that is my feeling at this phase of my life. In some ways, there are many things I regret having done and I am not able to go back and change them. Yet, how grateful I am for the Gospel of Jesus Christ in my life, and for knowing that through repentance I can become clean again through the atonement of our Savior, Jesus Christ.

I cannot write this story of my life without telling about my love for the Gospel because it is who I am now. I am no longer the person I was earlier in my life as I try to live like the Savior.

I joined The Church of Jesus Christ of Latter-day Saints on April 28, 1973, while living in El Paso, Texas with my former husband during the time he was stationed at Fort Bliss. Although I knew who the Savior was, I did not really in my heart know who He was in relationship to me personally. I am grateful to know now the love He has for each one of us individually. As I was writing this book, I was able to see that He was a part of my life in a very personal manner from the beginning. All the years I have been in the Church has totally changed my life. I came to know who Jesus Christ is and what my connections are with Him and our Heavenly Father. For me, knowing that they know me personally, by name, and know my weaknesses and my strengths, gives me so much hope of Eternal Life with my family forever.

The Pathway of Life

As I have gotten older, I have learned that no one really knows another person's heart. We do not know why someone does some of the things they do that causes hurt to another. I have become more understanding from my own limitations and have developed a more forgiving heart. Each of the periods of my life where abuse or difficulty had taken place gave me a strength and understanding that changed the path I was following.

Making the journey through life is almost like following the "Yellow Brick Road!" In the story of *The Wizard of Oz*, Dorothy followed the Yellow Brick Road and on the paths that she followed she found a new adventure and friends. After she and all her new friends traveled a challenging journey to see the Wizard of Oz, each of the travelers wanted something better for themselves—only to find that they had it all the time. The Lion had Courage; the Tin Man had a heart; and the Scarecrow had a brain. Each developed these attributes by loving another. As for Dorothy, going through the terror of being in the hands of a wicked witch brought her greater understanding of who she was, and it made her stronger and more loving towards her family and she wanted to be better.

Each one of us is on our own path, with choices every day that determine which path we want to follow. As for me, I prefer to look at the end of the road. My Dad taught me when I was learning to drive a car to always look far ahead to see where you are going and not to look right in front of the car. We need to look far ahead to see where we want to end up when we get to the end of the road.

The Path to Eternal Life and Exaltation is a definite direction. The Savior is standing there with His precious hands outstretched for us to come unto Him. At times I have made mistakes and lost my way on that path, but I am grateful because I have been able to repent and return to the path I want to be on which leads toward my eternal goal.

Family Beginnings and Blessings

Throughout my life I learned so much from my parents, Clair and Rosie Stockford. I have learned how to work, cook, and care for others, as well as creativity, patience, and a few other attributes that they taught me.

Dad and Mom had the most unique marriage. Dad's alcoholism and Mom's limited education were huge turning points for me. Their love for each other was not easy to see at times. Fifty-four years together is almost unheard of in society today. I am so proud of them for their devotion to each other. I wish that I was able to see it as I was growing up, but I am grateful that I am able to see it now.

As I look back at my life at home with Mom and Dad, I can see where they did their very best to teach us about the Savior. We went to church together as a family in Casselton, North Dakota until we left in 1959 and moved to Jamestown. As a family we joined the United Methodist Church when I was in high school. I still remember the Bible stories taught in Sunday School as a young child in Casselton. I can even remember the excitement I felt as I heard the story my teacher told us about Noah's Ark. I remember wondering how big that Ark must have been to hold all those animals and a family of eight people.

I give credit to my parents for my conversion to The Church of Jesus Christ of Latter-day Saints and I am so grateful to them for this blessing in my life. Mom loved the Savior so much, even though she didn't talk about the Lord very often, and yet it was obvious because she had pictures of the Savior all over our homes.

The Parable of the Iron Rod

The Iron Rod is a favorite song of mine (words at the beginning of the book), as well as a guide for me to follow in my desire to return to Heavenly Father's presence.

One time when life's challenges really seemed to be more than I could handle, I saw this vision of a rod going from before me and it extended all the way to Heaven. When I saw it, I grabbed hold of it and hung on with all my strength. The meaning of this vision is, as the song says, "The Iron Rod is the word of God." The Holy Scriptures are books of instructions given to us to aid us in surviving the challenges that we are to endure while here on Earth. So, when things get difficult in my life I drop what I am doing and pray, and then I read and ponder the Scriptures to help myself to gain control and feel the comfort of the Holy Spirit assure me that I can keep on going. Holding to the Rod is the only way we will be able to withstand the challenges of these last days prior to the coming of our Lord and Savior, Jesus Christ.

The words of the Prophets tell us of what people have done in the past that were unrighteous and righteous and the resulting consequences, so that we ourselves may know how to stay on the strait and narrow path to Eternal Life. When we read of people who lived before us we can see the consequences related to right and wrong choices.

This is a very dangerous and challenging world we live in today, with temptations at every corner. Pornography, alcoholism, smoking, drugs, even prescription drug addiction! The adversaries of God, the devil and his followers, want us to be as miserable as they are so they put temptations in front of us that will slowly lead us down to where there is no deliverance. The body is the temple of the Lord and Satan knows that by getting us to destroy our bodies he can get control of us. Taking care of our body is a commandment that the Lord has given us to help protect us.

The word "Gospel" means "Good News." The good news is "Repentance is possible!" We can turn around and take the necessary steps to recovery when we have made mistakes through the Atonement of Jesus Christ, which makes all things possible. How grateful I am for the Atonement of Jesus Christ!

I remember when my Sweetheart, Charles David, passed away and I was so afraid of being alone. Mom was not feeling well and I was afraid of losing her too. Within a short period of time, my sister-in-law, my mother-in-law, my Dad, and my husband Charles all died so close together, and the thought of losing Mom just completely overwhelmed me. While I was thinking about this concern, I heard the Spirit of the Lord tell me that Mom will be with me until I am able to handle it so I didn't have to worry. That thought brought complete peace to my heart. Mom was with me for four more years after Charles died.

Families can be together forever is an Eternal truth that I hold dear to my heart. I will see my parents again and Charles and hold my little girl in my arms, as well as my little brother and also see other family members and friends. With this knowledge to hold on to and treasure, life holds a whole new meaning. Knowing this truth gives me more reason and strength to Hold to the Iron Rod.

Writing My Personal History

I hope as you read my stories that you will enjoy them and realize that I am writing according to my memory. I could have errors that you may know about but it was not my intent to make errors, but instead to share my life account according to my memory and my understanding of each event.

A great deal of what I was able to understand in my experiences depended upon what I was able to hear, and later in my life, vision difficulties made things even more difficult to understand. As your vision goes, so does what you are able to lip read. So, if you can't lip read, you lose your understanding of what sounds you hear. At my best, I was able to "hear" 25 percent of sounds, and yet that does not mean I understood all of those sounds into words or knew what those sounds were. I have been embarrassed many times because of not understanding even one word in a sentence. That one word could have been totally opposite to what was being talked about. As a result, it is my hope that you will bear with any flaws or inaccuracies in what I have shared, but it has been done to the best of my ability.

Technology that exists today has allowed me to continue caring for myself and interacting with others. Also, it has made it possible for me to share my life story. Although my sister, Jessie, was so far away from where I lived, I am grateful for technology so that I was able to talk to her often through the Internet. Things were becoming somewhat difficult for me as my vision was failing, making it difficult for me to be able to read my emails from her and others, so that I began to feel so alone. On top of that going to Church was equally difficult. Not understanding the talks given at Church really caused me so much sadness. I felt like I was in a box losing my ability to see the people I love and hear their words. I couldn't tell who I was talking to and what they were saying. But then, a Cochlear Implant for my hearing opened a whole new world for me. I will tell about this blessing in my life later in the book. Although it took time to tell the direction of sounds or recognize voices, in time I was able to adjust to this also.

At one point in my later years, one of the good men of our Ward (church congregation) brought me a set of head phones and asked me if I would like to try and hear the Sacrament meeting (worship service) with them. I told him I would give it a try. It was so awesome to be able to hear the entire Sacrament meeting! I wore them every Sunday now Sacrament meeting. It doesn't bother me that I may look different with them on, because what matters to me is hearing the messages that the Lord wants me to hear and it is so wonderful to feel His Spirit as I listen to the words of the Holy Sacrament and the speakers. What a miracle!

The Talking Book has allowed me to be able to hear the Scriptures every day as I listen to them. I also get the Church magazines on Talking Book cassettes. Jaws, a program for the blind, helps me to hear the words that are in my emails and other documents. I use Jaws as I type this book. I absolutely love technology because it helps me continue to be a part of this wonderful life that the Lord has given to me.

I am grateful to have my brother, John, close by in my life. I am thrilled whenever he comes by to visit me or calls me. Technology helps me with hearing on the cell phone also. A gadget called ComPilot takes the sounds from the phone and connects them directly to my hearing aid and the Cochlear Implant. The Lord has truly blessed me.

I have lived through a variety of historic events and things that have had an impact on me and/or on our country. I have also experienced a few historic events in my Church as they happened in my life. I felt that these events were indeed a part of my life and my testimony of the Gospel of Jesus Christ. One of my biggest regrets is that when I was in school and college I didn't take classes to learn more about History so that I could understand how the events of History, and in the early History of religion, led toward the restoration of the Gospel on the Earth. I feel it is such a fascinating story as you take the Holy Bible, both the Old and New Testament, and fill in the pieces of History to discover the Lord's hand in world events.

My Story

A friend of mine visited me one evening and she asked me if I had written down the things I have learned in my life that I would like my family members, friends, and others to know and understand. I told her that I had not done so yet. We visited about a pattern of sharing stories that is explained in my faith's book of scripture, the *Book of Mormon*. In that pattern, two sets of records were kept to write down the history of the people. One set of records was used to write down the history of the people and included wars, contentions, and other items. The other set of records was used to write down the family memories and spiritual occurrences that were felt to be important for their loved ones and future generations to have for their knowledge and growth. My friend suggested that I should similarly create a record that focused on my personal memories and the spiritual things of my life. That is my intention with this personal record.

I feel that my Heavenly Father wants me to write a record of my experiences, for the benefit of my family and friends and others, that they may know how I have been blessed of the Lord. In the twilight years of my life, when I was uncertain about completing this task, a special friend came into my life to assist me and help me continue forward. This dear friend, Diana Berrigan, deserves special mention and would visit with me each week and have me share a story or two from my life while she recorded the details. She assisted me through encouragement, support and faith in the idea that my words could be preserved and passed on. She spent countless hours editing and arranging material in this process. There is no way on this side of the veil that I could ever express my gratitude to her for helping me understand that each of our lives are unique and precious in the Lord's sight. Her kindness and devotion to completing the process of recording stories in my behalf is a testament to her eternal perspective.

What I have chosen to write is true to my knowledge and memory. I have written it to the best of my ability at this time in my life. I have not chosen to record some things which are usually written about, but instead I have felt to share the things which are pleasing to my Heavenly Father. This is the story of who I am today and the experiences of my life that have led me to become the person I am now. This is my story.

Section 1

Family Beginnings and Early Life Experiences in Casselton

Shirley Ann Robideau was born in Fargo, North Dakota, in April 1947. She was born as the second child of Clair and Rosie Stockford. During the years prior to her birth, both of her parents were involved in the war conditions that occurred in this era, with her mother working on the East Coast in shipbuilding efforts and her father being a soldier in the United States Army for several years and being deployed for military service to Europe in World War II.

Casselton, North Dakota was the place that Shirley grew up in and experienced life as a young child. In that small town in North Dakota, she came to know family members, relatives and friends. She experienced the adventures and challenges of youth, learned from the example of her parents, and faced the struggles of life.

In the fall of 1948, a nationwide polio epidemic struck in the United States, and Shirley was one among the thousands of children who were afflicted by this dread disease. Soon, her body was ravaged by its terrible effects, and the medical doctors attending her believed that she would be paralyzed for life. Instead, with tender daily care from her mother and other medical assistance, she left the hospital—a year later. She would be followed by the health effects of polio throughout her life.

In the years that followed, Shirley's life took a variety of twists and turns. School in her early years was a struggle and so she was tutored at home for several years. She later navigated the difficulties of school in a multi-level building as a student with disabilities. Yet, her family life brought support and enjoyment, though it was not always easy to make ends meet. This section shares the story of her early years and life experiences from 1947 through 1959.

Chapter 1
My Turn on Earth

Our Pre-Mortal Existence with God

We lived with our Heavenly Father and our elder Brother, Jesus Christ, who was there from the beginning, in the Pre-Mortal Existence with God prior to our birth. At one point in our experience there was a sense of excitement in the air, as our Heavenly Father had announced that there would be held a grand conference. We learned that it was going to be a very important conference, in which we would learn what we must do to become more like our heavenly parents. All of us were spirit children of our Heavenly Father. Father created us in His image.

In this great conference, our Heavenly Father told us that we had gone as far as we could in this existence and we needed to progress to the next phase in our lives. He presented His glorious plan to us, a plan that would help us to progress and become more like Him. He told us that He would cause a new world to be created, a home where all of us would dwell, and we would go there to gain bodies created in His image and live in families. He told us that there were challenges ahead in this experience and we would make mistakes, and that He would also provide a Savior to atone for our sins and mistakes, thus providing us a way to return to His presence. The conditions of the atonement depend upon our Repentance, our willingness to turn from our sins or mistakes and follow Him.

This account of our pre-mortal existence with God is given in the scriptures of my faith, The Church of Jesus Christ of Latter-day Saints, and then recounts the pivotal moments that occurred. This great Plan of Happiness was presented to us by our loving Heavenly Father.

Then Father said, "Whom shall I send, and who will go for us?"

There was a brief silence but then with a loud voice our brother Lucifer cried: "Behold, here am I, send me, I will be thy son, and I will redeem all mankind, that one soul shall not be lost, and surely I will do it; wherefore give me thine honor" (Moses 4:1).

This powerful being who put himself forward, Lucifer, is he who became Satan and is known as "the father of lies." As part of His great plan, our Father extended to us the power of free agency, the gift of choice, and it was central to our ability to grow and follow Him. It was Satan's plan to destroy our free agency that Heavenly Father had given us. He also wanted to exalt himself above Heavenly Father. One third of the hosts of heaven rebelled when Father rejected Lucifer's plan.

But then a sweet, peaceful voice came of our brother Jesus and He said: "Father, thy will be done, and the glory be thine forever." Our Father then explained: "Wherefore, because that Satan rebelled against me, and sought to destroy the agency of man, which I, the Lord God, had given him, and also, that I should give unto him mine own power; by the power of mine Only Begotten (Jesus Christ), I caused that he should be cast down" (Moses 4:2-3).

All of us who ever were born, are now living and will yet live, have accepted Heavenly Father's plan of life and are now privileged to come to Earth. We chose to follow our Father. He promised that the Holy Spirit would be sent to us, to help us find our way back home. We shouted for joy and accepted His plan. If we follow the Lord's plan and repent of our sins and live to follow our Savior, Jesus Christ, we will each stand again before the Savior to be judged for our eternal reward. I am so grateful for the Plan of Happiness that the Lord gave to us in the Pre-Mortal Existence and to live in this time when the Lord's kingdom is upon the Earth.

After accepting the Lord's plan, then each one of us had to wait for our turn to come into this world where we would be tested to follow our Father. Adam and Eve were the first to come to Earth. They were our first parents. Then, finally, after waiting for thousands of years and watching others as they left to begin their lives on Earth, at last my time had come—***my turn on earth***.

Chapter 2
Parental Beginnings

Clair James Stockford and Rosie Mae Roberts

To begin the story of my life, I have to talk about my good parents—Clair James Stockford and Rosie Mae Roberts Stockford. My parents were amazing! With all the hardships that they faced together and the skills they possessed they accomplished a great deal in their lives. As you read about my wonderful family, I hope that you can appreciate who they were and the accomplishments they managed against all obstacles!

Family Beginnings of the Stockford Family

Clair James Stockford (1919–1998) and Rosie Mae Roberts (1921–2006) were married during the years of World War II. They were married just a few short months before my father was sent to Germany. These two special people were chosen to be my parents in the life before we came to earth (the pre-mortal existence). Also chosen to be a part of my family were my sister, Jessie Mae, born on October 24, 1945, and my two brothers, John, born January 28, 1954, and Kenneth Allen, born December 10, 1963 (died December 11, 1963).

Birth and Early Life of Clair James Stockford

My father, Clair James Stockford, was born on June 22, 1919, in Embden, North Dakota, to Amos James Stockford, Jr. (November 5, 1870–November 11, 1960) and Jessie Ann McKay (January 17, 1875–June 27, 1940). I remember many people calling my paternal grandfather, Amos Stockford, by the name "Grandpa Jim." Dad grew up in Embden and at some point moved to Casselton, North Dakota with Grandpa Jim. Grandpa Jim's father, Amos James Stockford, Sr. (October 14,

My father, Clair Stockford, as a boy.

1848–August 7, 1912), worked with Grandpa Jim as they were skilled Masons. They worked together and built many of the brick churches and brick buildings all over the state of North Dakota, including a "castle house" built for a wealthy family in Rolla, North Dakota. The cornerstone of that building had my grandfather and my great-grandfather's names on it. The "castle house" that they built in Rolla is called the "Coghlan Castle" and shows the masonry skill that characterized their work in construction. It is a great monument to their skill and ability. It makes me proud to think of their efforts to construct useful buildings across the state.

"Castle House" built by Stockford relatives in Rolla, North Dakota.

My father himself was a Master Plumber and taught one of his nephews, Kenny W, to become a Master Plumber. I remember in 1995, when Charles and I lived in Casselton, we went by the old house that was my Grandpa Jim's home. The people that lived there at that time told me that when they were digging things up to put in new plumbing pipes in the house in the earlier years, they found the hose that Dad had used to bring water into the house from the water pump in the vacant lot across the road. I thought that was so funny.

I don't know much about Dad's childhood nor do I know when he and Grandpa Jim moved to Casselton, North Dakota from Embden. I should note that my sister, Jessie, was named after our father's mom, Jessie McKay, and my middle name (Ann) came from her middle name. My dad joined the United States Army in June of 1941, in the same year as the Pearl Harbor bombing but before that event occurred. The war was very hard on my Dad. He witnessed many of his buddies killed and he served in the Army for four years.

Birth and Early Life of Rosie Mae Roberts

My mother, Rosie Mae Roberts, was born on October 2, 1921, to Johnson Roberts (July 14, 1881–August 14, 1974) and Alabama Curry (June 1885–1926).

Mom was raised in the coal mining town of Manchester, Clay County, Kentucky. My mother was an amazing woman.

She took me there to visit in 1972 before my Grandpa Roberts, her father, passed away two years later. It was a rough area, and very few jobs were available for women other than waiting on tables at a café or bootlegging. The men were coal miners most of their lives. The

Maternal Grandparents, from left, Johnson Roberts and Alabama Curry.

people were warm and very much fun to get to know. I had never met my mother's family until I went there with her and Dad. I will never forget that trip to meet my mother's sisters and her baby brother, Beve, and my Grandfather, Johnson Roberts.

Breakfast with our family in Kentucky was awesome! We had breakfast at my Aunt Lindy's home. She made about three dozen over easy eggs and had them on a huge platter. Alongside the platter of eggs were fresh sliced tomatoes, freshly baked biscuits, cucumbers, cream gravy, sausage and fried potatoes! The biscuits and cream gravy were a huge weakness for me! She had a huge counter top in the kitchen on which she left all the leftovers until they were all eaten up. So, there was food set out all day for people to help themselves. My Aunt Lindy was a quilter and had many quilts that she had made in the room I slept in at that time. I have one of her quilts on my bed to this day.

My mother was one of eight siblings and she was one of the youngest, being born second to last in her family. When Mom was five years old her mother died. She remembered being lifted up on a stool to be able to see her mother as she lay in her coffin. She told me that Grandma Roberts had long, beautiful hair. Her hair would go to the floor when she had it unwrapped from her head. Mom also told me of her mother sitting in a chair in the evening where she would brush her long hair as it was draped across her lap. She told me of watching her mother winding and wrapping her hair until it was all fixed up on her head.

My mother's mother, Alabama Curry, was called "Bammer" by my Mom all of my life. Then just before she died she told me that her name was "Alabama" and I thought she was making a mistake and thinking of the state. However, when we looked up the census records, sure enough her name was Alabama. I thought that was so neat that after all these years, Mom made sure that I knew her mother's real name.

Alabama's father's name was Thomas Bowling Curry, born November 1848. I have not located his death date but Mom told me that he was 108 when he died. I have not found proof of that as of yet, although there is some information that indicates he died in 1940. My grandmother's mother was named Susan Jones, and she was born in January 1849 and lived until 1916, according to existing records.

My mother's father, Johnson Roberts, was a preacher and as such he didn't make much money. So, from a very young age the children had to work to help earn money for the family. When my mom was nine years old she dropped out of school to work in the fields picking cotton to help earn money for the family. Somewhere during this time her father married again, perhaps around 1927. The story is told that he actually remarried a couple of times, but one of these women only lasted about two weeks with him because she couldn't stand all of the kids! Anyway, Mom and her new step-mother did not get along and this woman was quite hard on her, so at some time she moved to her older brother's place.

My mother only went to school through the third grade. She told me that back in those years, in that area, a third grade education was enough to be a school teacher. She had to work to aid the support of her family and schooling had to take second place.

I remember Mom telling me about one day when she was walking to school and she noticed a large dog following her. She had to get to school so she didn't stop and play with it. The dog followed her all the way to school and when she got to the school the teacher made all the kids, including my mom, run into the school and slammed the door behind the children. As soon as the teacher did that, the dog began running into the door repeatedly and running around the school trying to get in. Soon some men came with guns and started shooting at the dog. According to Mom's story as she remembered it, the men shot several times at the dog and shot the legs off but it kept on running on its stumps, and then eventually they killed it. The dog was rabid. Many people in southern Kentucky at that time died from being bit by animals with rabies, Mom said. I am so grateful Mom was protected and she didn't have any negative effects from that encounter.

When my mother was in her early twenties she, along with her older brother, went to Baltimore, Maryland to find work. World War II was still in force and many jobs that had previously been held by men had become available to women. The women that were working during the war time were often referred to as "Rosie the Riveter." My mom got a lot of ribbing about that since her name actually was Rosie. Such jobs were available and needed women to fill them because so many men had been drafted into military service. So, my mom became a ship welder and actually was a "Rosie the Riveter," and that was where she met my dad. She worked hard and earned money, much of which she sent home to her father to assist with meeting the family's economic needs.

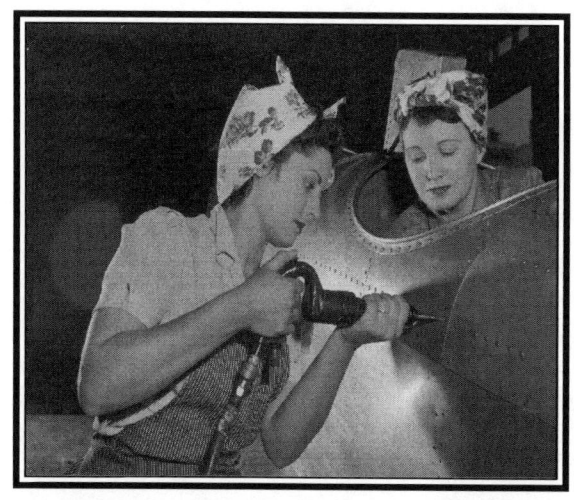

A photo of women working in World War II, which Rosie Roberts did as a "Rosie the Riveter."

In her adult years, my mother Rosie was tall (5'9"), and beautiful, with dark brown natural curly hair that was down past her shoulders. I remember how deeply my father loved her. He used to say that she looked like Loretta Lynn, a popular country singer in their day. Mom was raised in coal mining country, just the same as Loretta Lynn, and she seemed to have a red-hot coal of energy inside her, always ready when something needed to be done.

Chapter 3
A World War II Romance

A Meeting in Baltimore

Very little is known about the beginning of the courtship between my mother and father, Clair James Stockford and Rosie Mae Roberts, because they didn't talk about it very much. However, through pictures of my father as a soldier in Germany during World War II and some things that my mother talked about, I have put together small glimpses of their short courtship prior to getting married. It is a story that begins with a meeting in Baltimore, Maryland.

A Movie Date Leads to Marriage

My mother told me that when she first met Dad, Clair Stockford, he told her that he would take her out to a movie but he didn't have any money—so Mom paid for their first date to the movies!

At the time my parents first met in Baltimore, she was working there in the ship yards. She was a ship welder during World War II and that is why she was living in Baltimore. Her brother had taken her to Baltimore with him so that they could find work.

Dad once told me that he and my mother got married two weeks after they met while he was stationed in Baltimore, Maryland. However, Mom laughed and said that it was two months, not two weeks! Either way, they were married not long after they met, and their marriage was held in Baltimore, Maryland on December 2, 1944.

Rosie Ann Roberts, right, with sister Lindy as young women.

I am not certain how long my mother remained in Baltimore, but my father Clair was sent along to Germany to return to action in World War II not long after they were married. He had given my mother a black pearl necklace which she wore for their wedding. He was 25 years old at the time.

Deployed to Germany for Military Duty

My parents had about three months together in Baltimore after they were married before my father was deployed to Germany for military duty. They were married in December and he left on assignment in February of 1945. He served as an anti-tank gunner in the 397th Infantry Regiment, 100th Infantry Division in the United States Army. His unit was assigned to the European Theater of Operations during World War II and left the United States for service in Europe on February 26, 1945.

My father first enlisted in the Army branch of the military in June 1941, and then was inducted into service at Fort Snelling, Minnesota. He was assigned to the 397th Infantry Regiment, 100th Infantry Division, and his particular assignments included auto mechanic and 1st Class gunner. During his time of military training in the United States during World War II, he first went to service school for training as an automotive mechanic in Tacoma, Washington. Later on he was assigned to further training on the other side of the country as a track vehicle (tanks, etc.) engine mechanic, and this assignment took him to the small community of Aberdeen, Maryland. Aberdeen is located about twenty miles from the larger city of Baltimore, and so it was that he was located in the place where he and my mother first met while she worked there in the ship yards.

Clair James Stockford in the U.S. military in World War II.

When my father's unit was deployed on assignment in World War II, they went to Central Europe and participated in operations there during the last final and difficult months of the campaign

20

against Germany and its allies. His group arrived in Europe on March 27, 1945, and they immediately were sent to join other elements of the 397th Infantry Regiment that had been fighting on the European front in the Moselle region of France since November of 1944. The infantry group had been a stout part of the fight during the Battle of the Bulge, when Germany had made a significant effort to retake territory and change the direction of the war. The regiment began further advances in mid-March of 1945, and had just crossed the Rhine River into Germany at the end of March 1945 when my father and his fellow soldiers arrived in the area.

During the regiment's advances in Europe, it engaged in operations against German foes in the region of Heilbronn, Stuttgart, and Goppingen. Eventually, after the German forces had been defeated and victory in Europe was achieved, the regiment was then assigned as part of the occupation force and remained in Europe for over half a year as things stabilized and troops were rotated home.

When my father was getting ready to come home from Germany he sent pictures home as well as a few other items. Dad didn't talk about the war very much. However, I do remember seeing pictures that Dad had sent home to Mom of War Wagons that carried the many bodies of people that were being hauled away to be dumped into mass burial pits. He talked about a close buddy that had been killed right beside him while they were riding in a jeep to get back to base.

My father also sent guns, table cloths, and a few other things that he wanted to keep. What was really interesting to me was that they were not allowed to keep the table cloths, which were hand tatted, but were allowed to keep guns. So, Dad wrapped the guns in the table cloths so that he could send them home to Mom. The government allowed the table cloths to be sent home as long as they were being used to protect the guns!

A picture that was very touching to me was a picture that Dad had someone in Germany paint of my mother. He had given them a picture of Mom to have them paint it for him, and he had the artist draw her hair longer because he loved her hair. He then had a buddy take a picture of himself holding the painting of my Mom. He looked so lonely to me. There he was overseas, looking so very sad, holding pictures of Mom and I could just feel that he wanted to be home with her and my sister. I know that they missed each other and loved each other very much.

After a period of service in Europe that extended for almost a year, my father and his unit were allowed to return home. They returned to the United States via the Hampton Roads area of Virginia, which was a location where military personnel and cargo were moved overseas and back. My father's discharge papers indicate that he left Europe for the United States on December 31, 1945 and arrived back on January 10, 1946, having served overseas for 10 months and 15 days. All together, he had been in the service for over four years. His unit was released from active duty on January 10, 1946 at Camp Patrick Henry, Virginia, and then went through the process of de-mobilization, after which my father was able to return to our family for a wonderful reunion.

First Child Born to My Parents

My parents were together about three months after they were married and before my father went overseas in World War II. Their time together was rewarding and my mother became pregnant with our family's first child. Some time during her pregnancy my mother returned to Kentucky, and it was there in Kentucky that my older sister, Jessie, was born while my father was overseas in Europe.

My sister, Jessie Mae Stockford, was born on October 24, 1945, in the state of Kentucky while my father was still serving in Germany. Quite a few months passed before he was able to see her for the first time. Dad came home from Germany when Jessie was a few months old. I am sure that this reunion was one of great happiness as he met Jessie, his infant daughter, for the very first time.

After his release from military service, my father picked up Mom and Jessie and moved with them to Casselton, North Dakota. They moved in 1946 to live with my Dad's father, Amos James Stockford, who was known as "Grandpa Jim." The house was a small two-story house with the bedrooms located upstairs. I still remember crawling up and down the stairs in that house as a child. This home is the first place that I would come home to after my birth.

Chapter 4
A Blizzard Baby

A Baby Arrives in Fargo

It was late at night, during an early spring blizzard in North Dakota, that I came into the world. Being one of the babies that arrived during the "Baby Boom" generation, my birth took place on April 17, 1947. I was the second child born to my parents, Clair James Stockford and Rosie Mae Roberts Stockford.

A Perilous Drive to Fargo

A blizzard raged during the early spring in mid-April of 1947 and settled in on Casselton, North Dakota and the surrounding areas. My mother had gone into labor the previous night of April 16th, and the time had come to head to St. John's Hospital in Fargo, North Dakota.

The trip to Fargo was only about 25 miles but it was quite long and perilous that morning, especially to my mother, who was in labor. They drove through the ice storm on old Highway Number 10, the route of the old east-west highway, which was a narrow highway at the time. It must have been a very long drive.

I caused a bit of a ruckus with my arrival, not only due to the storm outside but because of the challenging journey to the hospital. During the trip to Fargo the ice built up on the windows and part of the way through the trip the ice jammed the windshield wipers and they stopped working. My father wasn't able to see the road outside without the window wipers working, so he recalled that he had to drive with one arm out the window in the freezing cold to make them work. He held his left arm out the window and moved the wiper back and forth by hand because the conditions were so bad. In the process of doing this maneuver, he ended up cutting himself quite badly on some ice and had a deep gash on his arm.

The Birth of Shirley Ann Stockford

When my parents arrived at St. John's Hospital in Fargo, they found it surrounded by water due to the spring floods and because of how close it was to the dam. The hospital staff had to lay down wooden planks for 200 feet to bridge the melting puddles for incoming patients. My parents had to cross over a makeshift foot bridge made of wooden planks to enter the building.

Once inside the hospital, both of them were put into wheelchairs. My mother was taken one way to the delivery room and my dad was taken the other to get his hand stitched up because of his deep cut. By the time they were done stitching up his hand and he saw my mother again, I had already been born!

I was the second child born to my parents, Clair and Rosie Stockford, and arrived in Fargo, North Dakota, on April 17, 1947. They named me Shirley Ann Stockford—a second baby girl but this time with blonde hair and blue eyes. My sister, Jessie, was a year and a half old. We returned home after my birth and so I began the first days and years of my life in Casselton, North Dakota, in the home of my grandfather (Amos James Stockford).

Picture of Shirley Ann Stockford as a young baby, left, with Sister Jessie Mae in 1947.

Chapter 5
The Polio Epidemic of 1948

The Polio Threat Hits North Dakota

In the summer of 1916, a strange new disease entered the metropolis of New York City. It seemed to affect children mostly, and one by one children became sick and caught the disease until thousands of children in the states of New York, New Jersey, Connecticut, and Pennsylvania had been afflicted. No one was quite sure what this disease could be. The first symptoms seemed to be the onset of a cold, such as a headache or chills, but then joints and other parts of the body became inflamed. The effects sometimes included paralysis, so that joints became stiff or even the whole body became immobilized, such that affected individuals could not swallow or breathe. If these symptoms appeared, death often followed quickly. Over nine thousand children were diagnosed with symptoms by the end of summer 1916.

This disease was almost a complete mystery in the world of medicine and public health. Some areas were more affected than others; children in rural areas were more likely to pass away than those in the city; it attacked strong children more powerfully than ailing seniors. What was this disease?

Although extensive sanitation measures were implemented across the city of New York and potential disease carriers such as stray cats and rats were disposed of, the disease continued to make inroads and cause problems and deaths. Public panic resulted and wild speculation ensued regarding the potential sources of the disease. Once a number of individuals had succumbed to the disease, autopsies were performed to assess what might be occurring and it was discovered that they each showed inflammation of the anterior portion of the spinal cord. Based on this information, the disease was given its dread name: *poliomyelitis*. However, the public labeled it with another name, Infantile Paralysis—the crippler of children.

The cases identified in the disease epidemic dropped dramatically as autumn arrived and temperatures cooled, but the damage had been done. Over half of the states in America reported polio cases in 1916, with over 27,000 total cases reported and more than six thousand deaths. Of the individuals affected, eighty percent of them were children younger than five years old. If an individual was affected by polio and survived, yet it often left them with weakened limbs, twisted backs, and bodies that were no longer able to run and play as before. Polio had seemed to come from nowhere, a phantom disease, and there was no clear treatment and no known cure.

The Polio Virus Spreads Across America

Once the polio virus arrived in the United States, each year a breakout would take place and children would be affected in locations across the country. Since nothing was known of how the disease was transmitted to others, extensive measures were often put in place to limit contact once an epidemic occurred.

If an individual was diagnosed, usually he or she was quarantined and isolated from others. Public events were cancelled, such as concerts and athletic events. Swimming pools, public schools, and day camps were closed. People avoided the movie theaters, stores, parks and other areas. Yet even with all of these measures, polio continued its deadly march on a yearly basis. A review of the polio virus and its history stated:

> It must have been profoundly difficult in that first quarter century of polio. How helpless parents must have felt to know that there was this killer that could come each summer, and that nothing they could do could safeguard their children. Every sniffle, every cold, every muscle cramp, every temper tantrum that a child exhibited in the long, hot days of summer and early autumn were potential symptoms of polio. How long could a family show good spirits in front of a child confined to an iron lung, or later, during the two or more years a child might spend in rehabilitative therapy.

Polio was never the worst disease in the nation. Many other contemporary diseases killed more. But polio seemed to go after the innocent children, and it left such powerful reminders of its passage. It was an affront to American technological and medical prowess and a denial of our new affluence and national strength. It had to be conquered, and the sooner the better.

The polio virus became feared, and eventually this fear reached such a degree that only atomic weapons were a greater concern for parents than the word "polio."

There were outbreaks of polio that caused paralysis almost yearly during the 1930's, 1940's, and 1950's in the United States. In 1933, there were five thousand cases. In 1943, there were 12,000 cases. In 1946, there were 25,000 cases, followed by 27,000 cases in 1948, and then 33,000 cases in 1950. In 1952, serious epidemics occurred in all forty-eight states within America at the time, and the numbers reached a high point of 59,000 cases. Eventually, medicine would celebrate the arrival of Dr. Jonas Salk and his polio vaccine, and the great epic battle against polio would change for the better, but not until there were many persons who yet faced its challenging effects.

A Polio Diagnosis

As noted in the previous chapter, I was born in the spring of 1947 in Fargo, North Dakota. I had a carefree, happy existence with my parents and sister in Casselton, North Dakota during that first year of life.

When I reached one and a half years of age, and autumn arrived in North Dakota, one evening I was outside in the yard playing and my father was raking up leaves in the yard. I was happily playing in the leaves that my father had raked into a pile. It began getting dark and the mosquitoes were quite bad outside, so Mom came out and picked me up and carried me into the house.

She was in the kitchen working and heard me begin crying in another room. She went in to see what was wrong. She said I kept asking her to pick me up and saying, "Hold me, Mommy!" She would then try and pick me up and couldn't do so because when she would touch me it was extremely painful and I would scream in pain. I would cry for her not to touch me and she would back up, and then again I would scream, "Mommy, hold me!" She told me that it was so difficult for her not knowing what to do to help me. I can only imagine what that must have been like for her to try and hold me and yet she couldn't because it hurt me.

My parents rushed me to St. John's Hospital in Fargo. The polio epidemic of 1948 had reached across Minnesota and North Dakota at that time, and St. John's was the designated place where all polio cases were handled. At that time, it was full of polio cases, and there I was diagnosed with the reality that I contracted polio. I was an innocent child, and yet, my life was changed from that point forward in many ways as a result of polio and its effects.

Treatment at St. John's Hospital

St. John's Hospital was the hospital where all of the children that were afflicted by the polio epidemic were treated, and so this hospital became my home for the next year. The doctors told Mom and Dad that I was totally paralyzed from my neck down and that I would never be able to sit up again. My mother wouldn't accept this diagnosis and determined to do all that she could to help me recover as much as possible.

In 1940, a nurse named Sister Elizabeth Kenny had arrived in the United States from Australia with a new treatment for those affected with polio. Rather than placing patients in casts, she advocated using hot packs on affected muscles daily and doing a program of assisted exercise in which a nurse, technician or other individual would move the paralyzed patient through a series of exercises intended to retrain the muscles. Her treatment approach met with much greater success than existing approaches, so this was the approach that my mother adopted in working with me.

Shirley Stockford in St. John's Hospital undergoing polio treatment in 1949.

Each day my father would drive her 20 miles into Fargo from Casselton, and then every day Mom would exercise my arms and legs. For a while I had to wear splints on my legs and arms to keep my bones from bending and/or breaking. Her efforts continued on a daily basis and brought some movement back to my arms and legs. When I left St. John's Hospital a year later, I was walking on crutches with braces on both legs up to my hips. The doctors told my Mom that it was a miracle because they expected me to never be able to sit up again—the miracle of my Mom and Dad who did not give up on me!!

Shirley Stockford with her mother, Rosie Mae Stockford, during her year of polio treatment.

Home to Casselton

After a year in the hospital recovering from polio, I came home to Casselton and was walking on braces up to my hips on both legs and I had crutches. I have been told that I could walk faster than many of the other children as I would run on my braces and crutches. I was constantly breaking the braces and so we had to go into Fargo to the Dover Building very often to get new parts for the braces. I was a tough kid!

I remembered this experience when watching a popular movie that the actor Tom Hanks was in a few years ago. The movie was called *Forrest Gump*. In the movie, Forrest also dealt with braces on his legs, but at one point Forrest was running from some guys chasing him in a truck and as he was running the braces fell off of his legs and he just kept on running!

Although my parents had been told by the doctors that I would be paralyzed for the rest of my life, I am grateful that my Mom particularly did not accept this diagnosis and through her persistence I was able to move and walk again. She believed that I could recover and each day my Dad drove her twenty miles from Casselton to the hospital in Fargo so that she could give me treatment. She was my nurse and my protector.

A Child's Reflections on Having a Body

My earliest remembrance of having faith in God took place when I was about four years old. We did not usually have a babysitter, but on this one occasion Mom and Dad had gone to town and asked a lady to babysit for us.

We were sitting together in the living room area and we were talking. I remember her telling us stories about when we died and she stated that we wouldn't have our bodies any more. She said that I would not have an imperfect body, but instead I would be a spirit, free to move around as I pleased. She told me that I wouldn't have my crippled body. I remember being very upset about her statement. I don't know if I didn't see myself as being disabled or what I was thinking at that time, but I do know it really bothered me. I didn't think there was anything different about my body at that time. I was too young to know that braces and crutches meant anything different. I could walk and that was all I knew.

Shirley Ann Stockford in 1949 with braces on her legs following polio treatment.

The next morning I was outside of our home in Casselton, swinging on the old box elder tree in front of the house, in a swing that Dad had made for us to play on. I remember talking with God and tears streaming down my face, and asking Him, "Why? Why won't I have my body? What is wrong with it?"

Many years later, when I learned more of the Gospel of Jesus Christ, I was taught that when we are resurrected at some point following death our bodies will be fully restored, every whit, and not a hair will be lost. That was so comforting to me to learn that, and it made me reflect on the anxiety I had felt years earlier as a little girl in my child-like desire to keep the body that God had blessed me with after coming to live on earth.

Chapter 6
A Tapestry of Family Memories

Early Memories in Casselton, North Dakota

As I continue with the stories of my childhood, I think you will be able to sense the devotion that my parents had for each one of their children. I never really appreciated my wonderful parents until I got much older. However, they were a daily part of my life during childhood and most of my early memories revolve around my interactions with them and other family members.

A Home in Casselton

I do not know all the details of how my parents moved to Casselton, North Dakota, but I believe it was for my Grandpa James Stockford. His wife had passed away in 1940 and my father had also worked with him in business. Also, living in Casselton gave them the opportunity to be close to other family members on my father's side.

We lived in a small house in Casselton with my Dad's father, Amos James Stockford, Jr. We always knew him as "Grandpa Jim." My Grandpa Jim's home was in the southwest portion of Casselton. The house was basic for the times, an old square, white, two-story house. Rooms were small. There was one bedroom on the main floor (for our parents) while the living-dining room was next to the kitchen, and Jessie and I were upstairs. The small town was divided by a set of railroad tracks.

As a child, I remember my Grandpa Jim so well. I loved seeing him sitting in the living room as he smoked his pipe. That is how I remember him. I will share more memories of him later on.

Memories of My Father

My father, Clair James Stockford, was a warm and friendly man who worked hard for our family. He was a Master Plumber and worked at being successful in that area of business. He was quite involved in the community and did a lot of things to build the community. He had some personal challenges but most important was his love for his family.

"Barn Dances" and "Witch's Pot Stew"

Next to my Grandpa Jim's house where we lived, my Dad built a large garage that he used for his plumbing business. I have so many memories of Dad's garage.

In those earlier years in Casselton, there were many times that Dad would do things to gather the neighbors together and we would have a wonderful time. He would take all of his plumbing gear out of the garage and put bales of hay around the sides for people to sit on and then have a "Barn Dance." He had many "barn dances" while we lived in Casselton. He would have a few people that knew how to play instruments come over and then they would put on a barn dance. My Dad certainly knew how to entertain and keep things fun.

Clair Stockford with daughter Shirley, on left, and mother Rosie Mae Stockford with sister Jessie Mae, right.

I also remember how Dad used to go to the neighbors and tell them that he was going to have a get-together for everyone and then he would ask what they would like to contribute to his "Witch's Pot." The Witch's Pot was a big round pot made of black iron that he would put on a fire outside in the yard and then he would fill it with water from the garden hose. Once he got started, he would go around and invite folks in the neighborhood to supper and he would put everything that he could gather up from the neighbors into the pot. Some of the neighbors were so used to my Dad doing this that they would tell him to help himself to whatever they had in their cupboards and refrigerators! He did so and cooked up the best stew anyone could ever imagine! Everyone would then gather in the front yard to socialize and have Witch's Pot Stew. I call it the Witch's Pot because it reminded me of the large round pot I saw on Walt Disney's *Snow White*. It was very big and Dad would build a fire around it and cook up a great stew in it. My Mom also used this pot to make lye soap! I never made the connection that she would use the same pot that Dad used for soup until later on in my life. I loved these neighborhood gatherings that he organized. It felt like we were a huge family.

A Gentle Disciplinarian

Once when I was quite young and we were making too much noise when we were supposed to be going to sleep, Dad warned us that if we didn't go to sleep he was going to come up and give us a "whipping." Well, we didn't quit giggling so Dad came up the steps and found us. He then put one of his big hands on our back side and with his other hand clapped his hands together to make a loud clapping sound. My Dad—he was a great man! He wanted us to make him look good to Mom but we were giggling, so I think that she caught on that he didn't really give us a whipping, but he was gentle and not harsh as he dealt with us.

Saturday Movies and Penny Candy

There was a movie house next to the bar in town and they always had it open on Saturdays for kids and others. It was a nice arrangement because when the adults were at the bar, we kids could go to the movie that was playing and have some fun entertainment. I remember many times that Dad would give us an extra dime so that we could buy some penny candy. I would always pick the candy that was two pieces for a penny. Smart kid! My favorite candy was licorice!

When we would run out of candy at the movie house, we would run next door to the bar and ask Dad for another dime to get more candy. If we bugged them enough and he had a little money, then he would give it to us in order to get rid of us!

Raising Dogs and Other Animals

One of the things that I remember with my father is that he seemed to have a way with animals. He raised a variety of animals while I was growing up, including some that we raised for food.

My Dad's first love with animals, however, was training dogs for hunting. He used to train Labrador Retrievers to be great hunting dogs. After a dog had been trained, he would then sell the dog and make a little bit of money. One of the dogs that he trained was a chocolate Lab that we called "Brownie." The man that bought Brownie put her in dog shows and she actually became a blue-ribbon winning dog. Once Dad told me that Brownie was a very wealthy dog and even had her own swimming pool! I don't know if Dad was kidding me or not, but Brownie's name was changed to Novak Lulu and she became well recognized in the dog show world.

Another memory related to animals we raised was that in our back yard my Dad built some animal pens. We used those pens to raise both rabbits and chickens while we lived in Casselton, which provided us with eggs and food. In addition to this, I remember that Dad even kept a large bull in the vacant lot in front of our house at one point. This big, black bull had a ring in its nose and was kept on a chain linked to a post in the ground, which was designed to hold the bull in place and keep it close by until it was ready to be butchered.

Memories of My Mother

Memories of my mother, Rosie Mae Roberts Stockford, remind me what a caring and generous person she was who took care of us children and many others. She very lovingly cared for me and my siblings, Grandpa Jim, and many other people who lived in the little town of Casselton.

Kitchen Memories

While we lived in Casselton, it seemed like every weekend someone in the family would come and be with us. Mom would be in the kitchen cooking and Dad would be in there making his famous Tom and Jerry batter. I remember being with my Mom in the kitchen often. One of my favorite memories of Mom being in the kitchen was when she would get out the big round dish pan and make bread. I still remember how she would take that dish pan and fill it with water about half way and put in big spoons of lard along with sugar and yeast. After the yeast was ready then she would add in lots of flour and salt. She always knew just how much flour to put in and it would make a huge mound of bread dough that would rise high in the bowl. I loved going up to it and slapping the dough and hearing the sound.

Sounds were important to me because I was hard of hearing and didn't know it at that time. My sister was also hard of hearing. My parents thought that she had lost her hearing when she had a very high fever when she was little. We found out much later in life that we both had *Retinitis Pigmentosa*, an inherited degenerative eye condition, which sometimes combines with hearing trouble and is a primary reason we both had trouble hearing and are legally blind.

Sister Jessie Stockford as a toddler with mother, Rosie Mae Stockford.

I was talking with Mom one day about my childhood and I told her that I really enjoyed the Tomato Soup that she used to make for us when we were kids. To my surprise, she told me that she hated it! I was so surprised and asked her why she hated it. She said it was usually the last thing we had left in the food pantry that she could make something out of and she would feel like she wasn't giving us a good meal. To me, however, that homemade tomato soup was a wonderful meal and I made it many times after I was on my own!

Once when I was talking with Mom about those days in Casselton I told her that it seemed like she was always in the kitchen. She said that she was always in the kitchen and it really got to be way too much, but she would keep on going because she really took care of her family members.

Donuts and Pickled Eggs

My mother worked really hard to help with taking care of family expenses and the kids. There was not always a lot of money to cover family needs, so while we lived in Casselton Mom started baking donuts, making pickled eggs, and also bread and cookies and other items to sell at the local bars. She was a very hard worker and in this way she was able to make some extra money for our family.

One time she made a huge batch of donuts to take to the bars in town. She had them sitting out on the kitchen counter and planned to wait until morning and then take them to be sold. My Dad went down to the kitchen to get something and heard quite a bit of noise. He went in to investigate and discovered that there were several mice in the kitchen that had come up from the cellar. They were moving and carrying the donuts down to the basement one at a time! He laughed quite a bit when he told me about that.

Caring for Others in Need

My mother seemed to be a natural caregiver. As we lived in Casselton and she became part of the community, she became familiar with many people and did much to reach out to those in need. She became aware that there were a number of elderly people who lived over the bars where she would sell food items. She began to give some care to those elderly individuals, and would take meals up to them whenever she made big meals at our place. In addition, when holidays came around she would take meals up to many of those elderly persons who lived above the bars. I always admired my mother for doing that.

As we were living in Casselton at my Grandpa Stockford's home, one day my mother noticed that he was off by himself in the vacant lot next door and wouldn't come home. She got worried about him and walked over to be with him. Grandpa Jim was getting older at this time, and he'd had some trouble with his ability to control his bladder or bowels, and he was so embarrassed that he didn't want to come home. Mom put her arms around him and helped him to walk home and she helped him to get cleaned up. After that she began taking care of him quite a bit and did much of the care for him when he could not care for himself any longer.

Shirley Ann Stockford with her mother, Rosie Mae Stockford.

There were also many ladies in town that were Mom's friends. Many times I saw her take care of their hair. She would cut their hair, give perms, or fix their hair in bobby pins or rollers. A person didn't need to have a beautician's license back in those days to do such things. What made my Mom so unique is that she never charged anyone for helping them to feel pretty.

The Forest Green Bedspread

One time Mom and I were sitting together and talking while she was crocheting a Forest Green and White Bedspread. I loved watching her as she worked on this bedspread. This was a bedspread that she had worked on for nine years. She had such a talent at moving her hands with the tiny hook that she used to make it. She told me that someday she would give it to me if she ever finished it. She didn't finish it in Casselton but did complete it quite a few years later, and I helped her to finish it as we both made the green and white tassels to tie on it. I loved working with Mom on finishing that beautiful bedspread together.

Mother's Meals

Mother's meals were very delicious. My family was generous and willing to share. Sometimes after a meal, my dad, my cousin Kenny W, who worked with my dad, and Roy B., a neighbor and good friend of my dad's, would all three lie down together on my parents' double bed and fall asleep with full stomachs. Pretty soon, we heard the first start to snore, then the second, and then the third. After a while, it sounded like one continual snore.

Memories of Grandpa Jim

Living in the home of my grandfather, Amos James Stockford, helped me get to know and appreciate him during the years that I was a very young girl. He had a number of children and had outlived his wife who died in 1940.

Grandpa Jim – A Hero

Grandpa Jim's home was located in the southwest portion of town, which was divided by a railroad track, and about a block from the house was a ditch along the railroad track to carry runoff from the rain. There was a huge drainage hole designed to keep the ditch from overflowing.

One time after a heavy rain occurred a number of children were playing by this drainage ditch that was near the railroad tracks in the center of Casselton. One of the boys fell into the rushing water in the drainage ditch and was quickly forced toward the huge drainage hole. Grandpa Jim was outside at the time and evidently heard the children hollering for help. He knew the plumbing system underground and so he took off running down the street as fast as he could toward the southeast part of town where the drainage ditch emerged. He reached the location where the ditch emerged and positioned himself over the drainage pipe, and then he managed to reach down and grab the boy by his shirt as he came out and pulled him up from the culvert.

Seeing that the boy was all right although badly shaken, he pulled him up and swatted him on the seat of his pants and told to go on home and stay away from the drainage ditch. It was not long after that incident that the City of Casselton invested in a cover for the drainage pipe so that it would never happen again. I have always thought of my Grandpa Jim as a hero in my eyes!

Twilight Years for Grandpa Jim

My Grandpa Jim provided a home for our family when my parents first moved to Casselton. He was a caring and supportive presence in a time of need. In later years, his personal health declined and there was an opportunity for my parents to return his goodness and care.

My Grandfather, James Amos Stockford or "Grandpa Jim," who provided us a home in Casselton.

As I mentioned in memories of my mother, when Grandpa Jim's ability to care for himself began to decline she took on much of the responsibility of caring for him. Grandpa Jim gave his house to Mom and Dad as a way of giving back due to her care for him. When Grandpa Jim could no longer climb the stairs, Dad made an area on the main floor for Grandpa's bed. Jessie and I then moved upstairs to Grandpa's room. He passed away in 1963 at 90 years of age.

Chapter 7
Adventures with Family Relatives

Memorable Family Experiences with Relatives

One of the important reasons that my parents moved to Casselton, North Dakota in my early years was to be with my grandfather. In addition, however, there was an added benefit of being close to some other relatives that were part of the community, particularly on my Dad's side of the family. Having close relationships with my uncles, aunts, and cousins was a fulfilling part of my childhood experience.

Cousin Kenny Wallak

One of the family members who spent quite a bit of time at our home in Casselton while I was growing up was Cousin Kenny. My cousin, Kenny Wallak (May 12, 1931–October 13, 2002), was at our house a lot because he was learning the plumbing business from my Dad. Kenny was the son of my father's older sister, Grace May Stockford, and her husband, Albert Joseph Wallak. Kenny was sixteen years older than me and so he was in his young adult years while I was growing up. Because my father was a Master Plumber, he was able to introduce Kenny to the business of plumbing and give him some mentoring.

I kind of think that Kenny was a favorite nephew of my Mom's because she had him teach her how to drive. Kenny told us at Mom and Dad's 50th Wedding

My cousin, Kenny Wallak, left, with father Clair Stockford.

Anniversary celebration that on their first day of driving lessons he told Mom to put the car into reverse to back out of the driveway. Mom did put the car into reverse and then the car backed up right into the side of Grandpa Jim's house! We laughed quite a bit at that funny memory. Years later when Mom gave birth to my baby brother, Kenneth Allen, she named him after Cousin Kenny and a friend of mine, Allan, who I had known in school.

The McKay Cousins

I very much enjoyed it when my McKay cousins would come and stay with us for a while. My Grandpa Jim's wife died before I was born, but her name was Jessie Mae McKay, and we had a number of cousins and relatives in the area from her side of the family.

Nicky, Terry, and Mike McKay were my favorite cousins to have come and visit. They were quite close in age to my sister Jessie and I. Terry was the oldest and he was approximately the same age as my older sister. I enjoyed them because we were all in the same age group.

One time when my cousin Terry and my sister Jessie were seven or eight years old, they got hold of some of the chickens that we were raising in the back yard. They used clothes pins to clip the chickens to the clothes line! Mom looked out the kitchen window and she could see the chickens flapping their wings out there and trying to free themselves from the clothes line! Many years later when I would visit with my cousin Terry, he and I would still laugh about Mom coming outside and chasing him and Jessie over that incident.

Uncle Grant Stockford and Aunt Isabel Stockford

My father's older brother, Grant Stockford, also lived in town with his wife, Aunt Isabel Stockford. They lived about a block away from our house. Uncle Grant had a shop and a car lot, which was located downtown in Casselton. Aunt Isabel worked at the café down the street, where she washed dishes, and they had one son who was seven years older than me.

In the early 1950's, Uncle Grant ordered a new invention to be sold in his store in Casselton. The invention was the Television. Dad brought one home and set it up in our front room. We were the first home in Casselton to have our own television. I remember looking at the blurry box and seeing a ballerina dancing on the screen and I got up on my braces and tried to stand on my toes to be a dancer like her. I remember telling myself, "When I grow up, I am going to be a ballerina."

My aunt, Isabel Stockford, lived not too far away from us and occasionally I was able to go over and visit her. One of these times was memorable.

The Fargo Tornado

In June 1957, when I was about ten years old, I was over visiting my Aunt Isabel while Mom and Dad were gone doing some errands. The sky got very dark and Aunt Isabel told me to look up at the sky and she showed me a long trail that was apparently a tornado. We watched it for a while and it moved east past us toward Fargo. When we heard the news a few days later we found out that a tornado had touched down in Fargo.

The date of the Fargo Tornado was June 20, 1957, and it was very fortunate for us that it did not hit where we lived only twenty miles away. It turned out to be a violent storm that was later rated as a "Category 5" tornado, the most severe level that exists, and it hit north Fargo in the early evening on that day. The track of this devastating tornado was over fifty miles long and began not far from Casselton. In Fargo it destroyed over 300 homes, damaged over 1000 more houses, and took the lives of ten people.

A picture of the destructive Fargo Tornado, 1957, witnessed by Shirley as a child.

A few days after the tornado occurred, Dad and Mom took Jessie and I to Fargo and we saw the area that the tornado had destroyed. I remember feeling very surprised that a storm could do so much damage. There were many people killed during that storm. It took Fargo a long time to recover from the damage. It seemed as though the houses had been built with toothpicks because they were totally shattered, but it was simply the awesome power of the storm that demonstrated the force of a severe tornado.

Further Memories of Stockford Relatives

Some of my Stockford relatives had a son, Jimmy, who was several years older than me. When he grew up and was of age he later changed his name but I will refer to him as Jimmy.

My cousin, Jimmy, was a Western loving kind of boy. He loved playing cowboys and Indians. One time he and Jessie were playing in the basement and Mom felt that she needed to go down and check on them. She got the surprise of her life when she saw Jimmy trying to put a noose around my sister's neck and they were standing on a swing that we had downstairs. Jimmy had put the rope around one of the rafters and if Mom hadn't listened to the Spirit telling her to check on them, my sister could have been hung! They were playing cowboys and Indians that day and evidently Jessie was the "bad guy" and was about to be hung.

I remember when my cousin Jimmy was quite young, about 12 years of age, his father bought him a rifle for hunting. I remember thinking a negative thought about him being so young with a gun in his hands. Jimmy went rabbit hunting in the 1950's with one of the neighborhood boys when he was 15 years old. While they were hiking in the fields, Jimmy tripped and fell to the ground, and the butt of the rifle hit the ground and went off. It killed the neighborhood boy, who I happened to know, and that was a very difficult time for the family. I always felt bad for Jimmy because he had to live with that incident on his mind all of his life. He was never the same person after that.

Uncle Grant Stockford with dog in Casselton.

Uncle Grant and my Mom were at a local cemetery in the early 1960's when they were working together to take care of the graves of some of our family members. Uncle Grant told Mom at that time that he was worried about Aunt Isabel and her health. It was almost

Memorial Day and they wanted the graves to have beautiful flowers and be ready for those who came to visit the graves. A couple of days after this excursion, my Uncle Grant died in his sleep next to my Aunt Isabel. She never was quite the same again. If I remember things correctly, Mom said that it was Memorial Day that they laid him to rest in the same area that he helped to clean.

In later years when Mom had her Home for the Aged, she took care of a couple relatives. I think that she felt good being able to provide some care to relatives that had been part of our lives. It was a blessing to have these family members living close and to be able to share some of the adventures of life with them. I remember my aunts, uncles and cousins with affection.

Summer Fishing Adventures

When summer came around each year my Dad loved to go fishing. To pursue our family fishing adventures, he and Mom would pack up the car and Jessie and I and we would go to Big Toad Lake or Little Toad Lake beyond Detroit Lakes, Minnesota. My Uncle Grant and Aunt Isabel and their kids went with us often, as well as other family members. We usually went in separate cars and met there.

One time when we were at the lakes with Uncle Grant and Jimmy, Uncle Grant had bought Jimmy a new fishing rod to use. Jimmy was very anxious to go out in the boat because he wanted to catch this large Northern Pike that was sighted near the dock. I remember the main lodge was rustic and had a plaque with a big fish on it. When we got there, Dad and his brother were told about a fishing contest being held. Uncle Grant was eager to go fishing, and soon after our group settled in the cabin, he drove over and backed his boat down the access ramp. I spoke up and asked to go fishing too.

Dad took his pocket knife and walked to a tree branch growing near the lake. He cut it off, trimmed off the leaves and excess, and then tied four feet of his fishing line to the end of my new pole along with a bare hook. He told me I could go fishing too. I went on the dock and was laying there on the dock with my hook in the water and looking down into the water at the little fish that were swimming around. The water was so clear that you could see everything.

After a while I saw this big fish come up by me and didn't think much about what I was doing, but I moved my hook and put it on the back of the fish. The fish was so mad that he did a quick turn around and grabbed my hook. I started screaming for Mom to help me because it was pulling me into the water. Mom came out and helped me and between the two of us we pulled in the large Northern Pike that my cousin, Jimmy, had wanted to catch. My Dad, Uncle Grant, and Jimmy were all watching from the boat at me fighting to get this fish that was almost as big as I was. Dad and Uncle Grant were laughing as they watched from the boat. Jimmy got so mad I caught the fish he wanted that he threw his new rod into the lake! Mine was the biggest catch of the day! I was about five years old at the time. Jimmy said it wasn't fair that I caught that fish with a homemade pole and didn't even have any bait on the hook—but I did it!

Fun Family Reunions

With so many family members on my father's side of the family living quite close together, we had many family get-togethers and reunions during those growing-up years. These gatherings would often take place in Casselton during the summer at the place that was at that time called "The Reservoir." It was like a park on the north end of Casselton where people could gather. This park-like area even had a section that was like a little waterfall and the kids would walk on the rocks and the water would go around their feet. This fascinated me because I couldn't walk on the rocks.

Shirley as a young girl taking a drink of Dad's beer!

The adults typically had games for the children to play, such as two-legged races, apple dunking, and running with a raw egg on a spoon. It was always a fun day when we got together. I loved it when all the family members were there. The Wallaks, the McKays, the Stockfords, and anyone who was anybody was there with lots of food and fun. Fifty years later, I went to a McKay reunion and all the kids that were there looked like the grown-ups that I knew as a kid! So fun! I have fond memories of growing up in Casselton surrounded by family relatives and their love and support.

Chapter 8
Heavenly Protection

Experiences with Danger and Divine Assistance

From a very early age in my life, I encountered situations in which I faced some personal danger or needed the assistance of others for protection. Each one of us encounters dangers and difficulties in life. While we are unable to avoid many of these life challenges, such as the experience I had in contracting polio, at times we receive protection from others or even divine assistance from the Lord. I am one who believes strongly that there are times when others around us are inspired to help or protect us. In addition, I am grateful for the times when God reaches down and gives us divine assistance or protection. In this chapter, I share a few childhood instances of "heavenly protection" that were both memorable and meaningful to me in my life.

My Dog Lady and the Train Incident

When I was probably about a year old or more, I had a German Shepherd dog that was named Lady. She would stay with me wherever I went. Our house in Casselton was located close to the railroad tracks (just a quarter block away), and there were about thirty trains that came through town each day.

One day Mom was outside with me and Jessie hanging up clothes on the clothesline. Mom heard the dog barking and turned and realized that I had wandered off and so she went looking for me right away. She saw the dog's tail wagging by the railroad tracks and knew that I would be close to wherever Lady was since she always stayed close to me. Mom went running and found me sitting on the tracks. She ran and grabbed me off of the tracks and quickly got away from the tracks as fast as she could and a train went speeding by! I feel that the Lord was watching out for me that day for sure!! I am so grateful to my Mom and Lady for saving my life.

Falling Into the Basement

It was mentioned earlier that one time when my mother was making donuts some mice came up from the basement and were taking them away. Well, after that incident, my Dad thought that he probably needed to put in a cement wall to cover the basement walls and keep the mice out of our home. He and his friend, Roy, carried a lot of dirt out of the basement and put in the walls. On one end of the basement was a drop area where a door opened to the outside and they would drop coal down through that door to be used for the furnace.

One day when I was about three or four years old I was riding my tricycle by this door to the outside where they would drop the coal for the furnace. The doors into the basement were open and I got too close and my bike tipped over and I fell into the basement. I remember looking around the basement, probably for the first time, and I saw the large furnace and thought it was a monster that was going to eat me up! My fearless father found me quickly and rescued me from the "monster" (the furnace). I still have a scar on my chin where my chin hit the floor of the basement when I fell through that door.

Shirley Ann Stockford on her tricycle as a young girl in Casselton.

The door that opened up in the basement from outside was just like what you see in the movies that you pull upward to get away from a tornado. I do remember many times that Dad would go and get several hundred pounds of potatoes and dump them down through that door. I remember it because when they would start growing sprouts my Dad would sit me on the pile of potatoes to pull off the sprouts!

A Snake Encounter

When I was about five years old, a circus came to Casselton and Mom and Dad took us to see the animals. I remember a partitioned glass cage with huge snakes inside.

The keeper began to feed them and left one of the glass covers back and open. I saw a huge snake looking at me from inside the cage. Slowly, the snake raised up to the opening and was looking straight at me. I froze to my spot watching him inch his way out of the top. The keeper then saw it. He pushed the snake back into the cage and slammed down the door just in time. I was really scared of snakes after that.

Sometimes as I was outside on the swing in front of the garage, I remembered the snake coming toward me and I would imagine a snake hiding in one of the holes in the tree that were near the swing. It took me a long time to get over that experience.

Protected from a Stranger

A potentially serious danger took place in my life a few years later when I was about six or seven years of age. This incident dealt with the brief intrusion of a stranger. As I have reflected, I feel that the Lord was watching out for me on this occasion when I was about six years old.

When this incident occurred, my parents and their friends, Roy and Marge, were at the bar downtown with us girls and just relaxing. Jessie and I liked to watch the people dance to the sounds of the jukebox. While I was watching some people dance, a man came up to me and began talking to me. In his conversation he said to me, "Would you like to come with me?" I felt the Spirit of the Lord, which can speak even to children in their mind or heart, tell me clearly that I was in danger and I said, "No!"

After he said that I quickly went away from him and sat in the booth near my Mom. Mom sensed something was wrong and asked me what was wrong. I told her what the man had said to me and that I had come over there to get away from him. Mom told me to stay right where I was and went to Dad and told him what happened. So, Dad and Roy picked up all of us kids and we went next door to the bar that served food. The man followed us there. When we were safely sitting in a booth, Dad and his friend Roy walked up to the man, each taking one of his arms and took him out of the dining room and out the door. I never saw what happened to him nor was it ever mentioned again. I felt blessed and protected on that occasion.

A few years later when my brother, John, was a baby, the same thing happened with him. A man tried to take him out the door and my Dad took John out of his hands, and then he and Roy took the man by the arms and out the door. I never heard the end of that story either!

Safety Concerns at the Medical Clinic

After I had been treated for polio and learned to live with braces on my legs and other challenges as a young girl, we made many trips to Fargo and the Dover Building when the braces would break or adjustments needed to be made. Children with special health needs are often more vulnerable and experience higher rates of child abuse. I learned about another safety concern years later from a classmate that I graduated with in Jamestown, which I had not know about earlier.

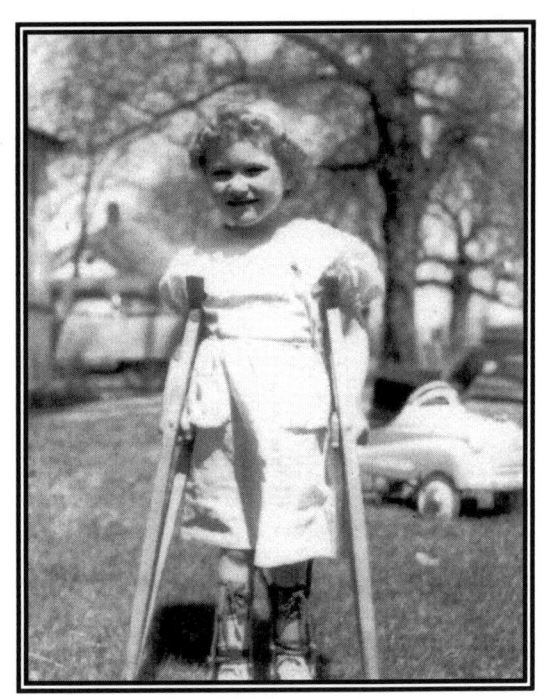

Shirley Ann Stockford with her crutches and braces as a young girl in Casselton.

My mother would always stay with me whenever I went to a particular doctor's clinic at the Dover Building in Fargo. She never left me alone there. My friend told me that she also went to this doctor's clinic and she was left there alone. She told me of how he would touch her in private places when she went to his clinic. Later on she lived at the Crippled Children's School in Jamestown and lived in the dormitory and felt safe there from this doctor. However, not long after she began school there, they began to have clinics right there and this doctor would come in and examine the children. When she heard this doctor was coming, she hid under her bed in the dormitory to try and keep away from having to see him in private. When I think about this experience of hers and the fact that I was vulnerable and saw the same doctor, I am grateful that my mother never left me alone at that clinic or with this particular doctor.

Chapter 9
Casselton Connections

Community Experiences Growing Up in Casselton

Growing up in Casselton, North Dakota, was a blessing for me since we lived close to many family members. In addition, however, it was simply a good place to live. Casselton is a small, tight-knit community just off of the main highway that runs through North Dakota and is located about twenty miles west of Fargo, North Dakota. During the years that I was growing up the estimated population in Casselton was about 1,400 people. The train tracks ran through town and it was large enough to have a few local stores and a downtown area. I have a few selected memories of living in the community of Casselton and ties to the larger community.

The Annual Fireworks Show at the Fairgrounds

One of the occasions that I remember taking place on an annual basis was the Fourth of July Fireworks Show. My father had a friend whose name was Otto who came to town every summer just before Independence Day on the Fourth of July. He would work with my Dad to set off the Fireworks Show at the fairgrounds in Fargo. My Dad and Otto were involved in the annual Fireworks Show for many years until our family left Casselton in 1959. I remember many times our family sitting at the old fairgrounds by our car in the center of the ring watching the shows. That was quite a thrill for two little girls.

When Otto would come to stay with us he always would give me a Silver Dollar. I would give the Silver Dollars to Mom and she would keep them for me. Then she would give me a dollar bill in exchange for it so I could have some spending money. When we moved to Jamestown in 1959, my brother found the Silver Dollars and took them to the little Mom and Pop Store that was nearby and he bought some candy and gave the store owner the Silver Dollars! The store owner called Mom and gave her back the Silver Dollars in exchange for the correct amount of money.

The March of Dimes Campaign

The polio epidemics that had affected so much of the United States and me personally were countered during my childhood by a new campaign intended to defeat the disease. The National Foundation for Infantile Paralysis, which was organized by President Franklin D. Roosevelt in 1938 to lead the efforts against polio, began an annual fundraising campaign in its first year to raise funds to use in combating polio. This fundraising campaign was titled the "March of Dimes" and citizens both young and old were encouraged to send in "dimes" or other amounts to raise money for research, treatment, and needed support for disabled children.

Local chapters of the March of Dimes campaign were organized across the country in the years that followed. My Dad was active as Chairman of the local March of Dimes chapter and so he would hold many fundraising activities to raise money for the campaign. He was so happy about what they did for me that he wanted to help the foundation.

I remember Dad having a number of slot machines in our living room that he was going to take to the bars to raise money for the March of Dimes. Dad told me that he had the springs wound so tight to keep them from paying off because he had to make sure that it was not considered gambling but indeed the money was intended as a contribution for the March of Dimes. He worked hard to raise funds for the campaign. I remember putting my nickels into the slot machine and it paid off! Dad laughed and said, "I guess I didn't get that one tight enough!"

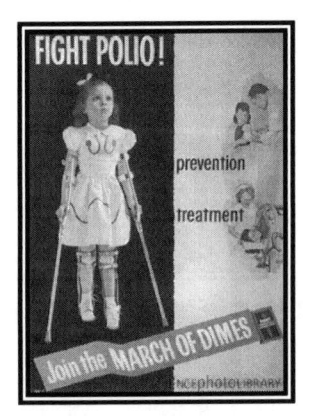

March of Dimes campaign poster from the 1950's.

Another time as part of a fundraising idea Dad wanted to put me on a blanket and carry me with a few other men holding the edges of the blanket. He thought we could walk around the neighborhood and people could throw money into the blanket with me. Mom got mad and told him he could not use me that way and she walked away with me! I can still hear my Dad laughing over that one!

First Encounters with Religion

Although my religion has been an important part of my life for many years, I was first introduced to religion through the influence of my parents as we lived in Casselton. Mom and Dad would take us to church at times in Casselton while I was growing up.

I remember the stories that the teachers taught us from the Bible. My favorite was the story of Noah's Ark. Later in my life when I began reading the Bible, I was surprised to find the stories there that I had heard in my youth. I don't know if I really understood that the stories taught to us in church while I was young were the stories of actual people recorded in the Bible until I read them for myself. Mom had purchased a big Bible that I loved to pick up and read when I was alone.

Other Casselton Memories

Most of the time that we lived in Casselton during my childhood we lived in the home of my Grandpa Stockford. However, in about 1956 we lost Grandpa Stockford's house to the bank, as my parents were not able to keep up payments on a loan. This meant that we had to move from Grandpa Stockford's home to an old house located near the high school.

After we moved to the old house, I remember Mom spent many days pulling off old dirty wallpaper. I watched her as she made a paste and put up fresh wallpaper in that home. I always admired my mother's many talents. She worked hard and made that old house a warm place to live.

One of our favorite pastimes took place on Friday nights as we lived in Casselton. Friday night was a time to watch television as a family together. I would grab a blanket and sit on the big floor heat vent and we would all watch the show *Maverick* together. The show first started in 1957 and went through 1962 and it was a favorite show in our home. I don't remember watching too much television as a child, but I sure did like the Western shows and *Maverick* was a family favorite.

There was an old out-house in our back yard and we had some bales of hay located around it. I went out there one time and there was a bucket sitting upside down on a bale of hay. I went over and tipped over the bucket. Suddenly, a huge rat jumped out from underneath it and it scared me so badly that I never went near that out-house again!

When I was about 10 years old, we had a pet parakeet that figured out how to get out of her cage. She took a liking to me. I taught her to fly to me by ringing a little bell. I also taught her to land on my out-pointed finger. One day I was sitting on my bed upstairs. I rang the bell expecting to hear the flutter of wings up the steps. Somehow, though, I fell asleep, surprisingly with my finger still pointed out ready for a landing. When I woke up, my finger was still ready, but I was sad to learn that one of our cats had nabbed the parakeet during her flight.

The Stockford family, left to right: Rosie Mae Stockford (mother), Shirley Ann Stockford, Jessie Mae Stockford, Clair James Stockford (father).

An interesting artifact that came into our family during the time that we lived in Casselton was a genuine arrowhead. My Dad and his friend, Roy, decided to dig out the basement under the house and began carrying dirt out of the basement. They dug it out and put cement on the walls and floor of the basement. When they were digging out the basement, Dad found an arrowhead made of slate and he cleaned it and gave it to Mom to keep. The arrowhead must have been there for many years. Mom gave this artifact to me a few years before she died, and I in turn gave it to my great nephew. It was an interesting link to the years that we lived in Casselton.

Chapter 10
Special Holiday Memories

Celebrating Holidays with Family Members

Holidays are a special time when we remember those we love and celebrate the blessings that are present in our lives. As with many families, we always enjoyed the opportunity to gather with others that came around when a holiday arrived. Two of the holidays that I have special memories about growing up included Easter and Christmas.

Easter Memories

Easter was always a special time in our home while I was growing up. Each year Mom would buy Easter bonnets for Jessie and I and also make us each a matching dress. We would all go to church uptown and when we came home Dad had an Easter Egg Hunt all ready for us.

During one special Easter time Dad had some pink, yellow and blue chicks and bunnies in Easter baskets for us to find along with the candy and eggs. It was so special to see the pretty colors on them. On one of these occasions I was holding a little chick in my hands (I was about four or five years old) and telling this little chick that I loved him. I hugged the chick so hard that it died. It broke my little heart.

Shirley Ann Stockford at Easter as a child.

Christmas Traditions

When the Christmas season came around each year, knocks at the door were a common sound as family and friends would drop by or come to spend Christmas Day with us at our home. We enjoyed the company and the sounds of laughter and conversation would fill the air. Grandpa Jim would come down from his room and sit in the over-stuffed chair with his pipe in his mouth and the house would fill with people.

Dad had the blender running in the kitchen, as his tradition was to make his own "Tom and Jerry batter" for the drinks. Jessie and I loved sneaking into the kitchen and asking Dad for a little taste of the rich batter. There was no liquor in it, of course! I can still remember the taste of that batter.

Of course, Mom would make a fantastic meal on Christmas Day. She always made a lot of food because people would keep coming throughout the day. There was always a huge turkey, stuffed with dressing, as well as mashed potatoes and gravy. In addition, Mom always had a large garden, which meant that we had endless possibilities from everything she had canned that year. There would be cranberries, pickles, carrots, green beans, tomatoes, and homemade jam. Also, who could forget the homemade bread, butter, pumpkin pie, apple pie, and all the extras that other family members brought with them to add to the feast. I would pile my plate high and sit on the floor with the other kids. Before long there would be another knock at the door and more people would come. I loved this time of the year and the people all around us at home.

Mom would also fix extra plates of food and have Dad take the plates down town to the apartments that were upstairs over the bars. There were elderly people living there that didn't have family in the area, so Mom would include them with our meals at holiday time by taking food to them.

Reindeer Noises and Grandpa Santa

As we enjoyed the Christmas season, there were also special memories associated with receiving gifts and anticipating the arrival of Santa Claus. To a child's mind there came the thought: "When will we open the presents?"

I remember one special Christmas in my childhood, when Dad was not there in the evening and we had to wait for him. Mom would say to us, "Wait for Daddy to come home." Then we suddenly heard a noise that sounded like something running on the side of the house. Mom came running in with excitement in her voice, looking toward the roof and saying, "Sounds like the reindeer are here! Yes! It is Santa! He is here!" Jessie and I squealed with glee!

Then the door opened wide and we couldn't believe it. Santa Claus came in the door with a big bag over his shoulder saying, "Ho, ho, ho! Merry Christmas!" Being about four or five years old, I thought it must be my Daddy. But lo and behold, Daddy came in behind him! My eyes were wide and the giggling was hard to control as Santa handed us our presents. Then Daddy gave us two big, tall dolls. They were almost identical, but mine had blonde hair like me, and Jessie's doll had brunette hair like her own. The two dolls were nearly as tall as I was and wore ball gowns, earrings and high heels. I thought they were so beautiful. I have remembered that Christmas all of my life because of how my Mom and Dad put so much effort into making it a special Christmas for Jessie and me.

The Stockford sisters, Jessie Mae (left) and Shirley Ann (right), celebrating Christmas with new dolls.

When I got older, I learned that Dad had been running around the house making it sound like reindeer were on the roof. I never did find out for certain who Santa was though. Years later, however, when I was ten years old, I was upstairs snooping around in my Grandpa's room. While I was digging around I found a Santa suit and knew the truth—Santa was my Grandpa!

Chapter 11
Public School Ups and Downs

My Early Educational Experiences

Education is an important pathway to growth and learning and has always been of great interest in my life since I was a young girl. However, dealing with physical difficulties that include challenges with mobility, hearing problems, and vision concerns has made that process more of a struggle in my life. As a young girl, I experienced a variety of ups and downs in regard to my early educational experiences in Kindergarten through the sixth grade.

Kindergarten and Hearing Aids

I began my education in Casselton at the Kindergarten level with the other children who were not handicapped. However, schooling was very difficult in those days for a person with a disability. Not only was I walking on crutches with braces, but both my sister and I had major hearing challenges.

Both my sister Jessie and I had a lot of difficulty with hearing, and when we began going to school they quickly discovered that each of us had this problem. I believe that I was about six years old when I got my first hearing aid. I only had one hearing aid in one ear at that time. It made things very difficult to understand where sounds were coming from and there were so many words I couldn't understand. As a result, when I went to school they told me I was "retarded" and kids made fun of me quite a lot. So, my entry into school in the public school system was quite difficult.

I can still remember my first hearing aid. It was about the size of one of the smaller cell phones that we have now. It was heavy and had a clip so that it could be clipped to our slips under our dresses. It had a long twisted cord that went from the box to our ear. I just hated it!

The next hearing aid I had was smaller and it would clip in my hair. It was heavy on the hair so I wasn't too happy about that either. As time went on, the progress of hearing aids was remarkable. Years later we were able to have two hearing aids and that development totally changed my life. I also took speech therapy which taught me and helped me to become an experienced lip reader.

Shirley Stockford, far right, at school with classmates in 1950s.

While I enjoyed the experience of learning, the challenges associated with attending public school were not always easy to handle. This was an era when accommodations for children with disabilities were just being explored and so there were still many things to overcome.

School Difficulties and Home Tutoring

My entry into Kindergarten happened in the fall of 1953 and I continued attending public school during that year but there were a lot of difficulties. I remember not liking school very much because of my hearing difficulty. In addition, some of the parents had misgivings about my having had polio and didn't want their children associating with me for fear of their child catching Polio from me. Some told their kids to avoid being near me. That made me feel lonely .

My parents kept an eye on my experience and supported me. However, one day during Kindergarten there was an incident that occurred which caused a shift in my early educational experience.

On this particular day, there was a parade being held downtown about three blocks away from the school. The teacher didn't feel I could walk that far and so chose to leave me at the school by myself. The teachers and the principal took all of the other children to the parade and left me in the school building alone. There were no other people in the school with me.

When they were all gone and I was alone, I was scared and so I went to the principal's office and found a phone. I picked up the phone and the operator was on the line. I remember that the operator's name was Jenny. I said, "Jenny, call my Mom." When Mom came to the school to get me she found me hiding under all the coats that were on the floor in the coat room. Needless to say, she was very angry at what had happened and decided that things needed to change. She was so angry that she pulled me out of school and arranged things so that a tutor teacher, Mrs. Jenro, could teach me at home.

I never went back to that schoolhouse again. I had four years of tutoring at home with Mrs. Jenro that was supported by my parents. I remember the three-line paper I used for copying her perfect letters as best I could. Letters turned into meaningful writing (and now this book!). Education was a priority for them and they wanted us to gain that experience.

Twenty-Eight Steps Up to Six Times a Day

In the fall of 1957, my parents decided to see once again if I could benefit from the public school experience and so I returned that year to the 5th grade. I had to try adjusting to public schooling once again. The classes were held at the high school in town.

On the first day of school, I was extremely nervous and asked the teacher if I could go to the bathroom. She told me that I had to wait until recess. Well, I ended up throwing up all over my desk due to the anxiety! If I ever asked her to go to the bathroom again, she did not hesitate to let me go after that incident!

Since my classes at the high school were held up on the second floor, my Mom brought me to school and carried me to class. My sweet mother carried me, with braces up to the hips, up 28 steps at least two to six times every school day. I remember her telling me later

Shirley Stockford, 1958.

on that she had to carry me up and down those stairs, "28 Steps" she would say, several times a day in order for me to go to school and get an education. Education was a really important priority for her, since she hadn't been able to get much education as a child, and she wanted her girls to have the best we could get.

I attended the 5th and 6th grades in Casselton at that school with Mom's help. If I stayed upstairs on the second floor for lunch then she didn't have to come as often. I remember looking out the window and seeing everyone outside playing as I sat alone during the lunch hour. On the days she came and helped me downstairs so I could eat in the lunch room, the other children would make fun of me and I would end up being alone anyway.

I remember once Mom came to help me downstairs so I could go outside for lunch break, and one of the school staff told her she couldn't park in front of the school because it was a bus stop. She said, "You fool with me, and I will drive that G-d damn car all the way up the sidewalk to get Shirley to school!" They didn't bother her about that issue again!

It was the parents' responsibility when they had a handicapped child to get them to their classes. I do remember once when the school had two high school boys come downstairs and they put their arms in a cross shape and had me sit on their arms and they carried me upstairs to class. That only happened once. So, it was a major task for Mom to assist me each school day.

Hopalong Cassidy and Other School Memories

In the last year that I was in public school in Casselton, they had created a special class on the main floor at the school so I didn't have to go up all the steps. There were also others there that had special needs. I liked that change because I could walk outside when the weather was nice and play on the swings.

I remember once during this last year that a boy came and sat by me and visited with me. This young man's name was Warren Albert. He was the same boy that my cousin accidentally shot in a hunting accident later on. I never forgot Warren for being kind and visiting with me.

Another special event I remember that occurred at the high school was when Hopalong Cassidy came to our school for a visit. I was so excited about that event.

Hopalong Cassidy was a major Western movie hero (played by actor William Boyd), had his own TV series, and was known for doing right and helping others. They took a picture of me and Mom as we were getting our tickets for the event, and the picture was shown in the local newspaper. So much fun—I saw a real cowboy!

I made it for two years in the public school system and then I had to have surgery on both of my legs. I missed a lot of school with the casts up to my hips and so they held me back a year. The surgery prevented my feet from dropping straight down and also made some adjustments to my ankles. After that surgery, I didn't have to wear braces any longer, which was great to me since I kept on breaking them anyway!

Shirley and her mother, as "Hopalong Shirley," when actor Hopalong Cassidy visited Casselton. Picture appeared in newspaper.

Birth of a Brother

It was during this period of my life that a new and exciting development occurred in the Stockford family. My brother, John Stockford, was born in January 1954 and became the newest member of our family. It was such an exciting day when John came home in Mom's arms.

My first remembrance of this little guy coming into our family was when Mom was changing him on a table and I heard laughing. I turned to look and saw this little fountain shooting up from the table! I began laughing as I saw him giggling. I loved him from that second on!

John, my brother, grew to 6'4" and reminded me of a young Tom Selleck, a favorite actor I had in the 1970s and 1980s, with thick eyelashes. John batted them just as Tom did. He was big and handsome like my dad. I will talk a bit more about John later, but he was a wonderful addition to our family. We would go on to have a lot of fun experiences together as siblings.

This change in our family life was just one of several major changes that were soon to take place for us at the end of the 1950s. We would go through a variety of changes and navigate the new chapters that came with them.

Surgery and Starting School Again

When I was in the 6th grade, doctors performed surgery on both legs and both ankles for me, fusing them so that I could walk without braces. I had casts on both legs up to my knees. The casts were on for weeks as my legs healed. Unfortunately for me, this kept me out of school for quite a long period of time and I was unable to make up the schoolwork that I missed. As a result, I started over in the 6th grade when we moved to Jamestown (see next chapter).

Sister Jessie, left, with baby brother John, right.

Once the casts were removed, I no longer needed braces on my legs, and that helped me to feel more freedom in the world. A neighbor had a steep driveway that kids loved to ride their bikes down and then go out into the street, and then they would coast on their bikes for several blocks down the street. It looked like so much fun. So, one day there was no around and I saw a bike on the driveway that had training wheels on it. I got on the bike, threw down my crutches, and began to coast down that steep driveway and on to the street. I very soon realized that I was in big trouble since I did not know how to stop the bike, which was picking up speed quickly. I turned the handle bars on the bike in the direction of our house and rolled up our driveway to the side of my dad's truck. I grabbed the door handle and was able to stop the bike safely. Never did that again!

Going to school in a public school setting had been my experience while living in Casselton, but there were other options ahead for me. Soon, our family would move and this opened up new opportunities.

Section 2
Transitions to Adulthood and Living with Disabilities

At the age of 12 years old, Shirley Stockford moved with her parents and siblings to a new location further west in North Dakota. In 1959, they moved to Jamestown where her father accepted a job with Montgomery Ward. Due to economic challenges, both parents worked hard and Shirley learned the importance of hard work from the example of her parents. Her mother found various work opportunities but ultimately established a care home for aging individuals and provided care for them. This became important training for Shirley as she assisted with care and would later care for aging or disabled individuals herself.

Another reason for the family move to Jamestown was so that Shirley could begin further education at what was known as the Crippled Children's School there. Later this facility was known as the Anne Carlsen Center, and Shirley attended several years of school and graduated from high school there in 1966. This educational experience helped her in adapting to some of her disability circumstances and also provided a setting where she could connect with peers and complete her high school education.

The transition to adulthood for Shirley brought its own set of challenges. Within a few short years, she encountered difficulties that challenged her significantly—a hasty marriage and eventual divorce; an infant daughter's birth and quick death; struggles in learning to drive; her siblings beginning their own adult lives; and a personal trauma that left her discouraged and fearful of others. Learning to navigate these transitions and challenges in young adulthood was the next chapter of her life.

Chapter 12
New Adventures in Jamestown, ND

Family Move and Experiences in Jamestown, ND

Our family moved to Jamestown, North Dakota in 1959, when I turned 12 years old. Jamestown was located directly west of Casselton about 75 miles and just off the highway. There were multiple reasons for our family to make this move.

First of all, my dad got a job working there in Jamestown for the Montgomery Ward company. Also, my limitations due to polio made education difficult, and there was a facility located in Jamestown that was specifically for children dealing with physical difficulties or other circumstances. As a result, my years from age 12 through graduation from high school primarily took place in Jamestown, North Dakota.

Parental Experiences Living in Jamestown

As noted, in Jamestown my father began working for Montgomery Ward. Dad found a nice green stucco house for our family to live in located right across the street from Roosevelt Elementary School where my younger brother, John, could attend.

While living in Jamestown, one day Dad was working with his friend, Marvin, in a deep hole that had been dug out to fix underground piping. As they were climbing out of the deep hole on a ladder, it caved in and they were in danger. Dad's legs got covered on the top of the ladder and Marvin was behind him on the ladder. Dad pulled himself free and yelled for help, then he immediately started digging as fast as he could, digging to free his friend Marvin. He used his hands to dig as fast as

Shirley's parents, mother Rosie Stockford and father Clair Stockford, in 1969 on anniversary.

he could. Finally, they reached Marvin and freed him. Marvin was all right because his helmet had slipped down just enough to give him a little bit of air until Dad and others reached him. That was quite a scare for all of us.

One time something happened that I missed my bus to school and my Dad took me to school in his pick-up truck. We were driving not too far from our house when a car came flying down the road. This was at the time when it was not required to wear seatbelts. Fortunately for me, Dad put out his strong arm across my waist and held me back in the seat as he slammed to a stop to prevent being hit by that car. I have long remembered this kind act of protection that he did for me and loved him more and more because of his kindness.

Mom also needed to work in supporting our family while we lived in Jamestown and she worked hard. Mom began working there at a small 12-unit motel as a maid. She was paid one dollar a unit for cleaning the rooms and doing the laundry. In addition, she also did cleaning for many people in town to supplement our family income. No matter what, however, Mom made sure that she was home by the time we got out of school. I so much appreciated seeing her when I would get off of the bus after school.

While living in Jamestown, Dad and Mom built our first house a few blocks away from the house we were renting. The home was located at 1104 6th Street South East. During this time, my father began having a lot of difficulty with alcoholism, and as a result his work suffered and we almost lost the house. Mom talked to our neighbor, Don, and asked him if he would be willing to lend her the money to save our house. Don was kind enough to do that and we did not lose our home.

The Stockford Home for the Aged

This was a time of economic struggle for our family. Mom kept working everywhere she could to support our family, pay Don back, and keep payments up for the house. Also at this same time, Mom started working at a nursing home called Green Acres. The administrator's name was Reverend Richards.

One night while Mom was working, one of the ladies had a bowel movement in her bed and Mom cleaned her up and washed the bedding out by hand and then took the bedding down to the laundry room. The next day Reverend Richards called her into his office and told her she was not to clean anyone up during the night. Mom said to him: "I will not leave anyone laying in a wet or dirty bed overnight." He fired her.

So, being the hard worker that she was, she decided to take care of elderly people in her home. That was the beginning of the Stockford Home for the Aged. It wasn't too long and Mom was able to have a second house built next door and she had a state license to accommodate 14 people for elder care. The address of the second house was 1108 6th Street South East. Both homes had double stall garages attached. Also, each house was 80-plus feet long. In one house there was one apartment and in the other there were two apartments in the basement, while upstairs there were about six bedrooms in each home. I lived in all of the apartments at one time or another while we lived there.

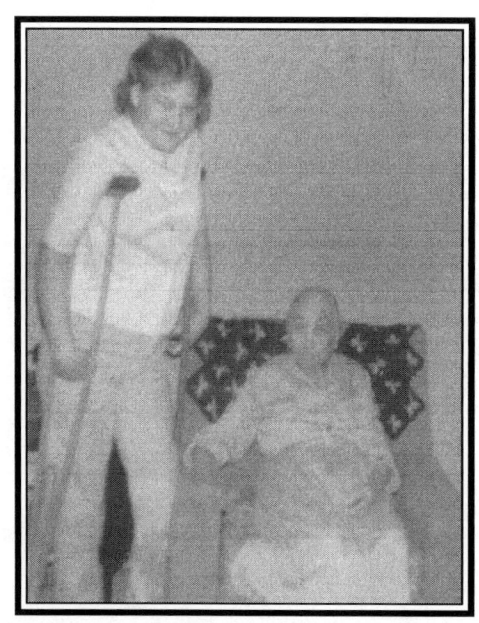

Shirley Stockford as young adult, left, in Stockford Home for the Aged with resident.

On these lots where the homes were located, Mom would plant a huge garden and grow a variety of vegetables, which she harvested and then did a great deal of canning and freezing to keep food for the year.

While running the Stockford Home for the Aged, Mom would hire help a few times but not very often. She let me help with many of the duties and I learned to love these people who had a variety of needs. One time, one of the men was in his room, but Mom was gone and I heard a strange sound so I went in to check on him. He was stretched out in his chair and his eyes were rolling back and I knew he needed help. I quickly called 9-1-1 and the ambulance came and the emergency workers saw him and took him to the hospital. After Mom got home, she asked me what happened and I told her about the incident. She then called the hospital and was told that "there was nothing wrong with him." Evidently, the air outside helped him to snap out of it and he recovered. I was afraid Mom wouldn't believe me, but she told them that she believed me and that they were to keep him overnight to make sure he was all right. He died that night. It made me feel so good that my Mom believed me.

Sibling Experiences Living in Jamestown

When our family moved to Jamestown in 1959, my older sister Jessie turned 14 years old, I turned 12 years old, and our younger brother John was 5 years old. Each of us had a variety of experiences while living there.

As noted, John began first attending elementary school after we moved to Jamestown and we lived across the street from the school. As he grew a bit older, John really liked putting together model cars and other types of models. The highlight of the models he built was a large ship (an ocean liner) that he put together by himself. He was about seven years old when he did the ship. I sure was proud of my little brother. The ocean liner was not the only model that he put together during these years, but it was the biggest project that he had done at this age and was a great accomplishment for a young boy.

It was during the time that we lived in Jamestown that Jessie got married to a man named Bill Meyer. They were married in December 1964

From left, siblings John Stockford, Shirley Stockford, and Jessie Mae Stockford, 1960s in Jamestown, ND

and Jessie was 19 years old. It was strange to not have her there at home with me. It was just me and John.

The Birth and Passing of Kenneth Allen Stockford

During the years that we lived in Jamestown, one of the more traumatic incidents of my young life occurred. This event was the birth and passing of my younger brother, Kenneth Allen Stockford.

Mom became pregnant once again during my junior year of high school in 1963. I was 16 years old at the time. She had such a difficult time with this pregnancy because the baby was very large. We were all excited but anxious as well.

When our little brother, Kenneth Allen, was born in December 1963, he weighed almost eleven pounds. I was at the hospital with Mom the night he was born. I had watched Mom in labor for so many hours and it was hard to see her suffering, and finally the doctor came in and said that the nurse had put a belt on her in the wrong way and it prevented the baby from being able to come. In any case, after it was removed then Mom was able to have the little guy.

I was waiting with Dad and while we were waiting a thought came to my mind that he was not going to live. I knew that he was going to die. A feeling? A prompting? I don't know—I only know that I knew. I said nothing to anyone. I kept the thoughts to myself. I got to see my baby brother Kenneth before we left the hospital and my heart was breaking. It was in December 1963 and it was very cold outside. Dad left the car running to keep me warm as he went into the bar to hand out cigars announcing the birth of another son.

While I sat alone in the car and waited, I prayed to Heavenly Father to take me and let Kenneth Allen live. I cried a lot that night after we got home and fell asleep due to my exhaustion and anxiety. In the morning, Dad told me that my baby brother had died in the night. His lungs had collapsed.

I never told anyone about the thoughts that I had because I was afraid they would think I was a bad person. I didn't understand why Heavenly Father let me live and took my little brother. I kept it to myself about what I knew the night before. I was afraid there was something wrong with me because I knew he was going to die.

We had learned in my history classes about witches being burned in the Dark Ages, and I honestly thought maybe I was a witch and that was how I knew. I didn't want to be burned at the stake, so I kept quiet. Kenneth's birth and quick passing was a sad event in our family.

Experiences in the Methodist Church in Jamestown

Our family began going to church at the United Methodist Church in Jamestown soon after we arrived in town. All of us as a family went to take classes for a period of time with Reverend McDonald, who was the pastor there. I liked the lessons that we were taught in preparation of becoming members of the church, but they brought to my mind many more questions. Then the day came that we were all to be baptized.

We all wore our Sunday best and sat in front of the congregation for our baptism experience. Reverend McDonald baptized us by sprinkling a little bit of water on our heads. I remember coming home and feeling puzzled. I remember sitting on a chair and looking at a picture that Mom had on the wall of the Lord Jesus Christ being crucified on the cross. I was so full of questions. My attention was drawn to the little sign above his head that said: "King of the Jews." Why was He crucified? If they knew who He was, why did they do that? I also remember feeling confused because I had just been baptized, and I thought to myself, "Why don't I feel different?"

Still, our experience with religion at the United Methodist Church in Jamestown was a positive one. We were welcomed and were able to worship together as a family in a meaningful way. As years passed, our church attendance dropped to just going on holidays and for my sister's wedding.

Chapter 13
Life at the Crippled Children's School

My Experiences at the Crippled Children's School

One of the reasons that our family moved to Jamestown in 1959 while I was 12 years old was because there were better opportunities for my education. Due to my difficulties arising from polio, my parents had looked for an opportunity to find a better educational setting for me. In Jamestown, there was a facility known as the Crippled Children's School that was run by Anne Carlsen. Anne Carlsen herself was born with physical impairments and yet she worked hard to make a positive life for others with such challenges. Through her work, the Crippled Children's School was opened in Jamestown in 1941 and it provided support and education to children with physical difficulties or other special needs. Eventually, it became known as the Anne Carlsen Center and continues its work today, but in my time it was known as the Crippled Children's School, and this is where I attended and received my education through the end of high school.

Early Experiences at the Crippled Children's School

I started attending school at the Crippled Children's School in Jamestown in 1960. I was then in the 6th Grade. My new school was across town. Most students lived there in dormitories. It had about 80 students with eight or ten at the same grade level and two or more grades in a classroom. We were provided school transportation each day. I remember feeling petrified going there in the station wagon that came to pick me up that first morning.

"THE CRIPPLED CHILDREN'S SCHOOL, JAMESTOWN, NORTH DAKOTA"

Postcard showing the Crippled Children's School in Jamestown, North Dakota, where Shirley Stockford attended beginning in 1959-60.

There were about five of us attending the school that were called Day Students. This meant that each of us lived at home with our family. The students who lived at the school full time were called Dorm Students. We arrived at the front of the school, and each step I took towards the door, I was closer to tears. The door opened and the first person I saw was Allen. He had a wonderful and friendly smile and my fears melted away. I secretly was hoping he would be in my class. He was!

I soon enjoyed classes at the school and was called in to Dr. Anne Carlsen's office to have some testing done. She told me that I was above average in intelligence after the testing was completed. She then sent me to Speech Therapy to help me to talk more clearly. It wasn't long until I had received two hearing aids and it seemed that the whole world opened up to me.

Dr. Carlsen then began teaching me how to lip read. I really enjoyed school even more then. I even was in an Industrial Arts class where I learned and did some carpentry skills, ceramics, and metalwork! I absolutely loved using the machines!

As part of my educational experience there, I also had Physical Therapy where they taught me to walk on shorter crutches that went halfway up my arms instead of under my arms. I had a little trouble with that because it was more weight on my legs, but I did the best I could for as long as I could.

The one thing that I did not like at the school was when they had doctors come in to see several of the students each month. They would put a pair of very short shorts on us and a halter-like top, and then have us individually go into the room with all the staff members present and these doctors as well. They would have me walk in front of them so they could see how crooked my body was. We had to do that twice a year. I realize that it was to see if there was anything they could do to make things better, but I just felt so "naked" in front of that crowd of people. I expect that they would do things more carefully and respectfully today.

My favorite experience was Occupational Therapy. The therapist that I had asked me what I would like to learn to do. I told her about the secretary that I saw in Dr. Anne's office whose hands were very crippled up, but she could type on the typewriter faster than I had ever seen before and I wanted to learn to do that. So, I began learning how to type. What a blessing learning how to type and developing that ability has been in my life. Now in the computer age, it is absolutely necessary and it has been a great aid to me throughout my life.

An Unhappy Encounter with the School Bus Driver

While attending school in Jamestown, myself and the other Day Students would get picked up for school by a station wagon (this was our "school bus"). On one of the days that I was finishing classes a few minutes before 4:00 p.m. when school finished, I began gathering all my books and headed back to the area where the station wagon was waiting for us to take us home. It was a very long walk back to the garage, so when I got there, I needed to sit down and rest a bit. I was the first student to arrive and others were not yet there.

The driver opened up the door for me to get into the car. He then climbed in and began touching me inappropriately, and lucky for me, the other Day Students came out to get in the car and the driver quickly got out.

All the way home I was confused why this man did this to me. When I got home, I told Mom about it and asked her: "Why did he do that?" She was so mad and she told me to get into the car. She then drove me to the school and made me tell Dr. Anne what the driver did. Dr. Anne first told my Mom that I must have made it up. Mom told her that I wouldn't have even known how to make that up and also told her that she would not bring me back to school until that driver was gone.

A few days later, Mom called me from my room and the driver was there, and he asked me to tell my Mother that I made up the story. I looked at him and said, "I did not make it up, you did do as I said you did, and you know it as well as I do." By the following Monday, a new van pulled up to pick me up and a new driver also. I was back in school. The "bus" was never in the back of the school any longer. Instead, they picked us up and dropped us off in the front of the school.

Fun Times with "The Wheelers"

I had a lot of fun and engaging experiences while attending school in Jamestown. On Wednesday night each week, I would go to the school to practice wheelchair square dancing. That's right, we had a wheelchair square dancing group and we were called "The Wheelers." The callers for the square dancing were Howard Clemens and his lovely wife, Evelyn.

I absolutely loved square dancing. I liked being at the school after hours and mingling with the students. The Wheelers square danced on *Polka Party*, which was a weekly television program, and we also performed in several other places in the area. The girls wore white blouses and red jump dresses while the boys wore white shirts, red ties and black pants, so we even had our own square dancing outfits and looked very professional.

All of us were in manual chairs, so when we would "Allemande left" (take left hands and turn halfway to the left) the guys would give us an extra spin, and we would have so much fun that the audience had a lot of fun watching us. Some of the dancers would rear up on their back wheels and balance as we started. I never did master that one. I got plenty of headaches trying as I reared back and hit the floor! So, I didn't do it when we were out professionally. We brought in a good amount of money for the school by performing and had a lot of fun doing it.

Shirley Ann Stockford in formal photo, teenage years, in Jamestown, North Dakota (circa 1965).

Other Fun Times at School

As I mentioned earlier, I really enjoyed it when I was at the school with the other students in Jamestown. The school was designed for students like me who had particular needs and I also enjoyed connecting with them socially.

They had a big area in the school near the dorms that was called the Day Room. It was a large room where we would all gather together. Some of them smoked in there occasionally but mostly it was a time of being together and socializing.

At the school, there were frequently tours that came through so that others could see what the school had to offer. One particular time two of my friends, Mary and Judy, were goofing around and saw the tour coming down the hall towards the Day Room. Judy was in a wheelchair and was able to stand up, appearing to be perfectly normal, while Mary was able to walk on crutches. Judy, while sitting in her chair was in front of Mary, and Mary placed her hands on Judy's head and said, "I command you to stand and walk!" Then, Judy stood up from her chair and began to walk across the room.

One of the people on the tour said, "They really do perform miracles here!" Everyone in the Day Room began to laugh out of control. That was an example of the fun and engaging times we enjoyed with each other.

Hearing Aids and Music Memories

Attending school in Jamestown brought some significant changes into my life, as I received assistance in how to manage some of my physical difficulties. However, it also stretched me because I had to learn new things and also had to adapt to new activities and resources.

I had some difficulties with my hearing abilities but at the school they worked with our family so that I could receive new hearing aids. This was helpful for me in being able to hear better. However, music began to be more intrusive to me after I received and adjusted to using two hearing aids that helped me to hear better.

I came to enjoy music and the different artists and programs that were popular in that era. For example, I listened to programs like *The Ed Sullivan Show*, *The Dean*

Martin Show (this was my Dad's favorite!), or any country and western shows. I remember when Elvis Presley first began to become popular, and oh, how I loved Elvis. Then on *The Ed Sullivan Show* they introduced the Beatles from England! That was another awesome event I remember to this day. Dean Martin and Jerry Lewis were my favorite comic team.

I enjoyed Country and Western music along with my Mom. She would buy albums and Jessie and I would lay on the floor by the stereo and listen to the music we liked. I remember many times that Jessie would write down the words to the songs and I would memorize the words with her. Jessie let me see the words she wrote and then I understood the sounds I was hearing in the music, which helped me to love music. Dad enjoyed evangelist programs on television, as well as a lot of Christian programs. We all watched the shows *I Love Lucy, Bonanza, Maverick, The Carol Burnett Show* and countless other wonderful programs.

Moments of Memory

During the time that I attended school from 1960 to 1966, there were occasional incidents that stood out in my memory. Here were a couple of unique ones that I experienced.

First, one year it was late March and we had a severe blizzard in which it snowed for three days. I had never seen so much snow in my life. When things were pretty much dug out so we could get to school again, I remember that we pulled up in front of the school and we had to go through a tunnel of snow to get to the front door of the school. There were people that tried to walk on the snow and sunk down many feet below the snow and they had a very difficult time getting out. What a memory!

Also, it was in 1963 when one of the most shocking and memorable experiences occurred. I was attending class in Mr. LaMont's History class (at the High School) and Mr. LaMont brought a television down the hall to our class. He turned on the television and the TV announcer said, "President Kennedy has just been shot!" My heart skipped beats as I listened and along with most of the nation joined in prayer in hopes that he would live. Everything seemed to move in slow motion as we waited to hear if he was still alive.

As the days went by, President John F. Kennedy slipped away from life and we all felt a great loss. When they caught Lee Harvey Oswald I thought everything would be more at peace; but then, when we were watching another newscast, we actually saw Jack Ruby walk up to Harvey and shoot him. I was in shock. It seemed to be unreal. I was young but I still knew that something was not right about what had happened and was afraid of what could happen to our country. I honestly believe that history was altered by President Kennedy's assassination. It was quite a dramatic and memorable event in my young life. It was almost too much for me to bear. For many years I could not get these images out of my mind, and even today, I can see it as if it were yesterday.

Miss Bergstrom and a Love for Shakespeare

My last few years at the school in Jamestown were spent completing High School. Miss Bergstrom became one of my favorite teachers in High School. She was a new teacher just out of college and she loved English Literature. My goodness! I had never even heard of Shakespeare and certainly did not understand his writing! Miss Bergstrom decided that our English class was going to focus on English Literature. My heart sunk! She had us read one paragraph and I could not understand one word of it.

She then gave us a quiz. I was lost! I happened to glance at the other students wondering if they understood this topic, and accidentally saw one of the other student's paper and I wrote down her answer. I felt awful.

I waited until after class and went to Miss Bergstrom and asked her if we could talk privately. We went to a room where no one else would hear and I confessed that I cheated and told her I didn't understand Shakespeare at all. She asked me if I would be willing to spend an hour a day with her and learn how to understand Shakespeare. I excitedly said that I would.

We spent the year doing just that and meeting regularly. By the end of the year I absolutely loved Shakespeare and many different types of poetry. We had our final exam for the course and it was easy for me because of our studies together. To my surprise, the next day there was no grade on my paper when she handed them back to all of us. After handing the papers back, she then came over to me and another student and asked us if we had cheated. I looked her in the face confused and said, "No, I did not cheat." She asked the other student the same question to which they said "no" also. She gave me an A on my paper and a zero on the other student's paper.

I can't tell you how many times that moment had such an effect on me. Not only did I never cheat on anything that I had accomplished, but I always wanted my name to be known for my honesty. I was grateful to the Spirit of the Lord for prompting me to go to her at the beginning of the year and being honest with her right from the start. As a reward, I received a great knowledge of Literature that I very much enjoyed. I would have never tried to learn that on my own. My experience with Miss Bergstrom was a positive experience and her teaching efforts blessed my life and gave me a knowledge of Literature that I have enjoyed ever since.

Taking Final Exams

During my Senior year of High School, I gained a greater appreciation for Mathematics. I really wanted to do well in my Final Exams. I decided beforehand that since we did not have a time limit, I was going to double-check my answers to make sure I had them right.

Mr. Arnesson was our teacher and he had no use of his arms. He was able to walk slowly with his hands tight against his body. He would use his toes to write and grade our papers. I always admired him.

When giving us our exam papers to fill out, we each went to our own desks and I began working on my paper. I worked hard to make sure that each answer was done correctly, and did each problem twice to make certain it was right. One student, that I also admired and was considered a genius, was also taking this test. His name was Gary. He was in a car accident a few years before and came back to school in his early twenties.

Mr. Arnesson would walk from classroom to classroom to make sure we were all being honest as we did our exam papers. It was not typical for me to be taking so long, so he walked down to check on me and saw that I was working on my paper. He walked behind me to find another student that was cheating and I heard what was going on but I kept working on my own paper. I finally finished and took my paper to his desk and left to go home on the bus.

When we got our exams back in that class, Mr. Arnesson announced that half of the class passed the test. My heart sunk! He gave Gary his paper back first and Gary got about 95 on his paper. When I got mine back I was so excited as I had gotten a 98! I was beaming and my had work had paid off. Gary could not believe that I got a better grade then he did! I had the highest grade of the class! He said, "You can't get a higher grade than me, I am smarter than you!"

Shirley Ann Stockford, HS graduation photo, 1966.

Taking final exams brought us to the completion of our High School experience and graduation. I was very blessed to attend the Crippled Children's School and receive a quality education, as well as association with fellow students and teachers who understood my physical and other needs. I enjoyed my time there and learned things that would help me as I moved forward.

Senior Prom and High School Graduation

The celebration for our High School Graduation in 1966 included a graduation party with a live band and a banquet. It turned out to be a very memorable occasion. This also was treated as our "Senior Prom" experience.

As noted, we had a live band for our graduation party. This event turned out to be my very first live band experience and I will never forget it. The school had been given a very pretty pink dress for someone to wear to the Prom and they helped me to have it fitted in Home Economics class. I felt like the belle of the ball! We had a banquet and listened to the live band afterwards.

My Mom rarely let me stay up very late and my ride was not going to bring me home until after ten o'clock at night. So, I called Mom and told her about the live band and that I needed to stay longer because Mary would not be bringing me home until later. She was quite upset with me, and even though she gave in and let me stay at the party, I remember feeling so bad that Mom was upset with me. I did enjoy my first experience with a live band however! It was a memorable event to commemorate our graduation experience.

I officially graduated from the Crippled Children's School in Jamestown in June of 1966. My small graduation class consisted of seven High School graduates. When I came home from graduation, it seemed so strange not to have to go to school again. I had much learning ahead but life would bring me many new experiences.

Shirley Ann Stockford, second from right, and fellow high school graduates in class graduation photo, 1966, in Jamestown, North Dakota.

Chapter 14
Into Adulthood and Its Challenges

Graduation and Marriage and More

I graduated from the Crippled Children's School as a high school graduate in June of 1966. My small graduation class consisted of seven High School Graduates. I was proud of that accomplishment and owe much gratitude to my fellow students and the teachers in Jamestown who helped me with my education.

Having been born in April 1947, I was nineteen years old when I graduated from high school in 1966. It was a turbulent time in America. There was political upheaval with the "hippie" movement and the assassination of figures like President John F. Kennedy and Martin Luther King, Jr. Many people questioned things like the Vietnam War and the civil rights movement made a major impact, as did the effort to focus on women's rights.

In my own life, the late 1960s were also a time of change and some turbulence. The transition to adulthood was not necessarily an easy one for me. In some ways I was an adult, but in many other ways I had much to learn and the world was not always friendly and supportive to me. My family also had challenges with things such as making ends meet and my dad's challenges with alcohol use. However, we loved each other and maintained good relationships.

For me, life as a young adult with some handicaps did not make things very easy. It was not easy for me to get around and I was no longer occupied by all the tasks of school. I was interested in working but most places were not willing to take a chance on me. It was a challenging time.

Searching for Work Opportunities

One of the major transitions into young adulthood involves working to support yourself and contribute to your family economically. I had learned to work hard growing up because both of my parents worked very hard. My mother, especially, showed me an example of hard work with all of her efforts to support us and in running the Stockford Home for the Aged. I had assisted her with many tasks for years while growing up and so had some experience in care for others and managing the tasks of daily living.

Shirley Stockford as a young adult with dog at home.

As already noted, I graduated from high school in 1966, and when I came home following graduation it seemed strange that I no longer had to attend school again. I soon went to the Employment Office to check on the possibility of getting a job to keep myself busy.

The job counselor that I visited with at the time was not very encouraging. He looked at me and without much reflection he decided that I would never be employed. He voiced his opinion about that and it just left me feeling down and discouraged. He did not really believe in me. However, he was right at that time to a point—people were just not willing to give me a chance to prove that I could work.

Although I helped out in our family care facility for the aged, I was not able to get a job on my home until several years later in 1975. At that time, I began working at the Tumbleweed Motel in Jamestown, North Dakota. I soon loved working there and did my best to be the best clerk that she had at the hotel. There are more stories from this period which will come a bit later. But prior to this experience, there were some other events and challenges in my young life.

An Unexpected Marriage

My older sister, Jessie, had gotten married a few years earlier in December 1964 at the age of 19. Similarly, my mother and father had married when she was still relatively young. So, it was not unusual for a young woman to marry quite young in those days, though it would be considered very young today. But back then? It was normal!

One thing I did not really expect at the time was getting married myself, but I did have a social life and I enjoyed positive relationships with others. Since I had graduated, I also wanted to "spread my wings" and have some adult experiences that seemed to be part of adulthood. During the year after graduation, I had a variety of experiences and also some frustration since I was unable to find employment.

Soon I met a man who became interested in me and his name was Andy Smith (pseudonym). We met in 1966 during an activity when I was at the Crippled Children's School. We became good friends and by March of 1967 we were pretty serious about each other and having a relationship. Andy was physically disabled in his walking ability, as he walked with his toes pointing inward (some referred to it as a "pigeon-toed walk"), though he was still able to walk long distances. He was a little guy about five feet and six inches tall and he weighed about 150 pounds.

One day Andy asked me to marry him. We went together to get our blood tests and then he brought me a ring. I went home to show my mother the ring and she was quite angry. She told me to give it back to him. I was quite surprised at her anger and refused to do that. Then, she took my crutches away from me so that I could not leave the house. The next day I told my mother that I would take the ring back to Andy and she gave the crutches back to me.

I began the slow, sad walk to Andy's house, where he lived with his parents and three siblings. It was not a long walk, just three blocks away there in Jamestown, but each step was painful for me as I didn't want to give him his ring back. For me, it seemed to indicate that this was a person who wanted and accepted me despite my physical struggles.

As I entered Andy's home, his mother and his father could see that I was feeling pretty upset. I told them why I was there. I tried to give the ring back to Andy and his mother said we didn't have to do that because I was of age. Then, right away his mother called her daughter and son-in-law on the phone in South Dakota. She told them that she wanted them to come and pick up Andy and I and to help us elope.

I was shocked but really didn't know how to respond to what was happening so quickly. Inside I was thinking this was not right, but thought it was because I was afraid of facing my mother. Well, their daughter and son-in-law arrived about an hour later and we were off to be married!

Shortly after we left, the police arrived at the Smith home and blocked all the doors and demanded that they let me come out. We were already gone at that point, but his mother also told them that I was of legal age and that I was probably already married to Andy. We were married by a minister that had been pre-arranged by Andy's parents. It happened so fast and suddenly I was married!

We did get married but not across the state line, instead it was in a little town in North Dakota, because we had to stay in the state because of the marriage license which we already had. I remember that when I was standing in front of the minister, I could hear a voice in my mind telling me to say "No" when I was asked if I wanted to marry Andy. But, I didn't understand why I was hearing it, nor did I realize that it was probably coming from the Lord. I didn't listen because Andy was there, as well as his sister and her husband, so I was too embarrassed to say no.

We had something of a "whirlwind romance" and so it was that we eloped and were married in March 1967. We needed to support ourselves and so we ended up going to Lawton, Oklahoma and looking for work there.

A Short Season in Oklahoma

While in Oklahoma, we were living with Andy's buddy Mitch, who was in the Army there, and his wife Bonnie. It was not the easiest situation. Mitch had gotten into some kind of problem and did not get paid his check for most of the time we were there. There was very little food and all of us were very hungry most of the time. For Andy, being disabled, it was difficult for him to walk, and so he was not able to find a job.

Outside our apartment window in Lawton there was a stairway that was a fire escape. We would go out there during the day or early evening just to be outside. I was sitting there by myself one day when one of the neighbor ladies came out and asked me if I was all right. I told her that I was fine and so she sat down with me for a while. She asked me if I was hungry and I said, "Yes, we all are." She went into her house and brought out a box of food and gave it to me. I went in and made dinner and when everyone came home there was a meal on the table waiting for them. The Lord blessed me so much when I didn't know where to go for help.

We were there for three months but did not end up doing anything in particular and so returned to North Dakota. It was during this time that I also became pregnant with my first and only child.

My Little Judith Ann

So, Andy and I met and married in March of 1967, and ten months later in December 1967 my little girl was born—Judith Ann. Judith Ann was born on December 20, 1967 and she weighed just five and a half pounds. Judith Ann lived just a day and a half but in that time she taught me a very special concept about life. She was a beautiful baby girl with long dark hair.

All of my life I had dreamed of the day that I would have my own children. I don't really think I understood what that meant but I wanted to have many children. When the day came that I found out I was pregnant with my first and only child, I was so excited. Andy, on the other hand, was not excited or supportive. He was very angry, as if I had done something bad, and this confused me. I didn't understand his outburst but the fact remained that I was pregnant. I didn't talk very much with Andy after that about things I thought about because he didn't seem to care much about communication between us. I just went through life one day at a time waiting for the day when my baby would be born. My cousin told me that I had a very bad case of morning sickness but I don't remember that. I remember being excited that soon I would have a baby in my arms.

I gave birth to her by Caesarean section and so was not able to see her until the next morning. When they began the delivery procedure, they tied both of my hands and arms out to the side and that alone was frightening to me. Next, they did something to attempt to deaden the area, as they were afraid to use a spinal anesthetic because of my condition of having had polio. They were concerned about whether my legs would be able to go back to normal functioning. As they began the surgery, the area was not anesthetized so that I couldn't feel it. I could feel everything. I felt the blood running down my side and I felt everything else. I remember screaming and I was terrified. I heard the doctor tell the nun to put me out because I was going into shock. She put a mask on my face to give me ether and told me to breathe slowly. I could not have breathed slowly if I wanted to since I was already hyperventilating as it was, so the ether burned my lungs because I inhaled it too quickly. I was so terrified that I began taking deep breaths in panic, and I began hearing the Lord's Prayer getting louder and louder in my mind.

I woke up and Judith Ann had been born. The next morning the nurse got me up on my crutches to walk down to see her. They had put Judith Ann into an incubator and she was laying in that incubator many feet away from the maternity window. The nurse beside her lifted her up so that I could see this little girl that looked just like I did when I was a baby. Long, dark hair—beautiful.

I could sense something was wrong. I knew she was in a lot of pain. I heard a voice in my heart, and it was her speaking to me through her spirit to mine, and she said "I am sorry, Momma." I didn't fully understand what I was hearing but I knew that she was going to die, just like my little brother Kenneth. I turned and looked at the nurse who was helping me walk and asked her, "What is wrong with her?"

She told me that there was nothing wrong with her, and that she was just in the incubator because she was a newborn baby. I turned back to my little Judith Ann and said, very calmly, "She is going to die." The nurse, of course, was stunned that I said that, but I knew from the words that Judith Ann's spirit whispered to mine that I would not be able to hold her.

The nurse helped me and as we walked back to my room, I noticed that they pulled the curtain shut where Judith Ann was in the nursery. A few minutes later, Dr. Lucy who was the attending doctor came in and told me that she was gone and had passed away. She died of a brain hemorrhage. She indeed was in a lot of pain. I didn't get to hold her and nor did I get to go to her funeral. The family decided since it was so close to Christmas that it was best that they didn't wait until after I got out of the hospital. Again, I had known a baby was going to die—my baby! I became a little more convinced that I must be an evil person because of this strange communication.

The concept that I learned from this experience with Judith Ann was that our spirits were able to communicate between each other. She indeed spoke to me and knew who I was—her mother. That had such a powerful effect upon me and I didn't know why.

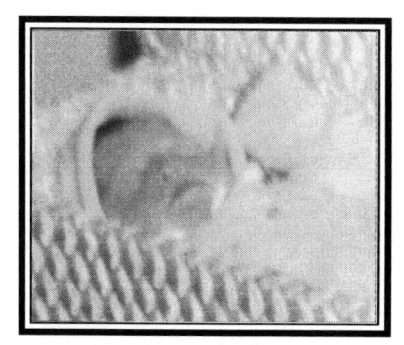

Baby Judith Ann, 1967.

The evening before Judith Ann died, they knew that she was going to die and so they called my minister from the Methodist Church to come by and baptize her. Reverend McDonald, who was from the United Methodist Church, came and did a baptism on her, and then he came in afterward and gave me a white handkerchief with a cross on it. My heart sunk. A handkerchief was all that I had to hold instead of my little baby girl. He told me after she died that Judith Ann would not go to purgatory because he had baptized her. I kept looking at the handkerchief and had a lot of confusing thoughts going through my mind.

I was totally confused and so hurt by his words. They didn't make sense to me. Purgatory? The Cross? Where was my little girl going? I never even got to hold her! My mind was spinning in so many directions that I didn't know what I was supposed to feel. I was numb and in shock.

My heart pondered those words from the minister for many, many years! I knew that I was supposed to remember this idea from him and get some comfort but the thoughts just could not come together. Instead, I felt confused. How could a little child sin? She was so perfect in my eyes—how could she have sinned? What can a little child do that would ever send them to purgatory if they died as a child without baptism? What about all those born dead (stillborn)? Were they condemned? This statement just didn't make sense to me.

I struggled with this statement until years later, when in 1973 I began listening to the missionaries from The Church of Jesus Christ of Latter-day Saints. Though this story comes a bit later, this portion of it is relevant here. The missionaries taught me that all children are "alive in Christ," and thus they are perfect and have no need for baptism. That made sense to me! Little children have no need for baptism for they are perfect! I learned that when a child is eight years old, then they are baptized in the Latter-day Saint faith because then they are old enough to know right from wrong. How beautiful this was to me!

Life began to take an unexpected twist for me as I discovered that the world I lived in was not as safe as I previously thought it was. I had a tough time coming home from the hospital without Judith Ann. When they wheeled me into the front room, I saw a picture on the television set that looked exactly like Judith Ann and I broke out crying. Mom said to me, "Stop it!" I looked at her in shock, confused at her outburst, but I turned off my feelings instantly. I was not able to easily show people what I was feeling after that. It seemed like showing my feelings was a sign of weakness.

I was filled with grief after Judith Ann's passing and it was a struggle to understand why she had died. It was very difficult to deal with that loss. My heart ached due to this loss and that I had not been able to hold her and raise her. I plunged into a deep depressive state where I didn't talk to anyone very much. I kept on going even though nothing felt real. But I had some comfort from my family members and also from my Heavenly Father.

Turning 21 and More Adult Challenges

In April 1968, I turned twenty-one years old and looked back on the past two years. I had graduated from high school, gotten married and eloped, struggled to find any employment, and dealt with my first pregnancy and the loss of a precious child. It had not been an easy time. There were some continuing challenges that occurred in my personal and family life during this period.

One of the challenges that I faced and then overcame at the time was something more simple for others—learning how to drive! When I was a very young girl, a friend of my Dad's named Ted was talking with me and I asked him: "When I grow up will I be able to drive?" He told me that when I turned 21 years old he would be there and have a way for me to drive.

True to his word, on my 21st birthday Ted came to Jamestown and he and Dad set up a car so that I could drive with hand controls. He invented them for me. What a guy! Dad was my main driving teacher and I will never forget him telling me to always look far ahead, in which he meant to look where you are going and not in front of the hood. He said that way you will always be all right if you look far ahead to see where it is that you are going. At other times I went to the cemetery and practiced driving there. I would practice parking between two evergreen trees there. I even broke off my car radio antenna doing that! Other people kept joking with me about practicing my driving efforts in the cemetery, and said at least there wasn't anyone I would kill there because they were already dead!

John Stockford, Shirley's brother, during service in the Marines.

Another driving lesson happened with a neighbor who took me out to the highway to practice. I had just gotten my car back from the service station after having new brakes put on it. We were driving and I saw a tractor on the lane I was in up ahead. I was not familiar with this type of situation and didn't realize that they were going much slower than the flow of traffic. I was about to go into the left lane to pass him when I saw that someone else was passing me, so I applied my brakes to slow down. I had no brakes! The car kept advancing towards that tractor and I had no idea what to do. I kept trying to pump the brakes with no success. I was in a panic and I leaned forward and accidentally hit the horn. The person in the tractor then moved over to the right side of the road just as my car was going to pass him! Everyone passed each other safely and I went back to the service station to have them bleed the brakes! That was a very scary event for me! I knew that the Lord had protected me because I would not have known to honk the horn.

For me, another challenge was that things were changing in my family relationships. Jessie had gotten married and so we weren't together very much, and then my younger brother John grew up! John joined the Marines about this time and he was to be in the military for at least four years. I really had a hard time when he left. By this time, I was at home alone with Mom and Dad and all the residents of the Home for the Aged. I enjoyed them very much but was so lonely for John. He was stationed in San Diego. California. He would come home on leave for a while but would always have to go back.

The most challenging thing for me during this time was trying to deal with and accept the loss of my little daughter, Judith Ann. I was suffering from grief and depression that made me sad much of the time. Life was a struggle. Many years have passed by since I was married to Andy and I have thought about whether life would have been different for me if I had not followed the words of my in-laws at that time. However, I have to admit that I likely would not have changed it, as somehow I felt like I was following a plan that was set out for me. The most important thing of all was that I had a beautiful little girl. I never had the blessing of holding Judith Ann in my arms, as she was taken back home to Heaven so quickly, but she will always be mine if I prove worthy to return to our Heavenly Father's presence.

The Assault and the End of My Marriage

During the year following my daughter's loss, life was difficult and things did not get any easier. I was making an effort in my marriage with Andy but things were not always really positive with us. Then, an incident occurred that left me with trauma and also factored into the end of our marriage in 1969.

Shortly after Judith Ann died, I was in a bar with my husband Andy. I always sat in the booth alone while Andy was up to the bar with the other men. I don't remember if I had a drink or not because I never was one to drink much because of my Dad's alcoholism. I didn't want to become that way so I was pretty careful about that. As I noted, Andy was handicapped also and walked with his feet turned inward, and he was a little guy. This night at the bar turned into a traumatic night.

Andy came over to my booth and introduced me to a very large-built man that was a truck driver. I had a very bad feeling about him. Andy told me that we were going to go home and have a pizza together. In the meantime, this man sat next to me and kept rubbing my leg. I tried to get Andy's attention that I was afraid but he didn't see it. I kept trying to move away from him and finally said, "Andy, I want to go home!"

He insisted that this man was going to go with us. My heart began to beat rapidly not knowing what to do. I was afraid not only for myself but for Andy. The man kept pushing me until we were out the door. The man dropped Andy off and told him that we were going to get pizzas. He would not let me get out of the car. He forced me to drive to a dark area and the night of horror began for me.

I do not now remember a lot of things about that night, except that this man attacked me repeatedly and raped me and I feared for my life. I was sure he was going to kill me but he did not. My clothes were ripped and I was badly beaten. By the time I got home to Andy, I was pretty scared and beaten up and angry at the same time. When I was able to say anything, Andy told me to call the police.

I called the police and the officer who answered the phone was a friend of my Dad, which helped me to be able to at least say something to him. To my surprise he said to me, "Shirley, go take a shower, go to bed and forget about it, no one is going to believe you." I was stunned. I never told Andy what he'd said.

I hung up and from that point on, I was not able to stand being around Andy or to talk with anyone about it. I was just so numb. I don't think I spoke another word for a few days. In my mind, I did not trust my husband anymore. We were soon to be divorced.

After I was assaulted following my daughter's death, my state of mind was pretty unsettled. I was afraid of everyone. I felt like I must have done something that made this man think it was all right to do this to me. It took me a long time to get over the fear I felt. Somehow, I don't think anyone ever gets over the fear of being attacked once they go through something like this. My emotions were at the limit. I had recently lost my daughter and then this happened to me. I left Andy and just wanted to be alone. Our divorce was finalized in 1969.

However, he and his friends (Mitch and Bonnie) wanted us to get back together. They came to see me one day and asked if I would go on a double date with Andy if they were with us. It was their hope that we would get back together. I then got a call from Andy asking me if I would go on a double date with him just to be able to see each other again. I gave in but really was not feeling good about the idea. We were then divorced and I didn't want to go back to that again. So, he came with his buddy and his wife and we went to a drive-in movie together.

In the middle of the movie, Andy kept trying to kiss me and then started trying to make out with me. It turned out to be a wrestling match. I fought with him and when he would not leave me alone I got angry and got out of the car. I was determined to walk back to the city. The outdoor movie theater was out of town and I just started walking. Suddenly, I felt pure fear in my heart. I looked around and realized that there was no way I could walk back to town safely. I froze right where I was standing, well aware that someone was watching me. Finally, Andy's buddy Mitch came and asked me to get back in the car and he would take me home. I never saw Andy again.

Section 3
Finding Faith and Battling Hardships

While still in her young adult years, Shirley Stockford met and married a man who she moved with to Texas. There, in El Paso, Texas, Shirley came into contact with missionary representatives of The Church of Jesus Christ of Latter-day Saints. She had already been engaged in a religious search and this encounter with Latter-day Saint missionaries led her to investigate their religious message. Her positive experiences and direction from the Lord resulted in a series of miraculous events that led her to become a member of The Church of Jesus Christ of Latter-day Saints in 1973.

Despite this positive development in her life, she also faced hardships and struggles in the time period that followed. Her second marriage did not last and ended in divorce, along with her loss of two step-daughters when that relationship was completed. She tried to pursue education but ultimately returned to North Dakota after an unsafe encounter. In the following years, she went through a period of personal wandering but eventually began working at a hotel in Jamestown.

While working in the hotel industry, Shirley met and married her third husband but it was a difficult marriage. She went through many ups and downs in her life and relationship from 1977 to 1985, when she finally took steps to free herself from an abusive relationship. For a time, they lived in Pelican Rapids, Minnesota, where she ran a group home for disabled or aging individuals. This was a successful enterprise but in time it became too much work to do on her own. Shirley moved to Fargo, North Dakota, and there took steps to begin a new phase of life via divorce and a new chapter. She also deepened her religious commitment in these years and was blessed by her faith-based associations.

Chapter 15
My Search for Truth

Searching for Truth and Finding Answers

In addition to the turbulence in my personal life and the difficulties that I had experienced since becoming an adult, there also seemed to be a religious turmoil going on around me at this time of my life. For example, common things that I heard at the time were references to "Jesus Freaks" and demeaning terms referring to the loving Lord Jesus Christ. It really bothered me and I spent a lot of time thinking about the things happening in my own life.

The loss of my daughter Judith Ann had left me unsettled and with many religious questions. In addition, I was dealing with fear and rejection in my life due to the other traumatic experiences and the divorce I had gone through. By 1969, I was single and living in Jamestown and trying to deal with these challenges. After my divorce from Andy, I spent a lot of time looking into different religions. I was confused at the way each of them taught different things and wondered why it was that they were different. If there was only one God, why wasn't everything similar? I was a member of the Methodist Church at this time, but felt like I was just not being told what I wanted to hear. So, I kept looking into other faith communities and hoped to find the right one for me. This is my story of searching for truth, traveling to Texas and starting a new chapter in my life, and finding answers to my religious search.

Living in Jamestown and Taking Next Steps

From 1969 forward I spent the next three years living in Jamestown and being involved with a variety of activities. Although I wanted to work, I still had very little success in finding meaningful employment away from home, and so I helped out my parents at the Stockford Home for the Aged and provided care for the residents. This experience was helpful to me for when I would work in this field a few years later.

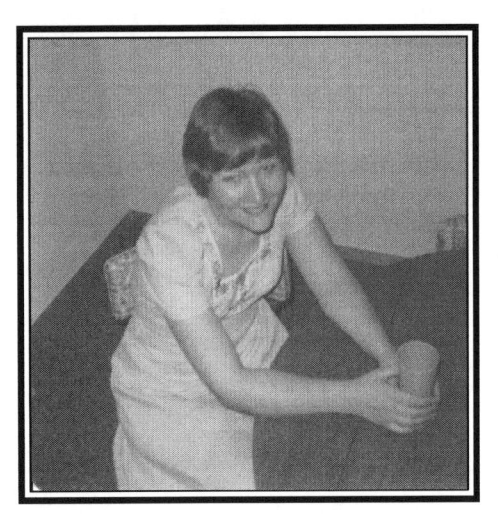

Shirley Stockford, 1972-73, living in Jamestown, ND.

My favorite place that I hung out was at Lil's Pizza Palace, which I remember well especially for the music and the great atmosphere. She had jukeboxes at each table in there, so I could go in and get a soda and then sit and listen to the jukebox as others put their quarters into it and made song selections. I used to love sitting there and listening to the music for hours at a time. Lil was very kind to me and would let me stay there as long as I wanted to visit. I usually stayed there until almost dark and then would walk the three blocks to my apartment.

On one occasion when I was walking home by myself, I was just about home when a car pulled up in the alley blocking my way home. There were two men in the car. Both of them looked at me and began getting out of the car and I felt very unsafe. I got scared and looked around to see if there was anywhere I could go to get away from them.

Just then, one of the local police officers came up on his motorbike and pulled in between them and me. They returned to their car and left. The police officer was familiar to me. He was getting married in a couple of weeks and was always very kind to me when he saw me. He came up to me and said he would help me get home safely. I thanked him and walked with him to my apartment. He opened my door for me and gave me back my key.

I went into the apartment and to my surprise he came in. I was pretty shaken up from the encounter with the men in the car and so I had to sit down. He came over and sat beside me and began kissing me. I began laughing hysterically. He asked me what was so funny and I just looked at him and told him, "You just saved me from God knows what, you are getting married in two weeks—and now you're hitting on me!" Needless to say, he got up and left.

It was also during this time that I had the encounter with Andy where he tried to see me again and start something by going on a double date to the drive-in movie theater. Of course, that did not work out but it was also a scary experience. Although these were uncomfortable experiences, I am grateful that I was somewhat protected and more harm did not come to me during these incidents.

When I was twenty-five, I met a lady who was a volunteer for The Salvation Army, and she gave me some pamphlets about the Bible. I so much enjoyed learning more about the Bible that I wanted more, so I began going to other churches to see what I could learn and maybe find a church that was the Savior's church. I went to several different ones and was surprised that they didn't teach the same things. I was confused. Why were they different? In fact, why were there so many different religions? I kept searching.

Marrying Levi and Moving to Texas

About three years after my divorce, I met Levi Walters while living there in Jamestown. It was a time of a lot of activity in Jamestown. The natural gas pipeline crew members were working in the area and so we saw them frequently. They were often in town and they were everywhere.

I was visiting at Lil's Pizza Palace one day, just listening to jukebox music, when I saw members of the pipeline crew coming into the place. One of the pipeline workers came over to my table and began talking to me. His was name was Levi Walters. This happened not long after the incident with Andy at the movies, and Levi told me that he was at the drive-in movie theater that night and saw me get out of the car and begin walking towards town. I felt comfortable talking to him. He mentioned that he was about to come and see if he could help me, when Mitch came over and got me back into the car and took me home.

Levi and I became friends after that conversation and we began associating with each other and started a relationship. We were married in 1972.

Levi began working at Haybusters Manufacturing and he was a welder. His boss was Joe Anderson, a brilliant man who invented the Haybuster Stacking Farming Machine. It was so amazing what that machine could do. I met Joe while Levi was working for him, a very nice man. Joe was murdered a few years later and his killer was never found.

Although he had been working on the pipeline crew and then in manufacturing, Levi decided that he wanted to go back into the United States Army and so he re-joined the military after our marriage. He was gone for three months in training and so I waited for him in Jamestown. While I was waiting for him, I continued to look around for a church to join. I visited several different churches but I just could not feel that any of them were right in my mind.

When Levi first was released from the Army he was a Sergeant, and he had thought that he could return and continue to be a Sergeant. However, he found out that he had to begin again at boot camp as an E-2. So, he spent three months in that training and we met up again in Jamestown after his boot camp experience. We drove together from Jamestown, North Dakota to where he was now stationed at Fort Bliss in El Paso, Texas. It was there in El Paso that I would have spiritual experiences that changed my life forever.

Touched By a Miracle

One of the things that I was looking for in my young life was the influence of our Heavenly Father. I was searching for more understanding of life and also the peace that comes from knowing God's love and truth. I was wondering if He had a plan for my life. Soon, things began to unfold in my life that continued my spiritual awakening.

Levi came to Jamestown after his boot camp training to pick me up. We packed up a U-Haul truck so that we could travel to El Paso, Texas. I hadn't told Levi that I was searching for a church at the time. I just kept it to myself.

On the way to El Paso, we were driving through New Mexico, which was a dry state as for alcohol, and they were doing a lot of road work so we were just driving on a very narrow, two-lane road. The traffic was awfully crowded and we had a couple of semi-trucks in front of us as well as many more behind us. Levi was impatient and eager to get ahead of the two semi-trucks in front of us, but he couldn't see in front of them to know if it was safe to use the oncoming lane to pass them.

Behind us, one of the semi-trucks soon pulled out into the oncoming lane and began to pass the other trucks behind us and us as well. Levi made the remark that they must be able to see further ahead than we could so he was going to pull out and follow behind that passing semi-truck. He assumed that if it was safe for that truck to pass then it would be safe for us as well.

As Levi pulled out to follow and edged into the oncoming lane behind the passing semi-truck, the semi-trucks around us closed in the gap we had just pulled out of in the one lane. Another semi-truck pulled into the oncoming lane behind us also. While Levi was passing, I looked ahead and I saw a red pickup truck coming head on at the truck in front of us!

We were trapped. There were four semi-trucks on our right, a semi-truck in front of us and also one behind us, and a red pickup truck headed straight for us all. I closed my eyes and NOTHING HAPPENED! I opened my eyes and our pickup and the semi-truck in front of us were still there, and the one behind us was still in back of us, BUT we were instead in the ditch on the right side of the road! The two semi-trucks that were on our right were now on our left and still on the road. I actually looked to my left on the other side of Levi and watched the red pickup pass by them on their left side with nothing in his way!

I have no explanation for this incident other than that we were touched by a miracle. Somehow, the Lord had picked up our pickup truck, as well as both semi-trucks in front of and behind us, lifted us up from the left side of the road, and safely placed us in the ditch on the right side of the road, away from the oncoming red pickup and over the two semi-trucks that had closed in the gap we had left!

Levi looked at me and said, "What just happened?!" He then saw that we were now in Texas and he saw a bar and pulled over into the lot and he was literally shaking. We went into the bar and Levi got a drink. Just then all of the semi-truck drivers that were almost in the collision with us came in to have a drink as well, and they also were shaking and saw Levi and asked him, "What happened?!"

I thought it must have been my imagination, but Levi saw the same thing that I did. The semi-truck drivers did too. None of them had any explanation for what happened either. They were all pretty shook up. All of them commented on how their trucks were literally picked up and moved to another place, and that there was no way we could have avoided that accident—but we did. I knew in my heart that the

Lord protected us and there was some reason that we were supposed to get to El Paso.

Living and Working in El Paso

We were living in El Paso, Texas when Levi told me that we would go to church on the military base because it would help him gain rank faster. I laughed but it turned out to be true. I went to church with him but it didn't feel complete to my understanding. I kept on looking for answers to my questions. I started taking Bible lessons by mail. I really enjoyed doing that. I wanted more though.

One time, Levi came home from the Base and told me that we were invited to go to a party on Base. It was a formal party and he needed me to get dressed up very fancy. I had a friend, Margo, who had a dress for me, and she fixed my hair so it was up and had many ringlets down the back. I looked pretty good! We went to the party and there were a lot of people there that were drunk and I didn't like that, but I was told by Levi to make a good impression so I kept smiling and talked with whoever came over to talk to me. There was one particular older man who had a lot of medals on his uniform. He and I hit it off pretty well. He was very kind and easy to talk to during the event. When we left Levi asked me if I knew who I was talking to, but of course, I didn't. He said that man was a four-star General! Needless to say, Levi was very impressed with me. He did gain rank quickly and was pretty proud of himself.

While we were living there, Levi wanted me to be able to walk better on my legs. I was having trouble with some braces that I was wearing on both of my legs, so he talked to the doctors at William Beaumont Hospital on the base and they decided I needed surgery. I had surgery on my left leg to lengthen the cord in the upper part of my leg so that I could stand a little straighter.

While recovering in the hospital, I was watching television and there was a spiritual healer on with a particular television program. I was so surprised at the things I was seeing her do on that program. The healer appeared to be healing people of all kinds of infirmities. It seemed really strange to me as I had never seen anything like it in my life. I sat wondering if the Lord really did still heal people like he did in the Bible. I didn't talk to anyone about it, I just kept thinking about the Savior and his healing efforts and wondered why I had never heard of this before. It gave me a lot to think about.

Finding the Lord's Kingdom

Also during the time that I was in the hospital, one day a beautiful Spanish lady came into the hospital and was placed in the bed beside me. She had an accident in which her wedding ring caught on a door hook as she was running out the door. It literally ripped all of the flesh and muscles off of her ring finger. I felt so sorry for her. I could not understand her because she didn't speak English.

Shirley, in 1974, living in Texas.

While she was there two young ladies came in and visited with her. These visitors came over to say "hello" and introduced themselves as sister missionaries for The Church of Jesus Christ of Latter-day Saints. They were kind and talked to me for a while before leaving. They asked me if I would let them come and see me when I got out of the hospital. I told them "yes" and figured that would be the last time that I would ever see them. However, true to their word, they did come to visit me several times after I returned home and while Levi was at work on the base.

Each time the sister missionaries came and visited with me, I listened to them and wanted to know more. They taught me about the Bible in a way that I had never known before. I was impressed that they carried their copies of the Bible with them. It reminded me of a Catholic funeral that I had attended many years earlier. At the viewing held on the evening prior to the funeral, a Catholic nun had a Bible that she was carrying. Later, I asked her about it and she told me that it had only been in the "last few years" (this was in the late 1950s) that the Catholic Sisters were allowed to read from the Bible and preach from it. That impressed me because I had been told by some that if we read the Bible from cover to cover, then we would die. Of course, that doesn't make sense. So, I began to read the Bible and I loved it! I was reading the stories that I had heard as a child in Sunday School! I enjoyed it when the sister missionaries came because I had been sending off for any kind of literature I could in search of the answers to my spiritual questions and they had many answers for me.

The sister missionaries continued to teach me until they told me that they were being transferred. They told me that the Elders would come to see me after they left the area. They were scheduled to come and visit on my birthday—April 17, 1973. I thought then that "Elders" meant some old men, plus it was my 26th birthday and Levi and I wanted to go out, so we left and missed that appointment. When we returned home to our apartment, there was a note on the door with a smiley face on it and it wished me a "Happy Birthday" and also that they were sorry they missed us. That impressed me. I was delighted and thought to myself, "That doesn't sound like old men!"

The next morning I was sitting on the floor of our apartment by the patio door and waiting for Levi to get home from the base, and I noticed two young men that walked by the patio door. I was so surprised that they were wearing full suits! In El Paso! About 80 degrees outside! I wondered what they were doing, but it didn't take long to get an answer because these two young men came to my door and introduced themselves as Elders from The Church of Jesus Christ of Latter-day Saints. I asked them: "Why are you called 'Elder'? You don't look old!"

These "old" men were not what I had expected. One was just 20 and the other was 26 years of age. I learned that the term "Elders" referred to their holding the priesthood of God. After giving me a cute smile, they told me that "Elder" is a priesthood office and doesn't refer to one's age. They were very kind young men and taught me some things and asked me when Levi would be home so that they could meet him also. We soon began taking some lessons from them and reading pamphlets about the LDS Church.

I had been searching for spiritual answers to my questions for some time. As they taught us, there were so many things that went through my mind as I listened and learned about the restored Gospel of Jesus Christ. As an example, Elder Horner and Elder Fry taught me more about the Bible and that little children were "alive in Christ." They taught me that little children do not have to be baptized as infants because they are pure and thus have no immediate need of baptism. Instead, they are not baptized until they are old enough to make that decision for themselves, and in The Church of Jesus Christ of Latter-day Saints they do not baptize children until they are eight years old.

This message and its truth touched my heart, as I'd had so many questions after Judith Ann's death as a baby. I had wondered how a little child could sin and why a child would be sent to purgatory if they died as a child without baptism. When I heard this truth, tears of joy ran down my face as I remembered the feelings I'd had about the handkerchief the minister gave to me when Judith Ann died. I felt strongly that what they told me was true. I had not told them about Judith Ann; the Lord and I were the only ones that knew. But as they continued to talk about the spirits of little children being sacred, the Holy Spirit witnessed to me in my mind that it had been Judith Ann's and Kenneth Allen's spirits that communicated to me all those years before, and not some evil power I possessed. My joy was so great, I could not talk anymore and broke down into tears so uncontrollable that the missionaries felt that they should go.

Another thing they taught us about that made an impression on me was about death and the resurrection of our bodies. Another huge question for me was whether we would ever have our own bodies again after we die. For me, with my physical handicaps, I had wondered about this question since I was a young girl. The missionaries taught me that when Jesus came back after his crucifixion and death, and then appeared to Mary, he said to "touch him not" because He had not been to see His Father yet. When He came again and visited his disciples, he was a resurrected being, which meant that He had his body and spirit restored to their proper form despite having gone through physical death. He came to show us that we will be resurrected just as He is.

These young missionaries, Elder Horner and Elder Fry, also taught us about living prophets and apostles, and that there was a living Prophet on the earth today. Harold B. Lee was the Prophet at the time in 1973. They taught us about the Bible and also about other scriptures that also were the word of God. One of these books of scripture, the *Book of Mormon*, told of a people that lived on the American continent six hundred years before Christ was born. This people came to the American continent from Jerusalem because the Lord led them away from there

LDS missionaries sharing their religious message.

before its destruction. The *Book of Mormon* also tells of another people that were totally destroyed because of wickedness, and who had come to this continent when the Lord confounded the language of people in the time of the tower of Babel. As soon as they taught me about the *Book of Mormon*, I began to read it that very night.

I mentioned earlier that I was troubled by the talk about "Jesus freaks" and such things during these years of my young adulthood. When I was baptized into the Methodist Church in Jamestown, North Dakota, at about the age of 15, Reverend McDonald explained to me about the death of Christ and many things prior to baptism, but it was quite confusing to me. Many things didn't make sense to me. Why had they crucified him when He had done so many good things to help the people? The Savior, had he been born anywhere else in the world, probably would have been believed in and not crucified. He performed miracles among the people so why did they crucify Him?

The missionaries taught me that when the Savior was chosen to come to the earth, He came as the Son of God and also the son of Mary (a mortal). Being born of Mary, He was subject to hunger, thirst, pain—just as we are. Being the Son of God, he was able to give up his life and take it again. The way that they explained it to me was so beautiful. Now, I knew that what happened to the Savior had to be done in order for the Savior to atone for the sins of the world. The sacrifice had to be done by one who was perfect in every way. His thoughts, words, and actions all had to be in perfect harmony with the laws of our Heavenly Father. He suffered in the garden of Gethsemane. If He had not finished what the Father sent him to do, all mankind would have been lost with no way to return to the Father's presence. These teachings clarified my understanding of the Savior and increased my love for Him.

There is so much more that I was taught in the two weeks of teaching that I then went through with the missionaries, but these are a few of the spiritual truths that touched my heart and made me feel that I had found the Lord's kingdom. With all the things that I had learned when studying other religions for the many years that I was searching, and then also with what I was then learning from the missionaries, I honestly was not certain of anything at the time. I felt the need to take another step and find greater certainty through asking God for guidance.

My First Vision

After I began reading the *Book of Mormon*, I soon told the missionaries that I had read some of it and they encouraged me to pray to our Heavenly Father and ask him if the *Book of Mormon* was true. Further, they asked Levi and I specifically to pray about whether or not the things they had been teaching us were true. They had invited us to be baptized but wanted us to take this step in searching out the truth.

I decided that if I was going to get baptized, then I had better do as James directed in the Bible (see James 1:5) and ask God, the Eternal Father, in the name of Jesus Christ, if the things that the missionaries were teaching me were true. The missionaries had taught me about a young man, Joseph Smith, who was wondering about the same things I was searching for when he was about fifteen years of age. He wanted to know which church he should join and what was right. In 1820, Joseph went into a grove of trees to pray and ask the Lord which church he should join, as there were so many that it seemed too confusing for a boy so young to be able to make such a decision on his own. He had been searching since he was about twelve years old and studying the Bible, and he was concerned for the welfare of his soul and didn't want to make a mistake. He went to the Epistle of James in the New Testament, and there he saw a scripture (James 1:5) that said: "If any of you lack wisdom, let him ask of God, that given to all men liberally and upbraideth not; and it shall be given him."

So, believing that he would receive an answer and that he could know for himself, he decided to follow that counsel. While kneeling in prayer and praying vocally for the first time in his life, he saw a glorious light descending from above until it fell around him. In the middle of that light, he observed two personages, and one of them called him by name and said to him: "This My Beloved Son. Hear Him!" (see Joseph Smith–History 1:17).

After hearing this account of Joseph Smith and receiving the invitation to pray from the missionaries, I decided to do exactly that and ask Heavenly Father if the things I was learning were true. So, I did that the very night that they asked me to pray. I had been reading the *Book of Mormon* and barely finished the first few chapters and I wanted to know the answer to a specific question: "Were the things I was reading about a real people? Did they really live?"

Also, the missionaries had taught me about Joseph Smith and his prayer, and that if one lacked wisdom, then if one asked God with pure intent and believing that he or she would be answered then the truth would be given by God. I wanted to follow that example. Was this why the Lord preserved our lives when we would have surely been killed when we were driving through New Mexico? Was this the church that I was searching for?

I went into my bedroom and got down on my knees and offered up a prayer, a very simple prayer, as I was not accustomed to praying. I prayed with all my heart to know if this church, The Church of Jesus Christ of Latter-day Saints, was true. Was this His true church upon the face of the earth and was it true that the Savior is indeed the head of it? I prayed and asked if the *Book of Mormon* was true. Also, I wanted to know if the Prophet who was leading and guiding the Church was indeed the Lord's Prophet.

A feeling of great happiness filled my heart as I kneeled down and prayed to my Father in Heaven. I felt a calmness and peace in my room that I had not felt in a very long time. My room glowed with such a warm, peaceful light as I finished my prayer and went to bed. I climbed into bed with a beautiful feeling coming over me. My bedroom seemed to shine so brightly that night. Levi came in and went to bed also.

I was laying there awake and thinking about the many things the missionaries had taught me, and suddenly I felt like I was not in my bed. I felt like I was moving in space and looking through something like an opening in front of me, and then I beheld what you would call a "dream" or a "vision." As I looked through this open space, I looked upon a beautiful wooded area that I had never seen before, and then I saw a young boy kneeling and above him stood two persons—and my heart knew. In this beautiful vision I saw Heavenly Father and Jesus Christ conversing with Joseph Smith, and I knew that the boy was indeed Joseph and these heavenly beings talking with him and teaching him were our Heavenly Father and Jesus Christ. I knew with all my heart that the Savior is the head of His Church, that Joseph Smith was a Prophet of God, and that the prophets who live today are indeed prophets of God.

I wanted to stay, I wanted to see more, I wanted to see my Lord. As I tried to reach to touch them, I was suddenly in my bed again. I knew I had just seen a vision! At that point in time, I felt someone wake me and the vision disappeared and I was back in my bed. I looked at Levi and he was sound asleep so it was not him that touched me. I laid down and pondered the things which I had seen and knew in my heart, for myself, that the Church was true. Joseph Smith was a Prophet of God and the *Book of Mormon* was true.

I woke up the next morning and was excited about the missionaries coming back. I told the missionaries about my experience that next day. I went into the front room and saw a pamphlet that the missionaries left behind for me to read. I read it and on the back it said: "Scheduled date of Baptism: April 28, 1973."

Baptism into The Church of Jesus Christ of Latter-Day Saints

I smiled when the missionaries came again and I asked them about that date on the pamphlet. They asked me if that baptismal date was too soon for me. I told them I needed to ask Levi first. Well, Levi was not sure, and since it was Easter Sunday on the coming Sunday, he wanted to go to church on the base. So, that is what we did.

We were listening in church that Sunday as they talked, and the minister began to laugh when he was talking about the Savior's crucifixion on the cross. I looked at Levi, and he looked at me in the same instant, and he said: "Are you ready to go?" I smiled and said I was. We went out of the base chapel and got into our pickup truck and went to the Eighth Ward of The Church of Jesus Christ of Latter-day Saints there in El Paso. The missionaries were surprised to see us there! After how I had broken down crying, they said that they were afraid they had lost us. I told them just the opposite, that they had won us. Both of us were baptized on the 28th of April, 1973—right on schedule!

Shirley Stockford, age 27, living in Texas at the time of her baptism in The Church of Jesus Christ of Latter-day Saints.

I knew! I knew it was true. The Gospel of Jesus Christ has been restored to the earth after being taken away following the death of the Savior and the twelve Apostles of the Lamb of God being killed. The Dark Ages, as I was taught about in school, were no longer on the earth. The Lord reigns again.

I was 27 years old then and a heavy smoker. The missionaries told me that I had to quit smoking or I could not be baptized. I asked them for a blessing and threw away my cigarettes. So strong was my faith in that blessing, that I did not have any withdrawal symptoms after smoking for about 17 years and up to three packs per day. Miracles one after another followed me in that time leading to baptism and in the period that followed.

At my baptism were two special people, Gerald and Marza C. Gerald was then a counselor in the Bishopric and his lovely wife, Marza, was holding two children, one on each of her hips. I was so impressed with this couple and was sad when they moved to Belgium for his job. The Lord blessed me that this wonderful couple moved back from Belgium in about 1986 to Fargo, ND, and our friendship continued until Gerald died shortly after Charles (my husband then) had passed away. Marza and I celebrated our birthdays together each April with another friend,

Martha O. The three of us were so close that I felt a sistership with them and love them so much.

I was baptized on the scheduled date, just ten days after my 27th birthday, and I can truly say that on April 28, 1973, I went into the font and was baptized by one having the authority to do that sacred ordinance. When I got dressed after my baptism and went outside, I looked at the sky and trees and all around me. I remember feeling that I was looking at the world for the very first time. I literally felt that I had been born again. The colors were radiant and alive. It was as though a cloud of darkness had disappeared and the light of life opened up a whole new world for me to see. It was a very special day for me.

First Steps in a New Faith

I began studying as much as I could about the scriptures. Not only did I study the Old and New Testaments, but the *Book of Mormon*, the *Doctrine and Covenants*, and the *Pearl of Great Price* (books of Latter-day Saint scripture). I had a lot of negative responses to my decision to join the Church, but I knew then and I know now, that the Church is true.

I learned from my vision that Heavenly Father and Jesus Christ have individual bodies just like we do. They are glorified but look very much like us. I was happy about that knowledge because I had been taught that they were all in one big body of gas or power that was floating around in the universe. The doctrine of them being all in one had never seemed right to me. How could Jesus be praying to himself? Also, prophets testified of seeing Jesus standing on the right hand of His Father (an example of this was when Stephen was stoned to death by non-believers in the New Testament times).

I learned without a bit of doubt that Joseph Smith is a prophet of God, that the *Book of Mormon* was translated by the gift and power of God, and that The Church of Jesus Christ of Latter-day Saints is the Savior's church. I live in the dispensation of the fullness of times! What a joyful blessing! I live when the restored Gospel of Jesus Christ is on the Earth. Can you even sort all this out in your mind? I have been blessed to be here in this time when prophets and apostles are again on the earth. I was led to find the Church at the border of New Mexico where our lives were preserved so that I could be baptized. How grateful I am.

I learned and gained my own testimony that Jesus is the Christ. He lives. He that was crucified is indeed the Living Christ and has redeemed His people. I am grateful for my first vision that gave me such a powerful testimony and enabled me to find the true church of Jesus Christ.

One early experience following my baptism that I remember so well was when a General Authority of the Church was coming to visit El Paso Eighth Ward. A General Authority is a spiritual leader in the Church, such as one of the Apostles. I didn't really understand what an Apostle was yet at that time and I was seated in the front of the chapel waiting for the service to begin. Many people walked by to say hello and shake my hand. I got to the point that I was shaking so many hands that I automatically put my hand up to shake hands with everyone without looking up to see who they were. Then, I put my hand up when I saw someone was standing in front of me, and I had a feeling fill my heart that I had never felt before in my life. I looked up and I looked into his face, and I knew that this man was an Apostle of the Lord in every sense of the word or calling. It was a memorable experience.

I love the programs of the Church. The women's organization is called the Relief Society, which is the largest and oldest women's organization in the world. Women are taught homemaking skills, cooking, child care, marriage and family relations, you name it—whatever a woman is responsible for, well, they have lessons to fit the need. It is a wonderful program. Priesthood organizations also exist and they teach men the things that they need to do to care for their families and communities. It too is a wonderful program. The Sunday School classes each week teach us gospel principles and we learn about the Lord's word and each work of scripture. Young Men's and Young Women's programs prepare teens for young adulthood, missions, education, marriage, or whatever they will face in life.

I was baptized on April 28, 1973, and became a Latter-day Saint in the Lord's Church. I thought I was safe for the first time in my life. I soon found out that being a member of the Lord's Church doesn't exempt you from the trials of life.

Chapter 16
Troubles in Texas

One Step Forward and Two Steps Back

In 1972, at the age of 25, I had married for a second time and moved away from North Dakota to live in El Paso, Texas, where my then-husband Levi was stationed in the military. We were stationed at Fort Bliss and things went well for us during our first year there. We became involved in life on the military base and Levi increased his rank status.

Perhaps the most consequential thing for us was that in 1973 we met young missionaries from The Church of Jesus Christ of Latter-day Saints. We studied the gospel of Christ with them and were baptized as church members in April 1973. Although this positive change came into our lives, there were also other changes ahead that challenged us and would lead to some troubles in Texas.

Fun with Mindy and Mandy

While we were there living in El Paso, I was introduced to Levi's two little girls and they came to live with us. One day we received a phone call from his ex-wife, asking us if we would take their two girls because her health was not good.

Their names were Mindy and Mandy and they were ages four and five. I adored Mindy and Mandy and tried to be the best mother figure I could be to them. I made dresses for them to wear to church meetings. They received a Priesthood Blessing at church giving them each their name and blessing. I was so proud of them.

Our favorite time was in the evening when they took a bath to get ready for bed. I would sit on the floor next to the bathtub and play with them. I would make sure I didn't have my hearing aids on as I always ended up soaked, as we would have fun together with the soap bubbles and toys they had in their bath. At that time, they were four and five years of age. Mindy went to school and she loved it.

One day Mindy came home and told me about a boy that was teasing her because she wore this long cap that hung down her back almost to the floor. I told her: "You tell him, 'I know you are teasing me because you love me'." She giggled and felt better. To my surprise, she did exactly that! She came home laughing and told me that the boy was so embarrassed that he wouldn't bother her any more.

I loved them talking with me and telling about their day. As I mentioned earlier, I had always wanted to have children of my own and this experience brought me close to that. I took care of them for a year in 1973-74. This was one of the choice experiences of my life.

Sign at Fort Bliss, Texas.

From Harmony to Hardship

When I first met Levi and we went to El Paso where he was stationed in the military, I remember not feeling for a while like anything was real. I was still working through my feelings of loss and depression, as well as the fear I had from being assaulted. Also, I was searching for something to hang onto in my life that felt real, and that was part of my search for religious truth.

At the time of my baptism as a Latter-day Saint in April 1973, I remember coming out of the baptism and looking around and everything just felt colorful, bright and real. I felt that at last I had something concrete to hang onto in my life.

Life with Levi that year together as active members of the Church was wonderful. We had his two little girls with us and enjoyed our new life in the Church together.

We went back to Jamestown, North Dakota for Christmas and we all flew home to spend some time with Mom and Dad. This was the first time I had ever flown on an airplane and was petrified! Prior to leaving for Fargo, Levi and I had brought several things for the girls for Christmas. The girls and I got into the pickup truck to wait for Levi to come out and drive us to the airport. Unbeknownst to the girls, Levi was setting up all the Christmas gifts so that when we came home and opened the door, then the girls would see their presents and we would have our own Christmas with them when we returned to El Paso again. We had a wonderful time in Jamestown for a week and returned to have a glorious time with the girls, as we had Christmas all over again when they saw the presents when the door was opened to our apartment.

Despite these positive experiences, things would take a negative turn and this stable situation didn't last. After a while, I started noticing some things that were happening with Levi. He started smoking and drinking alcohol again rather than avoiding those things. I had a feeling that life was going to change.

I thought that we were doing well but then Levi got military orders that he was to go to Korea. He wanted me and the girls to go with him, so we called Levi's ex-wife and told her about it and she asked if she could come to see the girls before we left. Of course, Levi let her come. She arrived shortly before Easter. Levi had guard duty and so she slept in our room with me that night. The next morning, I heard Levi come in the door and I felt for some reason that I should pretend I was sleeping. Levi came in the bedroom and went over to her side of the bed. I felt my heart shatter as I knew they were kissing. I got out of the bed without saying a word and went out the door and closed it. I was numb.

Just then, the phone rang. It was our Home Teachers from church. I knocked on the bedroom door and said to Levi that our Home Teachers were on their way over to visit. So, they came out and when our Home Teachers were there, Levi told them that he wanted to be married to both of us. They were honest with him and told him that he had to choose between us because he could not be married to both of us. I was not the one he chose, as he finally said that he didn't want to be with me any more.

Our marriage deteriorated and came to a rapid end. He was sent overseas and I felt crushed, confused, and alone again. Saying good-bye to Mindy and Mandy was the hardest thing I had to do. It literally tore my heart to pieces. I now felt like I had lost three children of mine. We had gone from harmony to hardship and once again I found myself divorced. Our marriage ended in 1974.

Even though Levi didn't want to remain married to me after a time, I am most grateful that I was led to The Church of Jesus Christ of Latter-day Saints during this time period in Texas. I continued to participate in the Church in El Paso, and my Bishop encouraged me to get a Patriarchal Blessing. Bishop Nations was a kind man and he helped me to set up the appointment so that I could receive this blessing. A Patriarchal Blessing is a special, one-time priesthood blessing that is designed as a personal, spiritual message of guidance and counsel from our Heavenly Father for your personal life. I made an appointment and received my Patriarchal Blessing on March 27, 1974, from Patriarch Gordon Romney. What a blessing that was to my life. I had no idea what a strength that would become for me at the time I received it.

Turmoils in Texas and Back Home Again

Although I was dealing with confusion and hardship, I tried everything that I knew how to do in order to pull myself out of the deep feelings that I felt wrapping around me and consuming me. I lived in El Paso thinking that perhaps I could put everything back together again, but it wasn't possible.

I went to visit the two little girls one more time before leaving El Paso and Levi was overseas now. To my surprise his wife, the girls' mother, was now living with another man. I realized then that she had deliberately broken us up to get her girls back and then was going to dump Levi again. My feelings were sure mixed up at listening to what was going on. I understood her longing to get her girls back because they were so precious. But, to destroy a marriage and go to such extremes to be so non-caring about the other people involved really was a mystery to me. So, she divorced Levi and just disappeared with the girls.

I literally lost my mind over all of this that happened. I went wild and was full of anger. In the midst of everything I was going through, I honestly didn't seem to know who I was or where I was going. I lived in El Paso, thinking that I would be safe there where I had been baptized, but I found that no matter where I was I could not get control of the feelings I had from losing Levi and the girls.

Assistance from Angels on the Other Side

This was a very bitter and painful time in my life. I was so hurt that Levi left me and took the girls that I didn't know what to do with myself. I had become bitter and angry and had so much to repent of as well. In this swirl of difficulties, one night I had an encounter with spiritual darkness and assistance from God.

I knew that I was struggling and needed the Lord's help. One night I kneeled down beside my bed and was praying for forgiveness and asking the Lord what he wanted me to do. Was it possible that I could be forgiven so I could be worthy to serve the Lord? There were many questions and I was determined to do the necessary repentance process that would bring me back into the grace of the Lord.

While I was praying, I felt something come into my bedroom. I looked up and out the window and the street light looked so weird. It was lit up but it did not shine like normal. Then I felt something behind me and turned and looked. It was evil and so black. I felt myself floating up in the air and my back went against the wall up above my bed. That thing was coming towards me. I heard myself barely say, "Help!"

Just then as I called for heavenly assistance, the light began to shine again in my room, but I was still up over my bed against the wall. I then looked down at my bed and saw the covers turning down and I was being lowered slowly into my bed. I could feel someone holding me on both arms and my feet were brought forward to go under the covers and then they pulled the blanket up to my neck. There was a peace in my room I had not felt in a very long time. I testify to you that there are angels from the other side of the veil who are watching over each one of us. I am so grateful for that knowledge and the help that came to me that night through messengers of Jesus Christ.

"Don't Stop!"

I decided to further pursue my education, so I moved over 600 miles east across Texas to the Dallas area and began attending school at Mesquite Junior College. I tried to keep myself busy but after a while I just couldn't do it. I took classes there and enjoyed attending college, but I was thinking constantly of the rape I had experienced and was also afraid in being so far away from home.

With the perspective that comes from hindsight, only years later did I come to realize that I was dealing with the trauma and fear that came into my life following the assault, along with the loss from two divorces and other losses. I did all right in my classes but I wasn't able to feel inside. I felt like I was being devoured piece by piece. As usual, I didn't tell anyone what I was feeling. I kept on holding onto the gospel by reading and studying the scriptures, taking classes, and trying to stay close to the Church. However, I was literally dying inside.

I found the pace of life in the Dallas area to be much faster than I was used to previously. I soon felt it was getting dangerous for me to drive home from classes without being followed. Then, one day I was coming back to my apartment from school, and two men began following me in a car. I did not want to go to my apartment and let them know where I lived.

As the men followed me, I felt the Spirit warning me not to stop my car. I kept driving but not near my apartment. I got to the freeway where there was an intersection with four lanes to cross and the light turned red. I heard the Spirit whispering to me: "Don't stop!" I saw that the light was red. Those two men were right behind me in their vehicle, so I said a prayer and stepped on the gas pedal and just kept on going. I knew that I was either going to make it across or I would die. Either way, I listened to the Spirit and drove into that intersection. Oncoming traffic was everywhere around me, but the Lord helped me and there was a break in all the cars on this freeway in Dallas, and I went across six lanes on a red light in open traffic. No small miracle.

Needless to say, the men did not follow me as they were unable to get through, but that was enough for me. I got out of there and went home and packed to come back to North Dakota. I flew home and decided that there was no place like home.

Chapter 17
New Steps in Jamestown

A New Chapter Back in Jamestown

Life in Texas had certainly brought a variety of changes into my life when I was there from 1972 to 1974. Moving to Texas itself was a big change in my life since I had lived all of my years in North Dakota prior to that move. The major changes during that time including entering marriage with Levi, raising his two young daughters, and getting used to life on a military base. Unfortunately, our harmonious life together did not last, and another significant change was the dissolution of our marriage after he decided to leave me.

I remained in Texas and sought to pursue further education and moved close to the big city of Dallas, which was another major change as I sought to manage life on my own. Of course, the biggest change in my life happened as a result of becoming a member of The Church of Jesus Christ of Latter-day Saints, which I consider to be the greatest blessing of my experience in Texas.

Due to some difficult circumstances in Texas, it made sense for me to move back to North Dakota and be close once again to family members and other friends. I was on my own again and needed to take some new steps. Returning to Jamestown allowed me to feel a bit more secure but it was still a difficult and challenging time period in my life. In this new chapter of my life, I ran into some life difficulties, gradually became more involved in my new faith, and began working regularly for the first time as an adult.

Family Travels

I returned home to North Dakota and was grateful to be close to my Mom and Dad again. I had the chance to do a little bit of travel with them shortly after coming back home from Texas. We flew to San Diego, California to see my brother, John, who was stationed there in the Marine Corps. I was able to go swimming at the hotel there and had a good time with my brother John. It was great to see him again. He doesn't know what a strength he has been to me during my life and still is today. I am very grateful for him.

Falling Down and Facing Fears

Coming back to Jamestown in 1974, it was not long before the stresses that had been overwhelming me from the experiences of the past several years took their toll. Despite my new spiritual roots in the LDS faith, that did not end the trauma I had experienced or automatically result in wise choices in my life. After I got home to Jamestown, it seemed like the gates of Hell were surrounding me and closing in for the kill.

I had pretty strong ties to the Church while in Texas as a new member and there were many local members there to help me take next steps. However, in Jamestown I had no idea if the Church even existed there, and didn't have any strong connection with it when I first came back to Jamestown. Although it is painful to admit, I definitely struggled during this time period and made some unhealthy choices. You might say that I "fell in with the wrong crowd," and those individuals got me involved in drinking alcohol and using some recreational drugs. One night, I ended up mixing beer with the drug LSD and ended up in the hospital with a serious health scare. I was not coping well with all of my difficulties. Additionally, I was not actively involved in church during this time period.

I am not going to pretend that what happened between Levi and me didn't bother me. I went through a very hard time losing him and the girls. I went through a period of depression and feeling sorry for myself and feeling that it was all my fault. I wondered how I could have done things differently, but in actuality there was nothing I could do. So, I went on with my life, one day at a time.

Realizing that I had to face my fears and feelings of low self-worth, I reached out and went to some counselors in the area in hopes of finding more direction in my life and also some healing. I wanted to let go of the trauma that had accumulated in my life due to the rape, the death of my daughter, two divorces, and just feeling like there was no place in this world for a person like me. However, no matter what I tried, the deeper my feelings plunged and I just struggled. It was a dark time in my life.

Finding the Church in Jamestown

Despite the difficulties in my life, I knew the strength that had come to me from my newfound faith and so I began to search for better answers. After a long period of grief and hurt from the divorce and not knowing what was real anymore, I began to put the pieces of my life together and to hold on to the Scriptures. I finally started to pull myself out of the pit of difficulty and despair that I was in and also discovered that there was a small but caring unit of the Church in Jamestown. There were only eight members—but they were there!

I had been less involved in the Church for some time but these local members in Jamestown accepted me with care and love, which enabled me to become more involved again in 1975. I had received a variety of spiritual experiences but really struggled with hanging on. Finally, with the help of my friend Sandra Horning, I came back into church activity and took new steps.

We met at Hunt's Funeral Home each Sunday for our services. I remember one day arriving to church early and there I saw our Branch President, Allan D., rolling bodies to the elevator to take them to the basement before the children would begin coming. That was a funny feeling for me but it was a logical thing to do—I just had never thought about it!

Those little meetings stayed with me in memory so strongly because of the loving spirit of those few members, as well as the feelings of the Holy Spirit that were strong. We grew slowly but the love between us was so powerful.

Loving Friends and Church Experiences

During this time period in Jamestown I grew close to a number of Church members. My wonderful friends in Jamestown were always there to give me blessings when I needed them and I had some lovely and memorable experiences there.

I recall one extremely special Sacrament meeting that we had in our church services that I would like to share. There was a young boy who was in a wheelchair. He could not talk very well and was severely mentally disabled. He was probably in

Shirley Stockford, seated row, third from left, in Jamestown, ND with members of the Handicap Club in the 1970s.

his teens at this time. The young Aaronic Priesthood boys were preparing the bread and the water to be used in the Sacrament. This young boy was very unsettled and kept trying to get out of his chair to go by the young boys and the Sacrament table. President D. took him out of the room and talked with him to help him calm down. When they returned, it was Fast and Testimony Sunday, and President D. had tears in his eyes. He bore his testimony and told all of us that this young boy wanted to help bless the Sacrament. He told us of how special this young man was and his appreciation for him. I felt a bond with this young boy after that. He usually sat beside me and one time we were singing a song that had several areas where the same word was repeated several times. I showed this to him and whenever all of us would sing that word, he would, with all of his heart, sing that word with us. Maybe some were annoyed by it but this young boy was so happy, and I looked at President D. and he was smiling with approval to hear him sing. It was such a special day for me.

Sister D. was also a wonderful support to me. I became so close to her and found that there was not much I couldn't talk to her about. Once we had an alumni reunion at the Anne Carlsen School (formerly the Crippled Children's School), and I had asked President D. to give the prayer at the event. At the dinner they had a fruit salad that they had put wine on. I found out that it had wine on it and apologized to Sister D. and told her I didn't know that they were having the wine on the fruit. She laughed and said to me that it is a good thing that we don't drink alcohol because it tasted so good! I just loved her sense of humor. She could take things that were bothering me and totally turn it around so that I felt so much better.

While in Jamestown, I moved into the basement apartment of one of the church members for a while. Her name was Vlasta. I just loved this wonderful lady. She had this beautiful, black cat named Sammy. I had a parakeet who was always in her cage. One day she got out of her cage and I spent a long period of time trying to get her back into the cage. No luck! I kind of jokingly said a prayer, asking Heavenly Father to use his Priesthood to put the bird back into her cage. I did not realize that the door to my apartment was partly open, and the next second I looked and Sammy the cat had my bird in her mouth! Just then, my Home Teacher stepped in and gently took my bird out of Sammy's mouth and put her into the cage! I was in awe! Heavenly Father had answered my prayer even though I was kidding around! He had his Priesthood holder put my bird back into her cage! I never kidded around like that again, but I realized that nothing is impossible for the Lord.

I became very close to one young lady. Her name was Sandy. Sandy and I became very close. When Sandy was pregnant with about her 7th or 8th child, we both had a garden space out by the Jamestown Hospital. The gardens were side by side. I was weeding my garden one day and had finished, so I thought I would help Sandy and I weeded her garden too. When I was just about done, she drove up, very pregnant and with three of her little ones, ready to weed her garden and found that I had finished it for her. When I saw how grateful she was, I felt so good about doing it for her. I was often blessed in receiving such small acts of service and I tried my best to also learn and do such things for others. In this way, I was taking new steps in following the Savior.

One of the members had come to Jamestown to marry a man named Doug H. She and I became very close friends. I received my first calling in the Church and was her counselor in the Relief Society. Quite a while after they were married and some years later, I was visiting at my doctor's office in Medina, North Dakota. I saw Doug there. He seemed so very happy. I didn't think about the incident again until a few months later when there was a shooting at Medina by some tax protesters (in February 1983). A man named Gordon Kahl had killed a police officer and was on the run. They finally caught him in another shoot-out where he was killed. It turned out that Doug and my doctor were both involved in this group of tax protesters. Dr. Martin was run out of Medina and Doug was arrested for tax evasion and sent to prison.

I saw Doug years later when I was in Fargo and he told me that he had come to know that "the Church was not true." He asked me if I wanted him to come and tell me about it. I told him, "No." He turned around and walked away and that was the last time I ever saw him. His wife soon left Jamestown and I only saw her once after that. She was a dear friend. I felt so bad for her that she had to be hurt like that. These incidents in my own life showed me the difference between following the Savior versus turning away from Him into other paths that led to hurt or sin.

A Blessing for My Father

After I got home from Texas, Dad's alcoholism was really bad at this time. He was really struggling. He had gone through so much with treatments at the State Hospital and any attempt to help him seemed to have been exhausted. He had even had to go through shock treatments at the State Hospital. That was awful for him. He told me how bad that was and how it had frightened him.

I remember one day in particular when Mom was calling the leaders at the Methodist Church and begging them to come and help Dad. I don't know what Mom thought they could do for Dad, but I knew Mom was at the end of being able to handle it and needed assistance. The minister there told her that he would not come and Mom broke down crying. I asked her if I could call my Branch President in the Church, President D., to come and give Dad a priesthood blessing.

Mom and Dad were very impressed with the Church when they came out to pick me up from Texas and met my Bishop there (Bishop Nations). When we were talking on the plane ride, Mom kept saying that she really liked my Bishop and that she would have joined the Church if she lived there. So, when I asked if President D. could come to provide a priesthood blessing, both she and Dad were glad to have him come.

President D. came over and talked to both Mom and Dad for a while and then told them what a Priesthood Blessing was and how it worked. He explained that in the Bible when someone was sick they would call for the Elders to come and give them a Blessing. He also told my Dad that he may not be aware of getting this Blessing because he had an awful lot to drink, but that my faith was very strong and that upon my faith he could be healed of alcoholism if he so desired. He then laid his hands upon Dad's head and gave him a beautiful Blessing. I felt the Lord's Spirit so very strong when he was blessing him. To the best of my knowledge, this was the last time that I saw my Dad drunk. I was very grateful for this spiritual blessing that was extended to my Dad in a time of struggle.

Work at the Tumbleweed Motel

It was not long after moving back to Jamestown that I faced another reality—finding a job. I needed a way to support myself as an adult. I knew that I needed to find extra help with my finances. However, since high school graduation in 1966 I had not been able to find any meaningful work, as people were just not willing to give me a chance to prove that I could work.

Finally, then, in 1975 I was able to get a job at the Tumbleweed Motel working for a local motel owner. The Tumbleweed Motel was a fifty-unit motel in Jamestown. This was the first job I ever had.

Postcard of the Tumbleweed Motel, Jamestown, ND.

My boss was Kim Tanner. I really liked her. She trusted me totally and I worked for her over a year.

I loved working there at the Tumbleweed Motel and did my best to become the best motel clerk that she had. I learned a great deal from Kim Tanner and respected her highly. I learned how to check people in and out, how to do some book work for the daily business, and how to schedule people coming in and take payment for rooms rented. I also learned how to operate the switchboard phone system and many more things about the motel business.

Kim told me that she had never had anyone that would not steal from her, whether it be money or candy. I couldn't believe anyone would do that. Although this story comes next, I married a man named Joe when I was working for her, who was also a motel owner. A couple of years after we had married she asked me to come and work for her again at the Tumbleweed Motel. I was a little surprised since I was now also a motel owner with Joe.

I did work for her, and while I worked for her she told me if the motel was full, then I could recommend our motel to people that came in. I knew that Kim wanted to get as much as she could for her rooms and I did a good job at arranging things as I was taught to do. One day her son had come in when I answered the phone, and he overheard me referring someone to our motel because Kim's motel was full. Her son misunderstood what was happening and called Kim and told her I was sending people to our own motel.

Kim came in and was very angry with me. I didn't know why but I would not say anything while other people were in the office. She pulled out a card that I had missed which could have been rented. I was embarrassed that I had missed that but I knew that was not what was bothering her. After I left I didn't hear from her again for a long time. Finally, she called me and said she wanted to see me.

I went to the motel and she told me what her son had said and realized afterwards that he was not right. When she had added up the income for that day, she saw that I had brought in more money than she had expected and realized that I had not done anything dishonest to her. She told me that she needed some help and asked whether I would please accept her humble apology and help her out. She and I were very good friends after that. This taught me a lesson about being honest in our dealings with people and it has remained an important value for me.

My work at the Tumbleweed Motel brought me into the world of paid work and I enjoyed the work very much. I felt valued for my work and I appreciated both the opportunity to gain skills and to earn a regular income. Kim Tanner was a very good boss and I learned to greatly respect her. My work there also linked me with another motel owner in Jamestown and this association would open up another chapter in my life.

Chapter 18
A Season of Struggle

Marriage and Managing Life's Challenges

The move back to Jamestown, North Dakota helped to stabilize my life although it took me some time to establish myself there. It helped that my family members were close and that I became more involved in my new faith as a Latter-day Saint. Working at the Tumbleweed Motel introduced me to the task of managing work and other life tasks but I enjoyed the opportunity.

The next near-decade of my life brought a new season into my life that would be a season of struggle. I turned thirty years old in 1977 and faced life as a mature adult. In this time period, I met and married for the third time. Life with my third husband would be challenging. Also, we had a variety of significant challenges with running a motel business, dealing with housing problems, and operating a group home in Minnesota. Fortunately, I had a supportive circle of family members and church members who were helpful to me during these years of struggle.

Into a Third Marriage

While I was working at the Tumbleweed Motel in Jamestown for owner Kim Tanner, I came to know another person in the motel industry. I met Joseph Duane Barton not long after coming home. He was another motel owner and went by the name Joe. Joe and I began dating and it was not long before he knew that I was going to be quite useful to him at the motel. We were married in October of 1977 not long after I had turned thirty. Joe was twelve years older than I was but we began a life together.

Ours was a very difficult marriage but I was determined to stick it out after going through two divorces. He had joined the Church before the two us were married, but yet had difficulty understanding why I would not do some of the things that he thought were right to do. I simply disagreed with some of the business practices he employed that I felt were not right and also felt that he did not treat others as well as he might. But, let me backtrack a little bit and explain how things began and progressed for us.

Although I have alluded to it, we had a very rocky beginning in a number of ways. Joe was the part owner of the Swanie Motel there in Jamestown, North Dakota. My earlier life difficulties still troubled me and I had difficulty with self-esteem and also in my fears of others. After we had been dating for a period, Joe approached me and asked me to marry him.

To tell the truth, I didn't really want to marry him and thought that I needed some help. I remember going to visit with my church leader, the branch president in Jamestown, because I didn't want to marry Joe and thought that he might support me. Instead, he advised me to marry him and in my heart I sunk. Nevertheless, I wanted to follow the guidance of this spiritual leader and didn't want to reject this priesthood leader's advice, so I followed his counsel and was married to Joe. Life didn't really start off well with him and in hindsight I likely would have made a different choice.

Shirley Stockford in 1980.

Struggle and Abuse

Joe owned the Swanie Motel and it had twenty-seven units available and so we moved in there to start our marriage. A couple days into our marriage, I asked him if I could rearrange the dresser so I could put some clothes into it and have a couple of drawers for my clothes. He told me that I could. As I was clearing out the drawers, I found little pieces of paper on the bottom of the drawer which were things similar to gum wrappers and stuff like that which I threw in the garbage. There was another little paper that had a picture of a Catholic Cardinal in a red robe. I didn't

130

think anything about it since we were both now members of the LDS Church and I tossed it in the garbage also. The maid came in and took out the garbage and evidently Joe went through the garbage before she put it into the dumpster. The little article about the cardinal was in there and he was furious with me.

A few minutes later Joe came in, very angry, and without saying a word he grabbed one of my legs and yanked me out of my wheelchair and dragged me out the door and across the parking lot of the motel. I saw a maid coming out of a room that she was cleaning and wanting to rescue me while I was dragged across the parking lot. I shook my head "no" to her because I didn't want her to lose her job. She went back into the motel and I knew that she was very upset.

He took me to the huge garbage dumpster and picked me up and threw me into it. I looked up at the dirty, filthy sides of that huge dumpster and began to scream. He tipped the dumpster and I got out of there as fast as I could.

I asked him what was wrong and he told me, "Don't you ever throw anything of mine away again." I looked at him totally bewildered and he pulled out that little article. I apologized to him and said that I didn't realize that it was anything important to him since he was not a member of that church any longer. I wanted to run!

Looking back, I wish that I had left. But like I said, I was determined to make it work. I prayed so hard for the Lord to help me not to make mistakes. Well, there were many mistakes, and many instances where he became angry with me and I paid for it one way or another. He was mean and abusive to me much of the time. My life with him after that was pretty much in fear for the eight years that we were married.

Running the Swanie Motel in Jamestown

Because of the work that I had been doing at the Tumbleweed Motel in Jamestown, I was somewhat prepared to help run the hotel business that Joe owned after we got married. My work with Kim Tanner had taught me many things about handling customers and running a hotel business. So, in 1977 I became heavily involved in running the Swanie Motel.

Although I was able to effectively work with Joe at times in running the motel, it was a difficult time trying to keep things going and dealing with the many concerns of managing a hotel. It did not help that I had ongoing concerns about his business practices. He was doing illegal things with a partner and I felt more and more uncomfortable being married to him. It was frightening at times.

As I already noted, during the five years that followed our marriage in 1977, Kim Tanner came to me again at one point and asked me to help her out at the Tumbleweed Motel. One day when I was working for her, one of Joe's regular people came into the Tumbleweed Motel. He was embarrassed to see me there. I told him to rest assured that it was fine that he came to another motel. He then confided in me about how Joe had been taking advantage of him. I told him I knew a bit about it but there was nothing I could do to change how he was treating his business people.

I never saw him again but I felt bad that people thought bad things about Joe due to these practices I disagreed with, but there was nothing I could do to change his heart. I hoped that maybe some day the Lord would be able to soften his heart.

While we lived in Jamestown, Joe also had a home property in the Minnesota "lake country" in Pelican Rapids, Minnesota. We were able to go there occasionally and it was a nice setting to get away from the pressures of running the motel. During this time, the pressures of running the motel got so difficult that Joe went to Pelican Rapids a lot to get away from things.

Once he left me at the motel alone and went to the lake home. I decided that I wanted a break too. I hired a couple to watch the motel and I went out to the lake home for the weekend. We were on our way home on Saturday afternoon, and as we listened to the news, it said that our Swanie Motel in Jamestown was robbed! We got home to Jamestown and found the

Swanie Motel in Jamestown, ND, circa 1980s.

couple was just frantic. They told us that a man came into the hotel at night with a knife. The wife in this couple screamed and her husband came running out of the back bedroom, and then the man with the knife grabbed the cash and left. If I had been there alone, who knows what would have happened to me. I was so grateful that the Lord protected me. I never stayed at the motel alone after that incident.

It was not long after that incident occurred that Joe lost his motel because of his partner foreclosing on him. They had been doing some dishonest practices involving the motel and other matters, and were not able to meet all of their responsibilities. We ran the Swanie Motel together from 1977 to 1982 until he lost it due to this foreclosure. That was a challenging five years.

Family Times in Foxhome

My brother, John, was married during this time period in the early 1980s and was attending classes in Wahpeton, North Dakota. Mom and Dad had gone to Foxhome, Minnesota, which was not far from Wahpeton, and they bought a house there in Foxhome. Dad just wanted to get out of Jamestown and Foxhome was a little town, and I think Dad liked smaller towns better than bigger cities.

Mom and Dad wallpapered their home in Foxhome with a vinyl wallpaper and it really looked nice. They had made an apartment upstairs and my cousin D. Nelson moved in upstairs with her children for a time. John had lived in this house for a while and also in a trailer home that Mom and Dad had brought with them. They had two trailers and a large building in the center of this little town. Mom wanted to make a second-hand store in the building but never got that done. She and Dad eventually moved to this house in Foxhome and lived there for quite a few years.

We had a lot of good times in Foxhome and I drove there often to see them. It was especially fun for me when John would come with his three kids, C., A. and J. One time when the kids were there, I was sitting in the rocking chair and just watching the kids playing in the front room. My brother didn't like it when Mom would give C. a bottle to drink her milk from, and on this particular day C. had a bottle drinking her milk, and Mom called out that John and his wife had just driven up. C., about two years old at this time, looked at me and said: "Aunt Shirley, hide

Shirley's father, Clair, who was injured by a fire accident in Foxhome, MN.

my bottle!" Then she tossed her bottle to me and ran to see her Mom and Dad! So funny!

We had one of the more frightening incidents in our family experience during this time they lived in Foxhome. Dad had bought a small camper to go camping with and had it parked on the yard in front of the house at Foxhome. This happened in the wintertime and my cousin D's husband, M., was visiting the kids and D. Dad and M. had gone out to work in the camper. I was in Fargo and had just called Mom to talk to her for a while. Suddenly, Mom started screaming and hung up on me. I had no idea what was happening. Pretty soon she called me back.

What had happened was that M. and Dad went into the camper, and the heat was not on in the camper, so Dad went to the back of the camper to light the pilot light and the furnace exploded. The force of the explosion threw M. out of the camper and he flew into a snow bank and he rolled around to get the fire out since he was on fire. Mom ran out to the camper and could see Dad walking back and forth in a daze in the camper, not knowing where to go. He was on fire and Mom went into the camper and grabbed Dad and led him out of the burning camper. Mom rolled Dad in the snow to put out the fire. The fire department came because the camper was near a large fuel tank and they were concerned about further fires or explosions but they soon had the fire out. Dad was taken to the hospital with M. M. was treated for some burns but was released while Dad had severe burns all over his body and on his face also.

He was in the hospital for a while with burns to his face and hands and they would give him whirlpool treatments to help the pain and help healing. When Dad was in one of the treatments he decided to sink his face into the whirlpool to help his face. Dad told me that the aides thought he was drowning and tried to pull him out and he came out laughing. That fire incident was quite a scare for me but I was so glad that Mom pulled Dad out and rolled him in the snow to put out the fire.

Establishing a Group Home in Pelican Rapids, Minnesota

Previously while living in Jamestown, I had supported my parents as they ran a care home for a number of residents and learned a lot about running that type of business. Also, it gave me a lot of experience in providing group care and taught me that I had the ability to do that kind of work. This experience would become very important to helping us in the next phase of our lives. I feel that through the Lord's help I was able to secure a house and a business to keep us going. Though Joe lost everything else that he had, I went and talked to another motel owner that I knew and was able to sell the hotel for what we owed on it, so that helped us a great deal.

Just before the foreclosure of the Swanie Motel was to go through, I went to the lake home in Minnesota to be alone for a while. The only piece of property that was left to us at this time was the lake home on Lake Lida, Minnesota. I had a strong feeling that it was just a matter of time and the lake home would be taken away also. While there at Lake Lida, I began talking with a realtor and he told me that he knew of a house that was for sale and that the lady would trade properties. I called Joe and told him about it. We decided to go ahead and the realtor went to file the sale of the lake home just in time. A few hours later the creditors were after that property and three banks tried to put a lien on it but it was too late—so we had a place to live.

This house was four miles outside of the city limits of Pelican Rapids and surrounded by a farmer's sunflower field. We had an acre of land and so we called it Joe's Acres. I went to the Lord for help and felt inspired to take care of other people. So, I went to the county and applied to be a foster parent. Soon we had two men that I took care of, "Bobby" and "Frank," who were brought to me from the State Hospital in Fergus Falls, Minnesota. Our facility, Joe's Acres, grew from being a Foster Parent's license to become the largest independent State Licensed Group Home in Minnesota.

I consulted the Lord often and He showed me many of the things I needed to do to keep us going. By the time I had our group home full with ten residents with my state license, Joe's mother needed a place to live and so her daughter asked us to take her in also. I was very busy taking care of eleven people, one of them being Joe's mother.

During the time I ran this group home in the Pelican Rapids area, Mom and Dad came out a lot to help me out because Joe would take off and would be gone a lot. One evening Dad and I were sitting outside and looking at how beautiful the evening was in the fall. Dad commented to me that the Northern Lights were bright and beautiful that night. I couldn't even see stars or the lights in the night sky and that worried me, so I decided to go into Fargo and get an eye check-up.

After my eyes had been checked by an eye doctor, the doctor told me that I a had a condition called *Retinitis Pigmentosa* (Usher's Syndrome) and that I was likely going to go blind. My fear was beyond what I can describe. So, I called my friend who was serving as a spiritual leader in the Stake Presidency (like a regional presidency in our faith), and he came over to Moorhead and gave me a Priesthood Blessing (this was in the early 1980s). In this blessing, he told me that I would not go totally blind. Even though I am legally blind right now over thirty years later, I can still see light and see enough to type for writing this book, so I believe very strongly in the power of the Priesthood to bless.

I continued in doing this work at the group home for three years from about 1981 to 1984. Though Joe could have worked with me in this effort, he was not able to accept the people who lived with us and began to have trouble being kind to them. He was too often unkind or even mean toward them. He began to be gone most of the time and left all of the work for me to handle mostly on my own. I was responsible for a variety of activities, such as: taking the residents to their churches; taking them downtown for coffee or just for some time on their own; taking them to their medical appointments, mental health appointments, or to Social Services; teaching them skills to be able to socialize; doing shopping, laundry, and taking care of our eight-bedroom home; cooking; and whatever else was involved with the business. It was quite a handful!

My goal was to help our residents learn how to be more independent and live more as a family. The oldest resident was 81, who died shortly after we sold the business and I attended her funeral. The youngest resident was 20 and had a long beard and mustache. Each had a list of chores made just for him or her according to their abilities. I helped them learn how to do their own laundry, shop for groceries, select clothes, and manage their money wisely.

I did enjoy it a great deal even though it was a lot of work. I loved the residents of the home so much. Each one had a special story to tell. We had the group home for about three years and during that time I had a huge garden in the back yard. Each year I canned about three hundred jars of tomatoes, and then two hundred quarts each of peaches, pears, plums and applesauce to help with

Home in Pelican Rapids, MN, that became a group home care facility run by Shirley Stockford, circa 1982-85.

feeding the residents. I had a sweet lady that liked helping in the kitchen, so between her and myself we worked miracles.

Our Home Teachers would come out to visit us, Jim and Pat P., who lived quite close by. I just loved them. They are still my friends. I learned so much from them. Jim's mother and dad lived right by them and their names were Ralph and Alice. When I would need a break, I was over talking with Pat and Alice, and that helped me during times of stress.

As long as we worked together, the group home was successful. Joe was often not there, or else he was usually looking for "something" to occupy his time other than taking care of our group home and the residents. After a while, Joe left and went to California with a member of the Church that did black-top work. Joe told me he would send home money to help keep our place on top of things. He was gone a long time. Work was piling up and there was no money from Joe to help pay for people to take care of the lawn and other things that I could not do. Also, this man in California was constantly trying to get Joe to sign over our property to him.

One day, while Joe was in California, his mother went down to the lower level of the house to go for a walk. It had been sleeting outside and I didn't know she was going out. She fell and when I looked outside two of the residents were trying to help her walk back into the house. She had broken her hip. I felt so bad for her. This was a turning point.

I loved the residents of the group home and tried to provide supportive care to them each day. However, this incident alerted me that there was too much going on for me to handle on my own.

Selling the Group Home and Making a Change

Joe's friend that he was supposed to be working with in California was trying to talk him into letting him have half of our business, so soon I began to worry about losing the house. I talked with Joe after much prayer to sign the house over to me to keep the house protected from his partner in California. Thank the Lord he signed the papers and returned them to me so the house was in my name.

Several weeks after the incident with Joe's mother and the continuing lack of assistance at the group home, I found myself running out of energy and ways to keep up with the demands of the work. I knew at this time that this was just way more than I could handle on my own. I called my friend and local Church member, Brother Howard O., to see if he could come out from Jamestown and do some repairs for me.

When Howard O. got there he saw that I was really struggling. He mowed the yard and took care of the needed repairs for me. He also built a sidewalk ramp for me to the trailer we had so that I could get in and out with my wheelchair. He stayed in the trailer a couple of days a week as he would go back and forth to Jamestown. Howard would come on Monday and leave on Friday for the weekend to be with his family. I think he was there for a couple of weeks.

This one day when he was outside working, I was making supper for everyone and I began to feel dizzy. I called to him and told him I needed to lay down and thought I was going to pass out from exhaustion. He told me to go to bed and he would take care of making supper for and feeding the residents. I got up in the morning and everything was cleaned up in the kitchen and Brother O. was making breakfast for the residents. There was loud, wonderful chatter with lots of laughter coming from the residents.

Howard told me he wanted to talk to me and that this was too much work for me to do alone. So, after breakfast he asked me if I would sell the business to him. I looked at him in shock. He assured me that he was very serious. We talked about the idea and he told me that he liked helping the residents, and with his wife Anna Mae and grown kids that lived at home, they could run it easily. He told me that I probably couldn't do it alone any longer without support from Joe. He suggested that I sell the house to him and Anna Mae and they would take over the business.

I thought about it and agreed and felt that it was a lifeline given to me at that time. It was the answer to my prayers at that time. So, I made out the contract with an attorney and sold the house to them. Then I called Joe and told him that I sold the house and the business! To my shock, he was back from California the next day. He was angry but there was nothing he could do about it, and I too was very angry.

Leaving Behind a Hard Marriage

In my first two marriages I had worked at the relationship but in both cases had been left by the men I married. In this third marriage, I also worked hard to make things work between us but went through many struggles. In the end, I was the one who made the decision to leave this third marriage.

I sold the group home in Pelican Rapids, then, in 1984 when Joe began being abusive to the residents and the workload became too much for me to handle alone. The residents were placed in my care and I made the decision that I could not let him hurt them. After I sold the house, Joe put me into a little apartment by one of the lakes (Lake Cormorant) out near Pelican Rapids and disappeared again. Things were not good between us. I sat there alone most of the time and decided I was moving to Fargo. Since he was gone all the time, the manager kept hitting on me and I knew that if I didn't get out of there, I would be in big trouble.

So, I finally called up some Church members in Fargo, and some of them came out and got me into a place there in Fargo. Soon, Joe came back and moved all of our things to an apartment in Dilworth, Minnesota. The problem with this apartment was that it was up three flights of steps! So, I needed to pull my manual wheelchair up and down the steps by myself since he was gone all the time. If he had been gone working on a job, that would have been different, but he would just go places just to have things to do.

Pretty soon, he had us evicted by bringing his four dogs into the apartment. He was warned but ignored the warnings. This began a pattern in our lives during that period. We were evicted out of two more apartments for the same reason. To tell the truth, I was so glad to get evicted out of the apartment that was on the third floor, since I was getting so worn out pulling my wheelchair up and down those stairs. Finally, we got a little apartment in Moorhead, Minnesota, so I began taking classes at Minnesota State College-Moorhead. I thought that perhaps I could get an education so that I could get a job and support myself. I knew I had to leave Joe but didn't know how I was going to do it yet.

It was at this time that I applied for a power wheelchair because I was attending classes at Moorhead State University, and wheeling back and forth from home to the school was extremely hard on my arms and back. I did get a power chair and was told by the doctors that I had better stop walking on my crutches as much as possible because my right hip was very bad and I was at risk of breaking it.

It bothered Joe that I was trying to get an education and he brought the dogs into our apartment again at this time. We were evicted and we had to move to a place in South Fargo. Getting to classes was much more difficult for me then so I had to stop. I was so nervous and having so much trouble getting along with Joe that I was at the end of my ability to cope any longer.

There were many things that happened to me during this marriage that I have not related. I have tried to let much of that go and extend my forgiveness. Eventually, I became tired of the abuse and was satisfied that the former residents of our group home were safe from him, so I planned to leave and divorce him. When I finally found an attorney to help me with my divorce, he told me that I needed to be in North Dakota for six months before I could apply, so then began the waiting game. That decision did not end the abuse, however, as I continued to receive harassment for some time afterwards, but I had made a hard decision and sought to get away from the hardships of this unhealthy marriage. It was hard but this decision was a turning point in my life and future.

Section 4

Life with the Man of My Dreams

By the mid-1980s, Shirley had matured into adulthood and undergone a series of relationships, life transitions and job experiences. The difficulty of living in an unhealthy marriage relationship and the stresses of running a group care home in Minnesota largely on her own weighed on her. She made a conscious break and sold the business and also sought a divorce.

After she moved into an apartment building in Fargo, North Dakota, Shirley became actively involved in social opportunities and there met Charles Robideau. He similarly had physical challenges and they became interested in each other. This interest blossomed into love and the two of them were married after Shirley's divorce had been finalized. Also, Charles became interested in Shirley's faith community, and chose to be baptized into The Church of Jesus Christ of Latter-day Saints.

These experiences led Shirley and Charles Robideau into a sixteen-year marriage that became the highlight of Shirley's life. Together, they learned to manage physical and financial challenges, grew in faith and service, and deepened their caring marriage relationship. They were able to obtain their own home in Casselton, North Dakota, and enjoyed their years together there. Also, they underwent a series of health difficulties that they endured with determination and mutual support. Eventually, Charles passed away after a period of decline and Shirley said farewell for a season to this sweet and good man who had so blessed her life from 1985 to 2002.

Chapter 19
Square Dancing and a Surprise Proposal

My Early Encounters with Charles Robideau

Since my rough and painful marriage was coming to an end in 1985, I moved to the New Horizons Manor in Fargo so that I would have a place to live and a new setting to move forward in my life. Though I was well aware of the need to get out of this difficult relationship, it was also a bit hard for me to take the steps toward divorce and envision a new and different future. While I made the move to New Horizons in hope that it would help with this transition, I did not realize at the time that this shift would truly open up a new door and introduce me to the man of my dreams.

Making the Move to New Horizons Manor

I learned about a wheelchair square dancing group while living in Fargo. I had loved doing that activity in school and thought that perhaps I would like it again. These wheelchair square dances were held at New Horizons Manor in North Fargo. I attended several times and really enjoyed it.

One day Joe came home in one of his moods and brought the dogs in again, and I knew it was a matter of time and we would be evicted again. I left in my car and was praying as to what I should do. I kept driving around, not wanting to go back home to my mean husband and those dogs! I found myself sitting in front of New Horizons and thought to myself, "I wonder if there are any apartments here?"

At that point, I got up and went in and saw the manager, Donna, and I asked her, "Donna, do you have any vacancies?" She asked me, "Who is it for?" I said that it was for me, and Joe would probably be coming also but I didn't know about that

New Horizons Manor apartment building in Fargo, where Shirley first met Charles Robideau (circa 1985).

yet. She looked at me and immediately said, "Shirley, for you, we have an apartment! You can move in tomorrow!" So, I asked her again when I could move in, and she said that I could do it the next day! So, I went home to pack.

Joe asked me where I thought I was going and I told him. I told him that I had another apartment lined up in Fargo, and where it was, and then told him that if he wanted to come, then he could—but I am going. I also told him that the dogs were not allowed! He told me I was not going to move, but with the Lord's help, I got my clothes and I left. A few days later, he came with his clothes. He decided that he didn't want to pay the rent there where he had been, so he came and moved in with me.

Then, he started stealing things from the residents there and began being mean to the residents, so I then told him to get out. He was very angry with me and showed his true colors to the residents, and the abuse became so bad that I went to my Priesthood leaders at church for help to get him out of my apartment. I am the type of person that never told anyone what was going on with the abusive treatment. Everybody thought that I was absolutely out of my mind because he was able to walk and get work and do things to take care of me, except he wasn't taking care of me.

Square Dancing and a New Partner

There was a six-month waiting period before our divorce could be finalized. While waiting for the divorce from Joe to be finalized in 1985, I kept myself somewhat busy by getting involved in this wheelchair square dancing group at New Horizons Manor. Again, I had moved there after we separated and was making some new friends. I enjoyed living there and soon learned that the square dancing caller was the same one I had when I was in high school, Howard and Evelyn Clemens. I was so surprised to see him and his wife Evelyn after all these years and it was so much fun to see them again. I had enjoyed being involved in square dancing back then and so got involved once again.

I became square dance partners with a fellow resident named Charles ("Chuck") Robideau, who was going out with another girl that didn't dance. He pretty much became my steady partner, as they had very few residents who square danced. They soon had a fundraiser for the Spinning Wheel Square Dancing Club (that was our wheelchair square dance group) and it kept me pretty busy. We would square dance every week on Wednesday night, so I made it a point to go down every Wednesday and to keep my positive attitude. These dance partners also became friends. On the nice days, a bunch of us would get together and go for hikes. Since we were all in wheelchairs, it would be so much fun to go to the parks on the trails. Chuck had trouble controlling his chair because he had Muscular Dystrophy. So, I volunteered to walk beside him and hold on to his chair to help him so that he wouldn't go off the sidewalks and possibly tip over and get hurt.

Due to our square dance interactions, Chuck and I became friends and did a lot of talking about the life and also about the LDS Church. He had told me about a period of time that he had been thinking of suicide. It was soon after that episode in his life that a resident named John K. had moved into the facility, and the two of them became good friends and could relate to each other because both of them had Friedreich's Ataxia, which is a neurodegenerative disease similar to Muscular Dystrophy that primarily affects the nervous system and the heart. John saved Chuck's life and gave him a better outlook on life. John and Chuck had been studying the Bible and attending another church together, and they kept asking Chuck to join, but Chuck never felt that he was supposed to do that.

One night when I was talking with Chuck, he told me that he had broken up with his girlfriend of many years. I told him I was sorry and asked what had happened. He then said that he could not continue being with her because he was in love with me. I totally lost my breath! I told him that I was still married and so we needed to remain friends. He understood and said he would wait.

Chuck was quite limited physically but he had a zest for life and did as much for himself as he possibly could. His mother, Cora, would come and help him with what he could not do for himself. He was originally from Moorhead, Minnesota. All of his family members lived within a two-block radius in Moorhead—his mother, his father, his grandparents, and his great-grandparents, and all of the nieces and nephews lived within a few blocks. I became friends with Chuck's sister, Sandra, and her daughters. I fell in love with his family. Also, his older brother lived in Casselton at that time and he had three other sisters as well.

Introducing Chuck Robideau to the Book of Mormon

We had gotten to know each other pretty well when Chuck began talking to me about religion. One day when I was at my apartment Chuck came to visit me. He wanted to know what it was that I had that brought me so much happiness in life. I told him about my conversion and involvement in The Church of Jesus Christ of Latter-day Saints. Also, I bore my testimony to him and we continued having a few discussions about the Church. I gave him a copy of the *Book of Mormon* and asked him to read it.

The next day his friends came to visit him. Many of them were involved in another faith community that was quite opposed to The Church of Jesus Christ of Latter-day Saints, and they had learned that he had begun investigating a little bit about the Latter-day Saint faith. They came to his apartment to talk him out of it. They saw the copy of the *Book of Mormon* there and they threw it in the garbage. I came up to see if he was all right and his friends were there and I felt a very bad spirit there that scared me, so I left and told him I would visit him another time.

The next morning I saw him and he seemed a little distant or reserved, so I just let it go. Then I felt prompted to go up and see if he was all right. I went to check on Chuck and he was busy, so I asked him if he wanted me to take out his garbage and he told me to go ahead. Lo and behold, there the copy of the *Book of Mormon* was on the side of the bag. I didn't want to embarrass him, so I asked him if it would be all right if I kept the book instead of throwing it away. He told me it was okay to do that and so I took his garbage down and took out the copy of the *Book of Mormon*. I didn't mention it to him after that.

Going Ahead with My Divorce

Things got so difficult with the process of my divorce during this time period because of continuing harassment. For example, I would look out my window and see him in the parking lot staring at my window. One day I was so discouraged and felt that I couldn't get away from him and so I might as well stay with him.

A few days later Joe (my then-husband who I was divorcing) came to ask me if I would walk to the park with him so we could talk. He was there to try and convince me to take him back. Since leaving him, I had felt good that the residents of our group home that I had grown to love so much were safe from his negative treatment, but I also just could not seem to feel that I had tried hard enough to make the marriage work. So, I thought that perhaps I should at least talk with him and see if we ought to get back together again. I prayed about it and asked the Lord to help me know what to do and say.

We walked together to the Trollwood Park that day and we talked. As we talked, I felt like I should just take him back and not consider or be worried about my own feelings. I had basically made up my mind that I would go back to him. I didn't tell him that but instead told him I would think about it.

I remember as we talked together that I felt like I was getting sadder and sadder. While we were walking back on a gravel road to the New Horizons Manor, there were cars coming towards me and I thought to myself that it would be easy to just quickly turn my chair in front of them and I wouldn't have to worry about anything any longer. Just before I was about to do that, I shook myself wide awake and paused. Suddenly, I thought, "My goodness, if I feel like killing myself over this man, I certainly can't be in love with him. If you are so unhappy with the way he treats you that you would end your life, this can't be right."

I suddenly began to smile and knew that it was the right decision to go ahead with this divorce and to move on with my life. When I got back to New Horizons, I then realized that the Lord didn't want me to be treated in an abusive way and that I ought to go forward with the divorce. I filed the papers and was finally able to put my life back into order again.

An interesting and somewhat challenging experience was that some of my friends in the Church were not very kind to me when they found out that I was getting a divorce from a man that they felt could support me. They felt that I was being foolish and they let me know it. I talked to Bishop Brad Leeser about it and he promised me that if I would live the Gospel to the best of my ability that within a year everyone would know his true colors. I didn't say anything negative about Joe to others because it was not my nature to tell people what I was going through. Just as Bishop Leeser had promised, within the year, his true colors were being manifested and many came and apologized to me for things they had said and thought.

Activities and Adventures

During this period of time, I kept doing the best I could to keep myself busy and occupied with positive activities. The Spinning Wheels Square Dancing Club really took a hold of my heart. I enjoyed being with the group and entertaining for other people. We would go to nursing homes, schools and other places to perform for organizations in the area. I also took up swimming, archery, and bowling with the Fargo Park District.

One time they had a trip to a river in Minnesota to go canoeing. A group from New Horizons went on the Park Board Bus, which included John K., Charles, myself and several others. There were several chaperones to help those that needed assistance with personal things.

On this trip I was in one canoe with several girls, Charles and John were in another, Sandy (Charles' sister) was in another canoe, and then there was one more, having four canoes total. The guides that were controlling Charles' and John's canoe came along the side of my canoe. I thought this was kind of dangerous since the water was unusually rough in this year. There were lots of rocks and extreme care needed to be taken. Just then, both my canoe and Charles' canoe hit rocks, and I felt a spiritual prompting to grab the side of their canoe. That action kept my canoe from tipping over and the other canoe went up in the air and I pulled it back down into place. Charles didn't get thrown out of the canoe but was knocked back under one of the seats. John, however, was thrown out of his place in the canoe. I yelled at the guide to grab John, as he had fallen out of the canoe. They grabbed him and put him back into the canoe. If I had not grabbed the canoe when I did, both canoes would have tipped over, and I doubt that the few guides we had would have been able to grab all five of us before the rapid current swept us away.

I know that the Lord guided me in hanging on to this canoe, and while I was holding on, I saw a vision in my mind that John had fallen out of the canoe and that his life jacket was pulling him down with the current. No one knew that he had fallen out of the boat nor where he was, but I was able to tell them and they got him. I was so grateful to the Spirit of the Lord for protecting us.

Charles Robideau, who Shirley met in Fargo (circa 1980s).

We had to continue down the river because our vehicles were further down the stream. As we were going, Charles' sister's canoe hit rocks and Sandy was dumped out of their canoe and her wheelchair was pulled downstream very quickly. They were not able to find it, nor were they able to find her walking braces, as they were also washed away. Needless to say, after this near disaster, they did not have any more canoeing trips after this!

I had also enrolled in Special Olympics and won several awards in swimming and archery. I enjoyed watching others as they did their best to accomplish a goal. There is no way to go to these events and not fall in love with the people and the staff that help each special person to achieve an award. This was an amazing experience.

From Friend to Convert to Surprise Proposal

Having realized that I was doing the right thing with my decision to divorce, I continued square dancing and other activities to keep busy until our divorce was final. These activities also kept me in further contact with Chuck Robideau and our friendship continued to grow.

On one occasion during this time, Chuck came to talk to me and told me that his friends had told him that the *Book of Mormon* was an "evil book" and that he should avoid me altogether. I asked him if he thought that I was evil. He then said that was something he didn't understand, because since he first met me when I began square dancing at New Horizons, that he could see there was something different about me but didn't know what it was.

One day, I saw that copy of the *Book of Mormon* and thought to myself: "I am going to wrap it up and give it back to Chuck." Which I did. He then gladly accepted it. He soon began going to church meetings with me and met Bishop Brad Leeser.

Bishop Leeser invited Chuck to come to his home for a cottage meeting. In the discussion they had, Bishop Leeser told Chuck about being married forever. He told him that he could be married not only for this life but for all eternity through the Savior and the ordinances of the Restored Gospel. Chuck really liked this cottage meeting and talked about it a great deal. From that point on, his whole attitude changed about so many things. When talking to me about that, he told me that he was thinking about ending his life. He had a girlfriend but didn't feel his life was worth living. After going to the first cottage meeting he felt a lift, especially when he heard about the Savior and the Plan of Salvation and Eternal Marriage. He began taking gospel lessons with the missionaries and attending more cottage meetings.

As the time for my divorce became final, Chuck had been taking the discussions from the Sister Missionaries. One day, he came to my apartment and told me that he wanted to be baptized and become a member of the Church (The Church of Jesus Christ of Latter-day Saints). I didn't want to comment because I didn't want him to join the faith just because of me, as he needed his own testimony whether it was true or not. I just said to him, "Talk with the Sisters." Well, Chuck had clearly decided that he was going to get baptized, and so he picked up the phone and called the Sister Missionaries and told them that he wanted to be baptized. The Sisters were so surprised that they dropped the phone. After they got over the shock of someone calling them and asking for baptism, they said that he had to have an interview with the Mission President and so they set up an appointment for him. He was so excited when they told him he could be baptized that next week.

He was baptized about three months before his birthday and joined the Church with a conviction that was so amazing to me. He asked me to give a talk at his baptism and I had found an article called "Finding John" which I read at his baptism. It was about two friends in the pre-mortal existence that were very close to each other, and one of them was going to be born into the Church and the other was not going to be in the Church. John was not going to be in the Church so he begged his friend to please find him and teach him about the Church. His friend promised him that he would find him. I spent the whole time crying! He was baptized in August 1985.

Charles' baptism was so special. He was baptized at the same time as another friend of mine, Virginia. After she was baptized, the missionaries carried Charles into the water, and as I watched Bishop Leeser baptize him, I felt the Spirit so strong that tears were flowing freely.

Finally, my divorce was final and I felt like I could breathe again even though my ex-husband kept coming by and trying to make me come back to him. I stood my ground with him. I kept busy with square dancing and going to Church meetings. I even went to Institute gospel study classes to keep myself busy. On the day that our divorce was final, I felt like a huge chain had been lifted off of my neck.

One day not long after his baptism, Chuck came up to my apartment and climbed out of his wheelchair in front of me and I wondered what he was doing! He struggled to get on his knees and he asked me to marry him. I was sort of surprised and yet I knew that it was coming because I knew that he cared a lot about me. I was trying to figure out this process because I had just been divorced and my emotions were up and down, but all of a sudden I knew that it was the right thing to do. I climbed out of my chair and got on the floor next to him and smiled, and said, "Yes!" This is how I met Charles David Robideau, who became my husband and the man of my dreams.

The Road to Marriage

Though I relate some of the beautiful details of our subsequent marriage in the next chapter, I describe here some of the bumpy road in getting to our wedding and related events so that they do not clutter that lovely event. However, there was quite a road for us in getting to marriage.

Since we were not sure how to go about this next step, we soon went and talked to our Bishop about the situation. Bishop Brad Leeser was then our Bishop, and he was a kind but firm leader. When we visited, he told me that Charles was a very nice man, and if I loved him then I should marry him. He also told me that my former husband Joe was not going to leave us alone until we were married, so we should make up our minds. Then he smiled and said he would perform the marriage. We were married by Bishop Leeser three months after Chuck's baptism.

True to what Bishop Leeser had said, my ex-husband Joe made that three months a run for our money. He came into New Horizons and stole many things from the building. He even went into Chuck's apartment and stole some records and other items. He talked with the Bishop to see if he could come into my apartment and get things that belonged to him. I agreed to allow this as long as Bishop Leeser was there when he came. Bishop Leeser watched as Joe took everything off of my walls and things like that. Then he was going to go into my kitchen cupboards and Bishop Leeser told him: "That is enough. You took every thing off of her walls, I have never seen anyone so greedy as to do that. The dishes and things like that stay!" He then escorted him out the door.

Chapel of The Church of Jesus Christ of Latter-day Saints, Fargo, ND, where Shirley Stockford and Charles Robideau were married, 1985.

Charles and I made plans to have our wedding held at the chapel for The Church of Jesus Christ of Latter-day Saints in Fargo, and then hoped to go to the Temple in the following year when Chuck was ready to enter the Temple. We set our wedding date to be on Charles' Birthday, December 14, 1985.

Well, without us knowing it, Joe (my former husband) came to the wedding with his own plan to walk down the aisle behind me and my escort during the wedding march to embarrass me. My dad was going to walk with me. Bishop Leeser found out about his plan to do that and had two elders sit next to him with one on each side of Joe, and then told him that if he even moved during the wedding then these two Elders were instructed to escort him out the door.

Next, Joe told Bishop Leeser that instead he wanted to sit with my parents. Bishop Leeser told him that they were no longer his in-laws and either he would sit with the Elders or be asked to leave. Not easily discouraged, then he thought that he would object when they asked if there was anyone in the congregation who objected to this union. However, they do not say that in the vows of a Latter-day Saint wedding—so he was out of luck!

When the wedding ceremony was done, we went to a different section of the building to have cake and ice cream. The people who were in the kitchen said that my ex-husband Joe had come into the kitchen and apparently stolen a large portion of the wedding cake. He also then went out to the van that I owned, took all of our clothes out of our suitcases which we had out there for our honeymoon, and replaced them with bags of garbage.

Well, even that wasn't the end of it. After we reached our hotel for the honeymoon, Chuck was very tired and so I helped him to lay down and I was going to get into the shower and then go to bed also. A few minutes after that somebody knocked on our door. Chuck said, "Are you going to answer it?" I said, "No, it is our wedding day!"

I didn't want any additional company. Well, it was my former husband and he had followed us. We didn't answer the door and he finally left. I opened up the suitcase and all our clothing was gone and there was garbage filled in it. I didn't know what to do and so I called Bishop Leeser When he heard my voice, he was totally puzzled and asked me what I was doing by calling him on our honeymoon?

When I told him what had happened, he began laughing, then he apologized and said, "Call the police!" I said, "Call the police? It's my wedding night!" He said, "Call the police and file charges." So, I called the police.

When the police arrived, they looked at Chuck laying in bed and me in my wheelchair in my wedding dress, and I could tell he thought, "What in the world?" I showed him the suitcase filled with garbage and he asked me if I knew who did it. I told him that someone had knocked on our door not too long before and I was quite certain it was my previous husband. I told him my ex-husband's name and I could tell he didn't quite believe me, so I told him to go ask up front if someone that stuttered came and asked what room we were in. They checked with the front desk and the clerk told them that a man had come to see which room we were located in and this man stuttered. So, sure enough, it was him that knocked on our door! The police asked me what we wanted to be done about the stolen clothes, and so I said, "Arrest him. He stole our clothes!"

In the meantime, Bishop Leeser had called my ex-husband and asked him if he did do that. When he was not able to talk because of stuttering, Bishop Leeser told him that he had better have our clothes back at our apartment that next morning or charges would be filed and he would be arrested. After the police left, we spent most of the evening laughing about what had happened. When we returned to the apartment the next day, our clothes were there—that is, everything except my new nightgown! Wonder what he did with the Red Nightgown!

Chapter 20
Temple Blessings and Being Sealed for Time and All Eternity

A New Marriage and New Chapters in My Life

As noted, I was divorced in 1985 but also met my future husband, Charles Robideau, and was courted by him during the period of time that my divorce became final. Charles chose to become a member of The Church of Jesus Christ of Latter-day Saints at that time, and this provided a foundation for us to build on common ground and pursue a future marriage relationship. To marry someone like Chuck, who was kind and loving to me, was like a fairy tale to me.

Getting Married and Moving Forward

I was thrilled with the marriage proposal that I received from Charles and looked forward to our marriage together.

We were married on his birthday, December 14, 1985. That was such a special day for us. Bishop Bradley Leeser married us at the Latter-day Saint chapel in Fargo with most of our family there with us. We had our honeymoon at the Holiday Inn in Fargo, North Dakota. We were married by Bishop Leeser and it was a very nice wedding. Bishop Leeser told us that we would go to the Temple later and be married for Time and All Eternity.

Bishop Leeser counseled us on a number of things at the time we were married. For example, he told us that we should never go to bed angry with each other, and that we should always talk things out before going to sleep. Fortunately, we never had to go to sleep after being upset about anything because Charles and I almost never had an argument. If we were unsure about anything, we would go to each other and tell each other our thoughts on the subject, and then after talking about it and praying about it, we would know what to do. He was such an amazing man. He let me know every single day that he loved me. I very much appreciate the wise words and counsel that Bishop Leeser gave to us on our wedding day.

We went to the Holiday Inn afterwards for our honeymoon, where Charles had rented a nice suite for us. During our honeymoon at the Holiday Inn, when we reached our room I found that Charles had a lovely vase placed in the room that had two red roses in it. One was wilted and dying, while the other was beautiful, large and vibrant red. He told me that the dying rose represented our past life and to let it go and let's move on. The beautiful full rose, he told me, represented our life together from here on and into Eternity. I had tears streaming down my face at the kindness of this good man and the love that he shared with me.

Again, for me, life with my Charles David Robideau was like a fairy tale. To be talked to in a kindly and loving manner was a wonderful change in my life. Oh, how I loved this kind man. He was the most romantic man I have ever met in my life.

Chuck's life with Friedrich's Ataxia, which at the time was considered a type of Muscular Dystrophy, was very difficult for him. However, he never let anyone know that. He wrote about these things in his journal. I had never really kept a journal much. It was hard for me because I had one while married to Joe but never wrote anything in it for fear of him reading it. I could not feel at peace with myself to put the feelings of my heart down on paper. However, in being married to Chuck I felt the darkness begin to go from my life—Chuck brought me out of darkness into light.

We shared everything with each other. He would help me with things that I could not do, and I helped him with things that he could not do. Between us there developed a feeling of oneness. We would help one another with tasks at home or church assignments and we enjoyed being there for each other. Chuck's way of viewing life was amazing and it brought joy. His sense of humor was the highlight of our marriage.

A Spiritual Moment for Charles

We went to Salt Lake City, Utah during the first year we were married. We could not be sealed together yet and Charles wanted to receive his Temple Endowment and do the temple ordinance work for his father. His Dad died when Charles found out that he had Friedreich's Ataxia as a teenager. His father Elmer died from a brain tumor. It was so hard on Chuck not having his Dad to talk to as he encountered many difficulties with the onset of the disease.

The Salt Lake LDS Temple, where Shirley and Charles Robideau first visited the temple in 1986.

Our friend Sidney Rodunce drove our van and took us to Salt Lake City. We had a wonderful time there. We were able to go through a live temple session at the Salt Lake Temple. It took us two days to drive there in September 1986, and I recorded these memories in a journal on the day we first went to the temple:

> My sweet Charles went to the temple for his endowments today. He is so neat and handsome in white. I didn't make it without crying. Charles' first words to me in the celestial room were, "You just glow." I felt him radiating so much right back. I did the temple work for a lady named Maria B. today. I really felt her spirit near me. She must be a very special lady. The temple workers helped us up the stairs in the manual chairs. I felt so bad that they had to carry us up those steps; but they assured me everything was ok. (Shirley Robideau Journal Entry, September 16, 1986)

Being able to participate in this sacred experience with my husband was a wonderful blessing in our lives.

As noted, the brethren working there carried us up the beautiful spiral staircase so that Charles could be baptized in proxy for his father. Charles was having trouble keeping his legs down in the water, so one of the Elders went into the font and put himself under the water and held his legs down while the ordinance was performed. When my sweetheart Charles came out of the water, he looked so proud and told me later that his father spoke to him during the ordinance and told him that he loved him. It was a very spiritual experience for Charles.

An Encounter with the Prophet of the Lord

One of the unique experiences that Charles and I had together quite early in our marriage on this journey to Salt Lake was when we met briefly with the Prophet of the Lord. Let me explain. In our Latter-day Saint faith, we believe in the concept of a living prophet on the earth today who leads and guides our church under the direction of Jesus Christ. The individual who serves as Prophet is supported and works with a group of Twelve Apostles, just as when Christ was on the earth and called his Apostles.

In September 1986, our friend Sid Rodunce took us for a trip to Salt Lake City, Utah soon after our marriage. Salt Lake City is the headquarters of our faith. We were touring Temple Square (the headquarters area of our faith), and one of the Elders (missionaries) was showing us around and became very friendly with us. He had a name tag on which said Temple Square Elder and I thought it said "Elder Square." I have called him Elder Square ever since. Anyway, in our conversation he told us that the Prophet of the Lord, President Ezra Taft Benson, goes to the Jordan River Temple every Friday. When I asked what time he attends, he replied that no one ever knows when he is going to be there.

I talked with Chuck and Sid Rodunce and we made plans to go to the Jordan River Temple ourselves on that coming Friday. I prayed earnestly that we could go at the right time and perhaps meet the Prophet, President Benson. We got to the Temple and I went into the dressing room to change into my temple clothing. Then, I went from there to the prayer room and waited. I didn't see President Benson and started to think that I would not get to see him. But, then the Holy Spirit whispered to me that everything would be all right. So, I calmed down and felt confident. We next went in for the temple endowment session and still didn't see him and I started to worry again. Again, the Spirit whispered that everything would be all right. So, again I calmed down. The Spirit of the Lord always speaks to me in my language and I found that he responds to me in the way that I can understand.

Following the temple session, I met with Charles and Sid in the foyer by the elevator and we were going to go down to change clothes back into our street clothes so that we could go down to eat in the dining room. Just as we entered the elevator, I felt the Spirit and President Benson's presence in a very strong way. The spiritual feeling that I had was so overpowering that I said: "He is here."

The Elder that was pushing my chair said, "Who is here?" I said President Benson was here. He said it was possible but that we could not be sure of that. I told him, "I know that he is here." As the elevator moved, I could feel his presence stronger and stronger.

President Ezra Taft Benson, the Latter-day Saint leader and prophet.

As the elevator door opened, I said again, "He is here!" We got to the floor where we were supposed to get off and the door opened and it was just like someone turned the lights on. The room just glowed and his presence was so strong. We turned the corner and there he was standing near the dressing rooms, dressed in white, the Prophet of the Lord. As we went to shake hands with him, tears streamed down my face at the goodness of my Father in Heaven's kindness to allow me to shake the hand of one of his chosen Prophets. I could not talk, as I was so emotional, but I did shake his hand. President Ezra Taft Benson shook our hands and then said: "What are you two doing here in your chariots on wheels!"

I loved that man instantly! I knew without a doubt that this truly was a Prophet of God. That was an experience I will never forget. To touch the hand of a Prophet and receive a sure witness for myself that he was indeed a Prophet of God. It was such a special feeling to meet him. This episode became one of the most memorable and touching spiritual experiences of my life and of our lives together as a married couple.

Other Experiences on Our Trip to Salt Lake City

The trip that we took with Sid Rodunce to Salt Lake City in that first year of our marriage was a wonderful experience. We also had a variety of other meaningful experiences while there.

Since Salt Lake City is the worldwide headquarters of the Latter-day Saint faith, there were many things to see and experience there. While we were in Salt Lake, we toured Temple Square and we really enjoyed that. We went into the famous Tabernacle building to see the Mormon Tabernacle Choir, but they were on tour and so instead we were able to hear the famous Tabernacle Organ. At Temple Square, we also went in to see the famous sculpture of Jesus Christ that is known as the *Christus* (by a Danish sculptor).

Other aspects of our tour while visiting Temple Square included a visit to the model that they had of the Sacred Grove where Joseph Smith was kneeling in prayer. This exhibit displayed the events of what is known in the Latter-day Saint faith as the First Vision, wherein Joseph Smith knelt to pray in the Sacred Grove and was visited by our Heavenly Father and Jesus Christ in answer to his prayer of faith. I loved this exhibit because it connected with my own conversion experience.

We visited other portions of Temple Square and were able to hear the stories of the pioneer Latter-day Saints who had built the temple and endured a variety of hardships. My favorite story was about the seagulls and the crickets, a miracle, in which the pioneers had crops that were being eaten up by crickets but their crops were saved by a large flock of seagulls that came and ate up the crickets.

Charles was so impressed about the Temple after his visit there and he was filled with the spirit of temple work and bringing spiritual blessings to our ancestors. He bought a family history program and began putting together his family ancestry on the program. I remember in that first year when he was going to be ordained in the Priesthood to the office of an Elder, and he was so nervous and he was hesitant to go to church that Sunday. But we went and I was able to hear it when they called his name to be an Elder. I had tears of joy and was so proud of him.

When we were in Salt Lake, Sid took Charles for a ride up the side of the mountain and Chuck was sitting alongside Sid while he was driving. Chuck was in his manual wheelchair and was not strapped down. As they went up the mountain, it got steeper and steeper and Chuck's chair veered back onto his wheelie bars. Chuck didn't think anything of it because he thought he was well balanced on his wheelie bars. But the road continued to get steeper and soon Chuck's chair tipped totally back into the van! So funny!

I so much enjoyed that trip because of all the things we saw on our way there and when we went on tours. We saw the Grand Canyon in Arizona, Old Faithful geyser in Yellowstone National Park, and much other beautiful scenery. In Salt Lake, we saw Brigham Young's grave, the Beehive House, the Church Family History library, and so many other wonderful things. I had never really been on a trip to see things like that and so it was pretty special to me to be able to share it with Chuck and Sid.

On the day we were driving back to Fargo from Salt Lake, Sid said that there was a problem with our van. We all prayed together that we would be able to return home to Fargo with no problem with the van. We took a long way home and went to Denver, Colorado so that we could go to see the new Temple during the open house. We finally got home to the border of Fargo, right by a gas and service station, and the van died! The problem was a clogged gas filter. Sid said that we should have prayed to get to our apartment because we did indeed make it to Fargo, but no further! Altogether, we drove 3,199 miles and the van quit just as we got home.

Being Sealed for Time and Eternity

Once we were married, living the Gospel of Jesus Christ and sharing it with a man that believed as I did and reading together each night from the *Book of Mormon* was such a treasure that I miss so very much. We had so many miracles in our short sixteen years together.

Our experience in being united together in marriage for time and eternity, which in our faith is described as being "sealed together for eternity," took place in the Chicago Illinois LDS Temple. At the time, this was the nearest Latter-day Saint temple for us living in North Dakota. We went to the Chicago Illinois Temple with our dear friend and fellow ward member, Sidney Rodunce, as he drove our van the many miles (over 14 hours) to arrive there. We arrived at the Temple grounds and

Chuck and Sid went one way and I went with the Temple Matron to the beautiful Bridal Room. On this day, August 21, 1987, we were sealed together as husband and wife for Time and All Eternity. It was the highlight of my life.

I cannot even express the feeling that I had as I was in the Bridal Room looking into the mirror and seeing myself dressed in white. I had been in the Temple a number of times prior to that moment but that day was so sacred. I looked into the mirror and saw myself, as a non-handicapped person, a daughter of God—I felt beautiful and alive in a real world. I saw myself as I will be when I am made whole after the Resurrection. I saw myself able to stand and walk and felt so wonderful. I will never forget that experience.

Shirley and Charles Robideau, as a married couple.

The Temple Matron took me to the sealing room for us to participate in the sealing ordinance that would unite us as husband and wife for eternity. There, I saw my sweetheart telling the temple sealer that he wanted to kneel at the altar as we were sealed together for Time and All Eternity and kiss his bride over the altar. That kind man helped him kneel at the altar and held Chuck there in place as he sealed us together and we did indeed kiss over the altar as Husband and Wife—a beautiful memory.

A Life of Faith—Together

Life with Charles was never boring. This man was so devoted to the Gospel of Jesus Christ that he taught me many things.

We would go to bed early at night so we could have time to read the *Book of Mormon* together. I loved reading to him and having him ask questions and talking with him about what we had read.

He began memorizing the Sacrament Prayers, the Thirteen Articles of Faith, and whatever else he wanted to learn. When we would read together, he would tell me which of the Thirteen Articles of Faith we had just touched on. He was amazing in his faith and devotion.

He was called to be the President of the Sunday School and held that position for a number of years. He began blessing the Sacrament often and from memory because he was almost blind and near the end of his life he was totally blind. He loved the gospel of Jesus Christ and lived it to the best he could and beyond his ability. He supported me in my callings and even helped me with a lot of my responsibilities.

One sweet spiritual incident occurred early in our marriage. We went to visit the Salt Lake Temple in Utah with a wonderful friend, Sid Rodunce. We stayed with some friends there. Judy and her children were without the children's father. On the last day we were going to be in Salt Lake, Judy asked us if Charles would give her son a Father's Blessing to prepare him for his school year (this is a special priesthood blessing). Charles, being so humbled by the request, went into the bedroom and changed his clothes to put on a white shirt and tie. This was not an easy thing for him to do. He then came out and I watched this young boy as he kneeled so humbly beside my husband, and Charles laid his hands upon his head and gave him a Priesthood Blessing. Tears flowed down my face as I watched and listened to this sacred prayer given by him.

This incident also reminds me of the special occurrence that happened when Charles received his ordination to the Holy Priesthood. Charles himself recorded this instance in his own writings and wrote:

> Another special moment in my life was a year before (Shirley and I) were sealed together at Chicago. It began at the church on September 7, 1986, after I was a church member for one year. I was found to be worthy and was ordained an Elder of the Church. My mother was present with me. She saw the Elders lay their hands upon my head and ordain me. She cried and left the chapel.
>
> Later when I asked her about it, she replied, "I saw Elmer." I knew my father was there, I know my mother saw him. He wanted her to know that he approved of what I was doing. The following week I had the sacred honor of

doing his endowments at the holy temple in Salt Lake City, Utah. My dad was there with me. I know that with all my heart and he approved all that I did in his behalf.

I would like my family to know this about their brother, cousin, uncle, or son. Know that I have a very strong testimony that The Church of Jesus Christ of Latter-day Saints is the Lord's Church here on earth; that Jesus Christ and Heavenly Father are two personages who together lead and guide this Church. I believe Joseph Smith was a prophet of God just like Moses, Abraham, Isaiah, and Adam were prophets of the Old Testament. I believe that just as in the Old and New Testaments, the Lord leads his people today through a living prophet. He guides a prophet of God and gives us divine revelation from the Lord today. (Charles Robideau Journal Entry)

Such experiences as this were important in teaching me that I was married to a special man and I sought to cultivate gratitude for the blessing of our lives together.

When Charles received his own Patriarchal Blessing, given by the Stake Patriarch, David Cobia, I also learned so much more about this special man who I had married. One line in his special blessing stated that Charles knew that he would come to Earth with the disabilities that he had and that he accepted them. I understood then that we all know the circumstances in which we are born and we accept them with glad hearts. This understanding has helped me to not complain when things get harder.

Church Service and Temple Experiences

In our faith, the regular ministering and teaching assignments are carried out by everyday church members who each receive a calling or assignment to serve. Charles received a calling to serve in the Sunday School Presidency shortly after we were married. In time, Charles served as President of the Sunday School for about eight years. I was very proud of him as he learned about the Church and the leadership responsibilities that he could exercise. He became an Elder in the Priesthood after the first year of our marriage, and then we went to the Temple to be sealed together for Time and All Eternity. As already noted, Sid Rodunce drove us to Chicago and was there to witness our sealing experience.

I held several callings in the Church prior to marrying Charles. I had been a counselor in the Relief Society Presidency in Jamestown as well as a Visiting Teacher. After we were married, I was called as a Stake Relief Society Secretary under Sister Pat Cobia as the President. I served there for three years. I remember so many special spiritual experiences I had in my calling as secretary at that time.

One really sacred time for me was when the Presidency met together to make decisions on the next two-day Stake Relief Society Conference. We were discussing the name of the conference theme and what it should be. We had difficulty deciding what it should be. Sister Cobia paused and read a scripture, and when she read the words, "Lift up your heads, and be of good cheer," all of us knew instantly that this was supposed to be the theme of this conference. Nothing was said, like, "Hey, that is it!" Instead, we just felt a strong spirit of unity—we all knew. It was a beautiful experience for me.

Other church callings I served in included being in charge of the luncheons for the missionary conferences, writing the weekly church bulletins, and other service opportunities. Chuck and I wrote and mailed out Visiting Teaching and Home Teaching letters each month. We did as many as 30 to 40 letters each month, sometimes more and sometimes less. We loved doing that.

Our closest available Latter-day Saint Temple at the time was the Chicago Illinois Temple, which was about a twelve- or fourteen-hour drive depending on the conditions. The way that church members made trips to participate in temple work was that the Fargo Stake (like a parish) would have a bus come and pick up members who could attend and we would go together for a few days. The trips we made in this way were very hard on Charles but you could not keep him

The Chicago Illinois LDS Temple, where Shirley and Charles Robideau made many of their temple visits together.

from going to the Temple. He loved the Temple as much as I did. Once when we went to the temple on such a trip, by the time we got there Charles' heart was racing so the other brethren with us tipped his wheelchair back so that his head was down and his legs were up. This action helped his heart to calm down and we went to the Temple and were there all day and he was so thrilled.

    The Lord blessed Charles and I because of our desire to be there in the Temple. We believe that the Temple is the House of the Lord and you can feel His presence and spirit there. It was such a sacred experience to visit the temple because of all the names that we prepared for temple work. Charles had done the preparation of many family names to receive gospel ordinances through temple work using the PAF (Personal Ancestral File) program. He had 900 names that he had prepared for temple work on the computer—one finger stroke at a time. We printed out all that we could and we took that information with us to the Chicago Temple. The other church members helped us to do the temple work for several of the names we prepared.

    I remember once such trip to the Temple and it was such a wonderful day. I had given one of the names that we prepared to my friend, Pat Cobia. Pat came back and told me that she felt very strongly that I was supposed to do the ordinances for this name. It was the name of my great aunt, Mary Hart. I took her name and went into the Temple and did the work for her. While I was in the Endowment session for her in the Temple, I heard her voice clearly telling me that she loved me. I cried the rest of the way through the endowment ceremony. It was such a special time for me at the Temple. I learned that the veil is very thin between earth and the spirit world.

    On a different trip to the Temple, we had to stay in our room the first day because Charles had a bad nosebleed from the bus trip. I think we were only able to go to the Temple about three or four times on the bus but we loved it. These were great spiritual experiences for us individually and as a couple.

    A somewhat related spiritual experience is a story that my Dad told me as related to him by my cousin, Kenny Wallak. Kenny was working as a Master Plumber and had been in an accident. He was walking on the roof of a meat packing plant when the roof caved in. Kenny had fallen through the roof and landed with a meat hook that punctured his lung. Kenny had been a cigar smoker ever since I can remember. The doctor told him that he was to stop smoking immediately. While in the hospital recuperating, Kenny said that our grandfather, Grandpa Jim (who had passed away many years prior to this), came to visit him. Grandpa was smoking his pipe and sat on his bed beside Kenny. He said: "Kenny, they aren't going to take you yet!" Then he left. The nurse came into the room and asked Kenny if he had been smoking. Kenny told her he was not smoking at all, but she told him that she could smell the smoke and to remember that the Doctor warned him that he could not smoke again. Kenny laughed and let it go at that. So, again this illustrates the closeness of the spirit world to our world here in mortality.

Another great experience in our lives happened when we went to the temple in Chicago in 1987-88 and were able to have my daughter, Judith Ann, sealed to us in our family for eternity. I was full of joy. I wrote in a journal record:

> I can't tell you in words the feelings that I had when I knew that my family on the other side was there with me in the holy temple, and sharing not only their ordinances with me but also sharing my joy in having my daughter (who lived just 1-½ days) sealed for time and all eternity to Charles and myself. When we went into the holy sealing room and I kneeled upon the sacred altar and held Charles' hand, I was aware that many people were in there with us, not just those from the stake but my family on the other side. Those wonderful spirits were there and they cried along with me as Judith Ann was sealed to us. Judith Ann was there and her love touched my heart so deeply that I didn't want to let go of her. My greatest joy now is knowing that I am no longer the only member of my family that is a member of the Lord's Church. This is the Lord's work and I am grateful I was able to contribute just a small part and to receive far more in return than I ever expected. (Shirley Robideau Journal Entry, c. 1988)

The transformation of my mother's grief at the loss of my infant daughter to joy as we experienced this family blessing in the temple was miraculous to me. Truly, our Savior Jesus Christ cares so deeply for us, in making it possible for us to be joined in family ties forever.

I am so grateful for the Temple. The peace you have there is like nothing in this world. It is a place of love and beauty. I love going there so much to do work to seal together members of my family to me and the rest of our family. My family means everything to me. I love them so very much.

Chapter 21
Life Adventures and Making Things Work

New Chapters in a Full Life

Getting married to Charles opened up a new era in my life and we had many positive and varied experiences together. We married in 1985 and were together for sixteen years before his eventual passing. In this section, I explain some of the memorable things that I learned about Chuck's earlier life as we got to know each other and also some of the life adventures that we shared.

Charles and I enjoyed doing things together and also shared a rich spiritual life. It was very meaningful to serve and grow together as we lived the gospel of Christ. We were able to also gain skills, work to support ourselves, and contribute to those around us. We spent the first year learning how to complement each other's abilities and filled in the gaps where we could. We made things work and our partnership made both of our lives better and more fulfilling. This was a significant and meaningful period of my life.

Getting to Know Charles and His Story

I was very happy to be married to my sweetheart, Charles David Robideau, and learned much more about him and his earlier life as we went further into our marriage in those early years. I remember a number of interesting and occasionally humorous experiences that Chuck shared with me about his life prior to our marriage.

Chuck told me about when he was in school and they were trying out for sports. He considered football and was told to run around this track a few times. He couldn't make it even once. He didn't know why he couldn't do it but he had to walk the rest of the way around. The coach asked him what was wrong. Chuck answered, "Oh, I have asthma!!" Chuck said that was the end of his football career!

So, next he thought he would try out for this sport where you run with this pole and push the pole into the ground and jump as high as you can with the pole (the pole vault). Chuck told me he ran with all his heart and pushed the pole into the ground and tried to jump . . . and his hands slid all the way to the ground holding the pole and his face hit the ground. He then said: "It was about this time that I totally gave up on being in any sports!" Chuck laughed when he told me about this experience. Though such sports were too much of a challenge for his body, he had a sense of humor about such things.

When it came to learning a trade, Chuck had actually gone to college to be trained as a book-keeper because he knew that he would need to have a sit-down job once the Friedreich's Ataxia began to take his walking ability away from him. One time when he was home for the weekend, his nieces painted his toenails bright red for fun. He didn't think anything about it and went back to the school the next morning, and since the bathroom was down the hall from his room he put on his robe and went down to shower. While in the shower, he told me that he was washing and looked down to the floor and saw his bright red toenails looking back up at him. He finished and went back to his room and realized that he had locked himself out! So, he knocked on the door and his new roommate was there and answered the door. A very large, football player-sized guy opened up the door to him. Chuck said of this moment: "I know that my face was as red as my toenails as this huge man looked down at my toenails as I came into the room!"

On a different occasion, Chuck was driving his car and he took it to the gas station and got new tires for the car. His Friedreich's Ataxia was getting very noticeable by this time. When you have this disease, your walk appears similar to someone that is drunk due to its effect on your nervous system. He left the service station and was on a one-way street heading home when one of the tires literally fell off of the car. The station mechanic had forgotten to tighten the lugs on one of the tires. So, Chuck got out of his car and went into the trunk to try and get things out to put his tire back on. While he was in the process of putting the jack under the car, a police officer drove up to check on him because one of the neighbors had reported a drunk trying to change a tire. Chuck was so embarrassed but kept his cool the best he could. It took him a while to convince the officer that he was not drunk, and then the officer helped him tighten the tire back on. These incidents represent just a few of the ups and downs that Chuck experienced in living with his disease and its varied effects.

Chuck told me that it was much easier on him when he was finally transitioned into using a wheelchair, even though he fought about even thinking that he would ever be in a wheelchair. Both he and his sister, Sandy, were diagnosed with Friedreich's Ataxia. It is common if there is one child with this condition that at least half of the family will have it. There were five in Chuck's family and two of them had the diagnosis of FA.

Dealing with Physical Challenges in Marriage

Of course, Chuck and I loved each other very much and in this way we were like most married couples as they begin life together. However, we were unlike most other couples because we both had physical disabilities resulting from polio in my case and from ataxia in Chuck's case, which made managing our lives a bit more challenging.

In so many ways, I felt as though my life had just begun when Chuck and I got married. When I told my parents that we were going to be married, they didn't say anything negative about it. Then one day Dad came to see me at my apartment and told me that I shouldn't marry Chuck. He was worried that we would not be able to handle our disabilities and the challenges that we would have to face. I assured Dad that we would be all right. Not long after we were married, both Dad and Mom told me how much they loved and respected Chuck. This righteous young man adored my parents and was a good example for them.

A few days after we got married, we were in our new apartment and Chuck had to go to the bathroom. I was in the kitchen doing some dishes. He came out of the bathroom and forgot to put his seatbelt on. You have to understand that when he sneezed the force would throw him forward and the seatbelt would keep him from flying out of his chair—which is exactly what happened. He had to sneeze and he literally sneezed so hard that he blew himself out of his power wheelchair! He went to the floor, hitting his face on the cement floor and his glasses embedded themselves into his face. I heard him fall and I went into the living room to see if he was all right. He had his glasses on and his face was full of blood from the glasses cutting into his face. I saw the blood on his face and I panicked. I couldn't get control of myself enough to remember to call the clinic to get help for him.

I asked him, "Chuck, what is the number of the clinic?" He broke out laughing and said, "Shirley, I am laying here on the floor with blood all over my face, and you are asking ME for the phone number?!" We broke out laughing, and when I calmed down then I called the clinic, and the nurse at the clinic walked across the street to help Chuck to get up into his wheelchair again. Chuck always knew what to say to help me to feel at ease no matter what the circumstances. His sense of humor helped us get through many challenges that we had to face.

Following that incident, we knew that we had to find a way to get him off of the floor if he fell. It was common for that to happen. So, we had transfer poles put up alongside the bed and toilet. A transfer pole is a pole that goes from the floor to the ceiling and you just grab it so that you can transfer your body from one spot to another. He would pull himself to a pole and I would get this one step stool that was about a foot high and go along side of him. He would then take both of his strong arms and pull himself up with the pole, as high as he could go. I would push the step stool under him. He would then pull himself up a little higher. I then would put my arm under him and grab the pole. He would sit on my arm and then pull himself up a little higher and I would go up with my arm to hold him there, and we repeated the process until he was high enough to slide from my arm to the toilet. Voila! We did this many times and didn't need help to get him off of the floor.

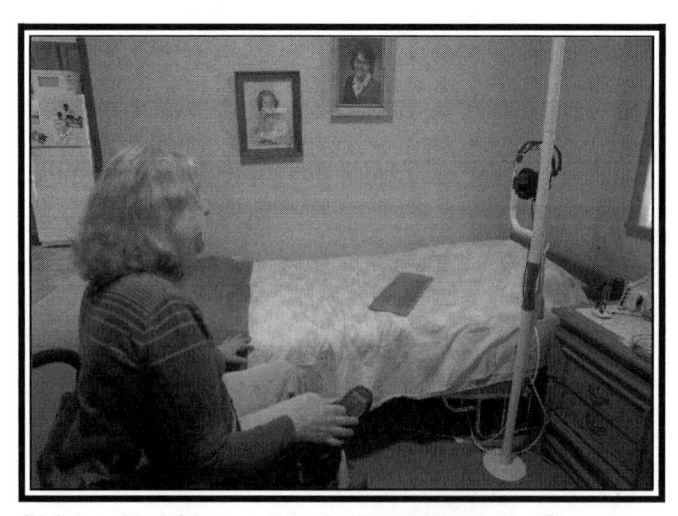

Shirley Robideau showing an example of a transfer pole in her living space to assist with movement from a wheelchair to bed.

The transfer process in the bedroom was more difficult because there was not much room, but we finally were able to get the bed positioned so that we were able to handle things there too. So, we figured out how to get him up off of the floor if he fell down. Later as his arms got weaker, we got a Hoyer Lift to help get him up. So, we found ways of doing things so that we could care for ourselves as much as possible. We made it many years by ourselves by just working together to handle whatever situations came up.

One time we were in bed sleeping and I felt the Spirit tell me that Charles needed help and then showed me in a vision what was happening. I saw him begin to roll to his right side and begin to fall off the bed. With the transfer pole along side of him as close to the bed as it was, he would choke to death as his neck got trapped against the pole. It was pitch black when I opened my eyes. I began to turn towards him just as he was beginning to roll over on his right side and was beginning to fall off the bed by the transfer pole. The Spirit prompted me as to where to grab him, since I could not see, and I did as I was prompted and was able to safely keep him from getting hurt. I learned to always listen to the promptings of the Spirit.

Another time, I was working downstairs at New Horizons in the kitchen and I felt that something was wrong, so I excused myself and went up to see if he was all right. He was in the bathroom washing blood off of his face. I asked him what had happened and he said that he had gone over to the grocery store and returned and was taking off his coat. The coat caught hold of his control for the wheelchair and sent him flying forward, and he lost his balance and the wheelchair ran him into the bread board and cut his face. We didn't have too many incidents where he got hurt so life was not always a difficult situation, but we had to manage a few of them.

Prior to our marriage, Chuck had fallen many times with no one to help him. He told me that he would lose about five pounds every time he had to fight to get back into his power chair. It could be a tiresome struggle to climb back into his wheelchair. His power wheelchair was an Everett and Jennings brand. He laughed as he told me that when he fell he would look at his chair from the floor and think to himself that he had to climb Mount Everett again!

Managing Financial Challenges

Now, financially, we didn't have very much. Chuck was concerned when we first got married about our finances. Chuck had given up his father's railroad retirement to be able to marry me, which had been about three or four hundred dollars a month. We didn't have much money. I think we were getting about six hundred dollars a month.

I tried to get some training so that I could get a job and so that we could have an extra income. It was office training and it taught me how to use office equipment, typing, telephone skills, and other items. I took that class for several months. Chuck prayed about it a great deal and I had begun taking these classes at the Adult Education Facility.

I was learning office skills which I dearly loved doing. I learned how to use the Apple II-E Computer and I was so excited about the things I was learning. I went home and told Charles about the computer and that he would love it. He thought there was no way that he could use the computer because of his hands. I assured him that he would love the computer and it would open up so many doors for him since he could not write any more. So, we invested $2,000 to get one. My dear Chuck took off with it!

After we bought our computer and I taught him how to use it, he just became so thrilled and from that point on until not long before he died he used it almost every day. He typed with just one finger but he could accomplish more with his one-finger typing than anyone else I knew. He kept a journal about almost every day of our married life. He bought an accounting program called Quicken and kept our financial records on that program. He even took care of a great deal of our Family History with a program called Personal Ancestral File or PAF. He and I put about two thousand names on that program. The computer gave him such a boost in life. I doubt that there was one day that he didn't use the computer if we were at home. This may not seem like a big task to others, but he did all these things with one-finger typing. It built up his confidence beyond anything I could have ever said or done for him.

As I mentioned, Chuck wrote in a journal almost every day and I have his journal with me still. It brings me comfort when I read the words he wrote about his love for me. He loved doing Home Teaching letters to members of our congregation and whatever else the Bishop could find for him to do. Chuck was called to be the Ward bulletin editor and Sunday School Leader in our congregation, and he held these positions for more than eight years.

When I finished my classes, Chuck had his family come over and they threw a graduation party for me. Such a sweetheart! Things were not easy for us but we found solutions and were helped by family, friends, others and the Lord.

Example of Apple II-E computer used by Shirley and Chuck Robideau.

Finding Ways to Support Ourselves Financially

Shortly after we were married, Chuck talked to Social Services about the possibility of me being paid for all that I did to help him so that I would not have to find work away from home. He knew that it was possible for individuals providing support as a caregiver to receive financial compensation. The Social Service representative told him about having me apply to be Chuck's home care provider. They worked it out so that we could get a little bit of extra money each month through this arrangement. It was not much money but it helped a great deal and I was able to stay home. I did that for about 12 years. So, by doing that I earned an extra four hundred dollars a month, which made up for the money that we missed due to the absence of his railroad retirement. That was a great blessing to us. We saved this money so that we could pay off bills and have money to do the things that we needed or to get necessary items.

We did not have enough funds to purchase an air conditioner, however, so Chuck bartered work with one of the church members who brought the air conditioner for us and Chuck worked his book-keeping in trade to pay him back. So, we found different ways to supplement our finances and support ourselves. Chuck liked keeping busy with the computer.

I then picked up a job working downstairs in the kitchen at New Horizons Manor and helping to set up tables for the meals that were served down there. I made seven dollars an hour doing that. I had never in my life earned seven dollars an hour and so it was a great amount to me. Nowadays, people might think that is awful because it is equivalent to the minimum wage, but I was pretty proud of that at the time. So, we began to be able to take care of our needs.

I worked for this Congregate Housing Program for New Horizons for about three or four years. I enjoyed doing that because it helped me to get to know the other residents of the apartment building. At the time we lived there, it was an independent living facility. I was responsible for setting up the tables, serving as the cook dished up plates, clearing the tables of the dirty dishes after the residents left the lunchroom, washing the dishes and stacking them in the dishwasher, putting them away when all was done, and reloading the dishwasher and washing all the tables. On the average, we fed anywhere between 35 and 50 people twice a day for five days a week and once a day on the weekends. I knew exactly who sat where in the dining room. I knew where everybody sat. I knew which ones drank whole milk and which ones drank skim milk. I had to have it all set up for them when they would come down. They would dish up the plates and I would take the plates to whoever they told me to take it to and serve the food to them.

I really enjoyed doing that job. It was six days a week and the number of hours depended on how many residents came down to eat and the length of time it took to clean up. Usually, it took about six or seven hours a day—it was a lot of work. However, it was perfect for me.

It was very convenient for me because I could take a break in between meals and go and check on Chuck to see if he was all right. I would get a feeling in my heart that there was something wrong upstairs and I would tell them, "I need to go and check on Chuck." I would go upstairs and there would be something wrong every time. He told me that I had an antenna that let me know when to come up and help him. Because I worked down there in the kitchen, we received our meals for free and I could take them up for us when I went up to our apartment.

Many times while doing this job I would also go in the elevator and deliver trays of food to people who were not able to come down for their meals. Usually, there were about 10 to 15 people that had their meals delivered.

One of the people that I had delivered a plate to was named Orah. I adored this lady. When I took her food tray to her, I smiled at her and talked to her a little bit and then left to get back to work. As I was leaving her apartment one day, the Spirit of the Lord spoke to me and I knew it would be the last time I saw her. I kind of shook that thought away and went down to work. The next day, I found out that she had died while she was eating. I try to listen to the Spirit better now as I have learned through such experiences. I don't know what I could have done or said differently but maybe I could have said something. Also, I later realized that what happened was a very sacred experience because the Lord let me know that this sweet lady was coming home and that I didn't need to do anything, just be comforted in knowing that she would be all right.

Service Through TOUCH and the Freedom Resource Center

Though we each had our struggles, Charles and I both desired to serve others because that was a central element of our faith and a way to follow the example of our Savior, Jesus Christ. Service activities also provided us with a way to give back to others and grow together.

Besides the Spinning Wheels Square Dancing group, Chuck and I were involved in an organization called TOUCH (Towards Our Understanding of Our Community's Handicapped). Through this group we went to schools all over the area and taught children about what it is like to be disabled and how we help ourselves to be independent. I really enjoyed doing this because the kids were so much fun and it was interesting to find out what they wanted to know about us. We would give them a half-hour talk about ourselves and then they could ask us anything. The children would send us pictures that they had drawn of us. Almost all of them would draw pictures of us holding hands!

Chuck and I pulled the Spinning Wheels square dance group into our involvement with the TOUCH program by having the Spinning Wheels come and dance for some of the schools. Then we would all go into classes and tell the

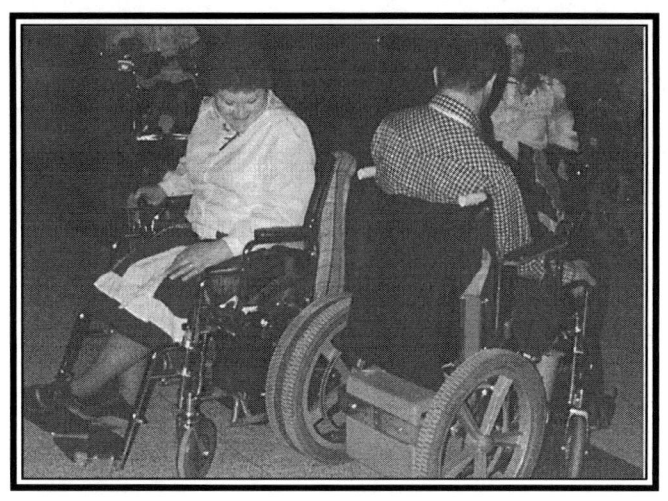

Shirley Robideau, on left, in wheelchair square dancing group.

children about ourselves. This was a really great gift that we were able to give to our community's schools. Transportation to these events was provided by the Fargo Park District. It was wonderful to me how the programs could be pulled together to benefit all programs. I was so proud of Chuck for organizing this wonderful project.

Another group we were involved in resulted in creating what is now the Freedom Resource Center for Independent Living. We actually were involved in the formation of this wonderful organization. We went all over North Dakota and talked to people and filled out grant proposals to begin this wonderful center. Today, I have been a client of Freedom Resource Center as I seek to solve many problems that I encounter as I strive to remain independent in my own apartment.

Adventures in Babysitting

A time that I dearly loved was when my brother, John, brought his three children over for us to babysit while he was working. We went to the park on every nice day that the weather would allow us to go. The children loved climbing on the bars that were there, the swings, the merry-go-round and playing in the sand. We would pack up a lunch and all five of us would go to the park together. Christina, the oldest, would climb on the back of Chuck's chair, Amber would get on the back of my chair, and Jonathan would be in my lap, he being the youngest.

We would go to the grocery store many times also with the kids on our chairs. People would smile when they would see us all together. We would play games on the days that we could not go outside and I loved it when they would laugh and have a good time. I absolutely love all my nieces and nephews!

I also did some babysitting for the manager of New Horizons Manor for a wonderful six months. Little James was two weeks old when I began to take care of him while his mother was working. I would put a pillow on my lap and lay James on the pillow, and then Chuck and I would take him to the park and he would fall asleep in my lap. His mother told me that he still falls asleep when he is taken for a ride in the car! I was so surprised at how smart this little guy was. He knew I was not a strong person and so he would not jump around in my arms. Also, when he would wake up from a nap, if he was laying on the blanket on the floor, then when I would go up to him he would reach his arms upright and when I began to pick him up he would stiffen his body so that he could go almost into a standing position so that I could pull him up to my lap. So smart!

Little children are naturally close to the Savior and have a strong spirit of love and I love being with them. I believe that they are so close to the Savior because they have left His presence not very long before. Perhaps one reason we can't talk as a baby is because we would talk too much about the things of the world we came from—from our time with our Heavenly Parents. It gives me such a warm feeling to hold children in our arms.

Friends and Funny Moments

As Chuck and I participated regularly in church meetings and activities, we found many friends and received a lot of positive support. We had great friends and some fun moments with many of them.

One wonderful experience that I had with Chuck took place when we were at church in our early married years. The Church takes some steps to make sure that things are accessible to those who have special needs. When we first got married, in our chapel there were the main men's and women's bathrooms and a shower room near the baptismal font. Since Chuck needed help when he went to the restroom, it was embarrassing for him to have to go to the women's bathroom and the same for me to go to the men's bathroom to help him. So, they made the shower room a bathroom for Chuck and I to use. They put a pole from the floor to the ceiling for us to grab on to for transfers. Also, alongside the toilet was the shower. They also installed an automatic door so that we could get out easily.

Once when Chuck was done using the toilet, he transferred back into his wheelchair and backed up to get ready to turn and go out the door. While backing up he accidentally bumped the valve for the shower—turning it on full blast! When the cold water hit him, he jumped and his feet hit his foot pedal in such a way that it pulled off one of his shoes and it flew up into the air and did a spin and fell directly into the toilet!

After getting the water shut off, Chuck was drenched and we went out into the hallway laughing so hard. There a friend, Steve C., saw us come out and saw Chuck soaked with his hair and clothes dripping and the shoe in his lap. He began to laugh so uncontrollably that he had to grab the wall to keep from falling to the floor and still continued laughing until he actually was down on his knees! That was such a funny day that left many people smiling as they left church that day, and it always brings a smile to my face as I remember it.

Two of our good friends were Brad and Minka Leeser, who would come and visit us often at our apartment. Chuck knew that Brad liked chocolate mint candy so he always kept a box in the refrigerator for whenever Brad would come. One time when Brad was at our place, Chuck went to the refrigerator to get some candy mints out for Brad. While he was getting the box, he dropped it and the mints all fell out of the box everywhere. Chuck was laughing so hard that when he tried to back off of the mints, his chair would rock back and forth with the pace of his laughter. As he went back and forth, he was also going over the mints! Brad was sitting on the davenport in the front room watching what was happening and broke out laughing and was not able to control it. The more Brad laughed, the more Chuck would laugh and his hand would make his chair rock back and forth over the mints, and they would both laugh all the harder. That was a fun day for all of us.

Giving and Receiving in Service

When Charles was ordained a Priest and then an Elder, and in time a High Priest in the Melchizedek Priesthood, it was very interesting to me to watch how he progressed in each step as he was ordained to a new office in the priesthood. He took his callings very seriously.

When Charles was called as a Home Teacher, we so enjoyed going to visit our families. It was important to Chuck that we see them every month. He would call and set up appointments to visit with them on a monthly basis and I doubt that we ever failed to make it to one of the appointments. One of these families was the Brian and Sue B. family. I remember the first time we visited them, it was on Valentine's Day and we brought a large Valentine cookie for them and had their name put on the cookie. I mis-spelled their name and it really bothered Charles that I didn't spell it right. They had two young girls named Leah and Janet and a son named Bernie. One time they came with the two girls and Janet was playing with a five-gallon jar that had all of our coins that we were saving to go on a trip to Utah. Somehow this little girl lifted that very heavy jar that was half full of coins and dropped it. The jar broke and had jagged edges of glass pointing upward near her. Brian stood up and took hold of Janet and gently lifted her straight up and away from the broken glass. I was so grateful that she didn't get hurt. Later, Brian brought over a plastic five-gallon jar so we had another jar for saving our coins in. When we went to Utah that next year, we had saved over 800 dollars in that jar!

Another family we visited was the Chuck and Joy Walen family. One time we went to visit them and they had a huge swimming pool in their back yard and all of them were swimming! It was so fun to see them enjoying themselves as a family.

Also, he was the home teacher in charge of letter writing to individuals who preferred receiving a letter to a visit, and he did as many as 50 letters a month for home teaching. He took that very seriously. He would have me proofread his writing and if I thought that he worded something wrong he would have me correct it. We did the home teaching letters together and printed them out, stuffed the envelopes, put on the stamps, and mailed them out.

He was the Sunday School president for about eight years in the Fargo 1st Ward congregation. To me, I could see in Charles the spirit of the calling and perhaps others did not, but I thought that the Lord knew what he was doing and I watched him grow in that assignment. He learned so much in that calling.

Charles received his patriarchal blessing a year following our marriage, and it said in his patriarchal blessing that he would have an insight into the scriptures. I thought about it and was concerned because I was trying to read to him and my reading efforts were not the best, and so I wondered how he would be able to learn anything by listening to me read to him. However, we read the scriptures every night and so we went through the *Book of Mormon* at least once a year. Once we were studying and he said to me about that section of the *Book of Mormon*, "Helaman, the son of Helaman, the son of Alma, the son of Alma, the son of . . .," and he just went all the way back on that family's ancestry. I asked, "Where did you learn all of that?" He answered, "Listening to you!" So, the Lord really was close to him because he certainly could not have learned all of that from listening to me since my reading was so bad. He was quite close to the Lord.

We have had many Bishops, Home Teachers and Visiting Teachers that came to visit us each month. I want to tell you that there has not ever been a change in either of these callings that we did not gain a witness that they were called of God. Every new Bishop was exactly who we needed at that time. The Lord has been very mindful of us and saw to it that our needs were met.

A part of Charles' responsibility to his Home Teaching families included taking the Sacrament to those who lived in our building. We had about four people that were church members that lived in our building that Charles would call together each Sunday and he would bless and pass the Sacrament to them. We would have a song from the hymn book, and then after passing the Sacrament, we would tell them what was talked about in Sacrament Meeting. We were so blessed to serve and be served by our friends.

Growing Together in Faith

Since both Charles and I were converts to The Church of Jesus Christ, we had much to learn and we also enjoyed growing together in our faith. We read the *Book of Mormon* each night and also read often from the Bible. We were married 16 years and 2 months, and we read the *Book of Mormon* more than sixteen times.

Charles said that as soon as we started out in our marriage that we were going to do that and read in the *Book of Mormon* every night while we were married. So, no matter how tired we felt, we read the scriptures together each night. I enjoyed that time because he would be laying there and I didn't have to worry about cooking or taking care of chores or anything else. That was our time together. He would lay on the bed and I would sit alongside of him and we would read the scriptures together and talk about it.

At first, he didn't seem to believe me in regard to some things and he would talk to Bishop Brad Leeser about something the next time he saw Brad. Brad would tell him

A copy of the Book of Mormon.

the same thing that I told him and he would say, "Hmmm, that's what Shirley said." So, he was a little surprised that I knew quite a bit about the scriptures. We focused on reading the *Book of Mormon* together, as he knew the Bible already and it was more difficult for me to read. In addition, Charles said that according to Joseph Smith, we could become closer to God by reading regularly from the *Book of Mormon* than by following any other book. He liked the *Book of Mormon* because I would explain things and we could talk about it.

Shirley Robideau working on a home project putting varnish on a cabinet.

Chapter 22
Our Own Home in Casselton

A Special Home in Casselton

Living together at New Horizons Manor in Fargo, Chuck and I were happy together and had lots of support. We had access to needed resources, the opportunity for making a living, and a lot of connections with friends and others in the disabled community. It was a supportive setting for us to live in. But I had also had a dream that eventually we might get our own home together. This chapter relates the story of how that dream came true.

Dreaming of a Home and Finding an Answer

Chuck and I went for many walks on the streets around the New Horizons Manor and we would talk about the houses that were for sale. I told Chuck that I had a desire to have my own home someday. We would wheel down to the McDonald's place and have an ice cream cone together and then wheel back home again, taking a different route so that we could see all the houses that were for sale. We would talk about what it might look like inside each home. Of course, we would build it in our minds so it would be a fit for us.

The desire for having our own home got stronger and stronger. One day when Chuck was reading the newspaper, he saw an ad about FMHA (Farmers Home Administration) financing for a new home for low-income families. He told me about it when I came up from working in the kitchen at New Horizons.

"Let's call them," I said. Chuck said, "Are you serious?" I told him that I was very serious. We called them and they said that we would need at least $2,000 to make a down payment. I said, "We've already got it." We called and received an application and we filled it out and began the process. We had saved enough money to be able to make the down payment from all of my odd jobs, so we thought, "Why not go for it?"

Creating a Floor Plan and Finding a Location

Then it started—the waiting game. I think it was three or four months before we heard anything. We finally got a call and they told us that we needed to come up with a floor plan. At first, they gave us a very small amount of square footage and told us we needed to add a laundry room and two bedrooms. They only gave us about 800 to 900 square feet for the house. The apartment that we lived in was about 900 square feet. We were trying to fit the plan into that size of an arrangement but it did not fit because they wanted us to put two bedrooms in and also a laundry room. We just couldn't figure out how to do it. So, he told us to look for an architect.

I thought, "Holy cow, how much does it cost to get an architect?" I started to panic but we called this one architect in Moorhead and he said, "That is okay, I will come and do it for nothing to help you guys out." I cannot remember his name any more but he was super. His company drew up floor plans and so they came over and talked with us.

They had many ideas but felt the square footage was way too limited for two persons in wheelchairs. So, they talked to FMHA and were able to get more footage added to the plan, and then we were able to make a floor plan according to what we wanted. They helped us design a beautiful home that would have enough room for two wheelchairs and allow us to be comfortable. It was so much fun to work with them in designing and creating our own house.

At last, the floor plan was accepted and we then had to find a place to build it. Our choices were either in Harwood or Casselton. Harwood was closer to Fargo but it was beyond our limit with the cost of the lot. The reason that we went to Casselton to live is because FMHA is oriented toward more rural communities and so we had a choice between going to Casselton or Harwood or another area further away. So, we called Chuck's brother, Joe, who was making plans to move from Casselton to

Fargo. It seemed ironic to us that we were going to move there and Joe was moving to Fargo!

Joe came and picked us up and we went looking for a lot where we might build in Casselton. We found one right by the golf course. Things were sure getting exciting for us now, as we had a lot and a contractor to build our new home. We spent the entire summer going back and forth to watch the progress on our new home!

It was at about this time that Chuck began to get a bit nervous about moving to the new home since he had lived at New Horizons for about 15 years or more. For eight of these years, he and I were married. So, it was a safe haven for the both of us. He began to get worried.

Financial Concerns and Spiritual Answers

We got a call from the contractor, just before the actual building of our home began to take place, and they told us that the house was going to cost more than FMHA was able to allow. The amount that we would have needed would have been much more than we could afford. We once again faced financial pressures and sought help in asking the Lord for some guidance.

We talked to the Bishop and they took the matter to the Elders Quorum and they talked about the problem. The Elders Quorum leader, Mike Buxton, came and talked to us as well as to FMHA, and asked if they could do some of the work to accommodate the extra cost. To our surprise, the contractor and FMHA approved this approach. Once again, my friend Howard came to our rescue, as he did all the sheetrock work and texturing with help from the members of the Elders Quorum. It was truly a blessing. Their contributions were truly an answer to our prayers!

The Elders Quorum helped with that part of building the home as well as putting in the shingles on the roof. It was an awesome sight to see our friends all pitching in to help us to have our own home. It was a very cold day when they were up on the roof but we were able to move in the next week.

We took pictures of every aspect of the process. I was able to drive at that time so we went out in the van and we would go and take pictures of the house. First, we had the lot and then we took pictures of the square that was on the ground, which was the foundation where they poured the cement and everything. It was fun to look at it and recognize that it was the beginning of our little house. They put up the walls and we took a picture of almost every board that they put in it. It was just so exciting. Chuck kept saying, "We are really going to have our own home," and I would say, "Yes, we really are." He said, "You know, Shirley, I never thought in my lifetime that I would be getting married, and yet I got married. In addition, I never thought that I would ever have my own home, and we are going to have our own home." It was pretty exciting and special for us.

When it came time for us to move out there, it was bitterly cold and they took all of our stuff and put it in there and made our beds so that we had a place to sleep. The Elders Quorum moved all of our things to our new house and the first night there we were both a bit nervous.

Chuck said to me at the time, "I am scared." He was scared being out there in our home since he had never had that experience before. We were so protected at New Horizons facility because the doors were locked at six o'clock and we just felt very protected from every threat. So, we felt a little bit vulnerable suddenly when we were in our own home. I said that we could lock the doors and that we would be all right. It didn't take long and we began to feel that it really was our home and we absolutely loved it.

Gardening and Landscaping and More

We got everything put away once we moved out to our home. I sewed my own draperies for the windows. I had learned how to sew draperies when I lived in Pelican Rapids, so I made my own drapes. We had an eight-foot patio door in our bedroom and I made the drapes for that also.

During the first summer at our new home in Casselton we were able to put in a potato garden. Our friend, Owen Sivertson, came out and brought a truckload of dirt and straw and everything that we needed. It was wonderful.

We decided that we needed to have a garden the next year that I could take care of without having to ask for everyone to help us all the time. So, we talked to Dave Clawson, our home teacher from church who lived nearby in Mapleton, and he really got excited about the idea. In the spring he brought over a bunch of railroad ties to build a raised garden so that I could take care of it myself.

In the springtime, our friends and fellow church members put the garden together by making an 8-foot square in the center so that I could reach all the way around. Then, Dave made a four-foot walkway all the way around that and a border on the outside, and there was a four-foot opening on one end so that I could go in and go all the way around the garden on each side. It was so neat and we really enjoyed that. They hauled in beautiful black dirt and later put in a sprinkler system in the frames. I planted a garden and it was the most awesome garden you could imagine. I had never seen anything grow like it did in that garden. I put sticks on my tomatoes and the tomatoes would grow as high as the house. It was absolutely beautiful and the produce was unbelievable.

They had a late flood in the area a couple of years after that and our friend, Alan Miller, who was a newscaster for Channel Four News, was in a plane flying over our place to film the flooding areas and he told us that our garden looked pretty awesome from the air!

Home of Charles and Shirley Robideau, Casselton, ND, 1992.

I enjoyed working in that garden so much. Every once in a while, I would be in it weeding and I would think that something was in my garden but never found anything. Years later, the present owners of that house told me that they took out the raised garden and there were hundreds of garden snakes under that garden! So, there were little visitors in my garden. I am sure glad that I didn't see them when I was in the garden!

The Elders Quorum members came over during our first Spring and leveled out the grounds and planted seeds for grass. I was so humbled at all they had done to help us have our own home. When they finished building the house, Lee Allen and Dave Clawson came out and planted the grass so that we had nice green grass all around the house. It was so nice. I never wanted to leave there.

We moved into our house in October 1992. We had many Church functions held in our back yard by the garden. We had a lot of parties out there with the members of the ward.

Once we had a party for Pioneer Day, and Brother Doney was in charge of that, and then he came up to me and he said, "All of the speakers that were supposed to come are not here. Can you do me a favor?" I said, "What is it?" He said, "Say a prayer because I know that whenever you pray everything works out." So, I said a prayer and about fifteen minutes before it was time for them to give their talks they had all arrived. He said to me, "You can always count on Shirley's prayers!"

Our next-door neighbor in Casselton was good to us and took care of mowing the grass and snow shoveling. That was a great blessing.

Our home in Casselton was pretty neat because it was totally accessible. The bathroom was amazing because we designed it, Chuck and I did it together, and we told the architect what we wanted. It was a very unique bathroom due to the design we put into it. We had everything arranged just exactly as we needed it so that it would work for us. For example, in the bathroom we had a full-length mirror on one side over the sink and it was slanted so that we could see ourselves. If it is straight you can see it only at the level above the sink, but since it was slanted we could be back from the sink and see our entire profile. It was a really unique home.

In our bedroom we had a walk-in closet so I was able to go in easily and get our clothes and come back out. The patio door was located in the bedroom and we had a big patio outside. When they brought the dirt in to put the topsoil on for the yard they made sure that it was level with the sidewalk so that we could just wheel right out the door and not worry about tipping over.

Alan Miller was the Channel 4 news anchor and he came over one day and he said, "Is it okay if I bring out the news crew?" I said that was just fine, so all of his crew came out and they took pictures of us in that home. He talked on the Channel 4 news about how our congregation members came out and helped with completing the work on the home to minimize costs. Also, the Relief Society all got together and put together an album with pictures. They had an open house for us and took pictures of everyone that came and made an album for us.

Family and Friends and Our Home in Casselton

Mom and Dad would come out often and stay overnight with us. Mom would bring plants to put around the house. We had an apple tree in the front yard as there were many apple trees in the area. Mom also brought some horseradish plants and planted them in our back yard, as well as raspberry bushes, plum bushes, strawberry plants and other plants. There was a short tree in the back that was so ugly, and I asked Mom what we could do about it, so then she went and took a saw and cut off all the low branches. It looked so nice after she did that and it grew to be a beautiful tree. I just loved it. I just felt like it was my own little Eden. I really miss it.

Once when Mom and I were going for a walk, we went by a sand pile that was sitting along a driveway. Evidently, they were going to put cement in the driveway but never got around to it. Mom looked at the weeds growing on the pile and said to me, "Look, Shirley, there is a Wild Rose growing on there." So, she took that Wild Rose and planted it on the side of the house on a rack to help it grow up the side of the house. It was so beautiful.

Chuck's Brother, Joe, came out and did landscaping, and we had a huge rock brought in to put in the center of the landscaping. It was so much fun to watch our home be put together for us. There were many things that Joe had done for us with our house. He and Nancy were always there if we needed help.

We had some Christmas parties where our family all came out to be with us. I had made curtains and drapes for the windows and the patio door and Joe hung all of them for us. We felt so much love and support from our family and friends as we lived in Casselton.

On the day that we were moving to Casselton, we found out that Alan and Ana Miller from our ward at church were also moving to Casselton. That indicated to us that we would not be alone out there in Casselton because we would have fellow church members close by in Casselton. So, even though Chuck's brother moved away from that area, the Lord provided someone to be there to help us if we needed help. I thought that was a tender mercy from the Lord. Those two people were sent there by Heavenly Father. I know that so well. We watched their children grow up while we were there. I felt their love so strongly and they never failed to support what we were trying to do.

One day when I was over at the Miller home, they had their family scripture study while I was there. I was amazed at how they taught their children to read the scriptures. The littlest one would sit on Alan's lap and Alan would tell him what the words were as he pointed to the words, and then this little boy would read the words back to Alan. I loved their family so much.

The Miller Family moved to Casselton at the exact same time we moved there and moved away at the exact same time we did. Brother Miller would come over and help Chuck get ready for the day and then he would go to work. Alan and Ana were such angels in our lives, and I know without a doubt that the Lord knew we would need help and provided them to be there while we needed them.

Chapter 23
Health Troubles and Hard Times

A Season of Health Concerns and Hard Challenges

Our adventure in building a home where we could live together as a married couple in Casselton, North Dakota was one of the great highlights of life for Charles and I. We loved our home and appreciated living in the Casselton community. We had several years together there that blessed our lives and united us in ways that we could not have otherwise experienced.

With our inherent health circumstances, however, both Charles and I were to face a season of health troubles that made life much more challenging. This time period involved dealing with health issues that threatened our well-being and also needing to access greater support for managing our needs. And yet, Chuck and I faced these challenges together as we did other things in our lives.

Adjustments and Adventures in Casselton

For the most part, we didn't have too much trouble with getting in and out of our place at Casselton. In the years that we lived there, I remember just one time that there was a bad snowstorm that kept us inside. We were safe inside our house but the snow was coming down so hard and for so long our little house was buried in the snow. We weren't too worried about it but it was so weird to not be able to even see out the windows! Our neighbors brought out their tractor and dug us out and all was well!

In the spring of that year the flooding was so bad all over the state and we were no exception in Casselton. There was a hill on our west side and there was water up to the top of that hill on the other side. I felt so confident when the local police told me that they were watching everything, and if there was any threat to Charles and I, they would be there in a flash to get us out. It was nice to live in such a wonderful community.

The grocery store was not far from our home and they would bring us groceries whenever I would call and tell them what we needed. Also, our neighbors and fellow church members Alan and Ana Miller were always checking on us as well. Once our garbage cans blew away and they came and went across the field and golf course and brought them home for us.

I felt so much love in Casselton and was grateful to the people who remembered my Dad and Mom and would come and visit us. It was a wonderful experience for the both of us.

About this time, Charles' sister Sandra had a heart attack and we went into Fargo several times to see her at the hospital. It was so hard watching her because she had the same disease that Charles had and I loved Sandra so much. We square danced together in Fargo before moving to Casselton until she was not able to do it anymore.

I saw her cry when she finally realized that she couldn't see enough to square dance anymore. It was so hard on her. It is a difficult thing for those of us with disabilities who watch and experience, one by one, things taken away from us that we enjoy doing. I well understand how she felt at the time. For me, to see her lying in the hospital bed with her health concerns was extremely hard. I wanted to know the words to say, the feelings to share, and yet words would not come. It was very hard.

We had gone into Fargo one particular afternoon to see Sandra and had just returned and gotten into bed back in Casselton when the phone rang—she was gone. I held Charles that night as he and I cried together.

Shirley's Bout of Encephalitis

In 1994, Chuck had his physical therapist there at our home one morning and for some reason I was just freezing. I could not get warm no matter what. His therapist covered me up with a heavy blanket and I kept on shivering. Later that day, I got up and I was in my wheelchair and Chuck said that I was moving back and forth and not talking to him. He said, "If you don't talk to me, Shirley, I am going to call the ambulance." I didn't respond and he thought to himself that it was really serious, so he called the ambulance and they came over. He was worried and called 9-1-1 and told them what I was doing.

I remember the ambulance personnel coming into the bedroom but I do not remember much of anything else. I remember that they asked me who the President of the United States was, but I didn't give them the right answer. Then they asked me what day it was and I didn't know the answer, so they said, "We are going to take her in the ambulance to the hospital."

Shirley Robideau during her married years to Charles Robideau.

They took me out in the ambulance and Chuck called his mother to come out and stay with him. In the meantime, I came out of my haze briefly and looked up and saw the Elders Quorum President from our congregation, Mike Buxton, standing there. He and someone else had come to the hospital to give someone a priesthood blessing, and they passed by the Emergency Room and just happened to see me laying on the cart by the door. I quickly asked him to give me a blessing and also to take care of Chuck. Then, I was out of it again and unaware of my surroundings.

I did receive a priesthood blessing and both the Elders Quorum members from our church and Chuck's mother took good care of Chuck. What was wrong with me? Well, it turned out I had encephalitis.

Encephalitis is an illness caused by a virus which brings about inflammation of the brain tissues and symptoms can include brain swelling, headache, stiff neck, light sensitivity, mental confusion and seizures. It was pretty frightening to me. One minute, I was aware of where I was, and then in the next minute I was not. The illness can last a few days to a few weeks but the recovery can be gradual and take time.

I don't know how long I was unconscious, but the next thing I remembered was waking up and there was someone holding me tight against the bed by my shoulders and my feet. They were doing a spinal tap and apparently I was fighting them and screaming, which I don't remember. Then I went into sleep mode again and woke up a few days later.

When I woke up again, a doctor was in the room and told me that I had encephalitis. He explained that it was an infection in my brain. I was in the hospital for a month around February 1994. They called encephalitis the "sleeping disease," so that even though I was awake and looking at everybody I was out of it. I didn't know where I was and did not know what was happening.

Our friend Sidney Rodunce came out to pick up Charles and took him to Fargo so that he was not out in Casselton alone. He brought Chuck up to the hospital to see me. Sid accidentally was lowering the lift as Chuck was coming out to get on it. He tried to get it up as quickly as he could, but Chuck came out and his wheelchair tipped over and Chuck's head embedded into the floor of the lift, so he had a cut on his forehead. Since they were in the Emergency Room entrance at the hospital when it happened, he had help immediately. Weighing about 400 pounds, the wheelchair pressed his face into the metal mesh of the lift, and the grid was diamond-shaped so it made an interesting pattern with the stitches. After they stitched Chuck up he came up to see me, but I didn't know who he was because he had gauze around his head. Actually, it took me a while to recognize who anyone was.

I was in the hospital for a month before I was able to come home. They gave me double antibiotics for the whole month. As I was starting to come out of the effects of the illness, I was very emotional and I would cry at the drop of a hat or express other emotion. There were no feelings clearly associated with my interactions. So, if you know me you tend to find that I have a deep love for all those that I know, and I just love little kids, but I couldn't feel that when I had encephalitis. I could look at somebody and know that I liked that person, but there were no feelings within as I encountered a person. Charles would come to see me and I wouldn't show any feelings toward him at all. I didn't really realize that he was my husband.

When I came home from the hospital and went into my new home, I didn't know my house very well. I didn't know where the bedrooms were or where the laundry room was located. I was in our home with Chuck and I didn't even know where anything was. I didn't recognize my home. I was afraid of the stove and microwave and was very paranoid. I kept everything to myself because I didn't want anything to happen to us so that we couldn't be in Casselton. I didn't even tell Chuck how fearful I was. It was a very challenging and fearful time for me during this episode.

Eventually, my memory came back but the illness had affected my emotions and ability to feel them, and so feelings of love or any kind of feelings at all were so slow in coming back. It took me a long time to be able to smile, cry or whatever. I just had no emotions whatsoever during this period and for a significant time afterwards. There were just no feelings. No sadness, no happiness—no emotions. So, it was very hard when I had that experience. However, I didn't tell anyone what I was experiencing because I didn't want anybody to know that I wasn't feeling love toward them any longer. I knew that I did in my mind, as I remembered that I loved Chuck at one time, but I couldn't feel emotions in my heart and experience. So, I started praying to Heavenly Father to let me have my feelings back again, and that gradual return of my feelings took about a year. So, in association with overcoming encephalitis, the hardest thing that I went through was the loss of my feelings and not being able to feel the love that I had for people or other normal feelings.

It was after we moved back to Fargo that I went in for a psychological test. They wanted to examine me with regard to the effects of the encephalitis on my brain. My brain was still not functioning right. They told me that I needed to keep a watch on all of the time. The reason for that was because I could be sitting in one spot and thinking that I was there for a couple of minutes when in reality it would turn out to be three hours later. I had no conception of time. So, there were a lot of negative effects due to the encephalitis that have stayed with me over the years. That whole experience was hard on Chuck.

Also, I was not able to drive our van anymore because my vision was getting too bad to drive safely. It was a tough time on my ego at the time to not be able to drive any longer but I knew that it was the right thing. For a while, our helper Rick drove us to Fargo to attend church meetings, but for the most part Alan Miller and his family would drive us. We were so grateful for their assistance.

Help in the Home

Since I had experienced encephalitis and its negative effects on my health, I was not able to work for Family Home Care anymore. The family home care program had been providing us with $400 a month due to my care for Chuck, but that ended as a resource once I got encephalitis and experienced its effects. That option was removed from us once I got encephalitis because the program said that I was not capable of taking care of Chuck any longer. My strength was not very good after being so sick. This meant that I was not able to provide as much help to Chuck and we needed some assistance. In reality, I was still taking care of him but the program indicated that they would not pay me any longer for doing it, so we still had to get his care managed and keep going forward.

So, we had to search for someone to help with care for Chuck after I had returned home. We had advertised for a live-in aide and a man named Rick P. applied for the job. He was young and was an awesome caregiver. He would help Chuck and talk with him and they became buddies.

One time Rick didn't come home when he said he was going to be there, so I helped Chuck get to bed and Rick came in pretty late. He told us that his car stalled on the highway. He was so worried about Chuck that he walked about ten miles to get home to help Chuck! He left his car on the highway and just walked and it was very cold outside. What a guy!

Rick helped us for about five years in Casselton. He lived with us and provided good care and support for Chuck as a live-in aide. Generally, he did a good job and for a long time he gave us rides to church and he would drop us off there for our meetings.

Then we didn't have anybody for a little while, but Alan Miller from our congregation came by and said that he would be willing to help with Chuck's care. He did all of the paperwork so that he could be his health aide and so he did it for a while. Whenever he came to our home, he would bring his albums of the Beatles and so we recorded the Beatles songs onto audio cassette so that he could listen to them in his car. It was fun. I liked listening to the Beatles. You could hear Alan in there working with Chuck and singing along to the Beatles. We had a good time with him.

One time it was twenty degrees or more below zero outside and it was Alan's day to come and work. Alan's car did not start and so he got on a bike and pedaled from north Casselton to south Casselton, perhaps a mile or two, in that twenty-below zero conditions on a bike to be there for us. He got to the door and came in and he was about half frozen. He was so devoted to Chuck.

The care provision eventually became too much to do along with Alan Miller's job as a news anchor with Channel 4 news, so we advertised again and the neighbor that lived on the other side of us began coming over and helping with Chuck. She helped us until we left that home.

Chuck and Heart Concerns

Chuck had a variety of health challenges due to his diagnosis of Friedreich's Ataxia and a major one concerned his heart health. Chuck's condition definitely affected his heart, which is common with FA. We tried to pay attention to this issue and be aware of any concerns. In 1996 or 1997, Chuck started having trouble with his heart. At first, he would just have these spells during which his head would drop back and his eyes would roll. If I took a wet washcloth and put it on his head he would usually snap out of it.

One day Chuck told me that he had to go to the bathroom. I helped him in there, and normally I would have left his chair alongside of him, but this time I moved the chair out of the way and I sat alongside of him talking with him. Just a week prior to this incident, Chuck said that he wanted to have a telephone installed in the bathroom right by the toilet. I asked him why and he said, "I don't know, maybe I will want to make a phone call while I am in there, but I want to have a phone there!" I said okay and we had a phone installed in the bathroom by the toilet. I thought it was a strange request but we had one put in.

Anyway, while I was helping him transfer to the toilet, I had a feeling come over me and I decided to move his chair away from his side. Usually, he would finish and transfer back in the chair by himself, but this day I listened to the feelings I had and made this adjustment and moved up beside him. While I was sitting beside him and we were talking, he suddenly stiffened out on the toilet and his eyes began rolling and I grabbed him and held him so he would not fall. I feel that the Lord directed me to get alongside him in the way that I was so I could catch him. I panicked because he was turning blue and I didn't know what to do, but then I saw the telephone and so I picked it up and every number on there passed through my mind. I could not remember what to call because I was really anxious, but finally I remembered 9-1-1 and dialed it and the dispatcher knew my voice because she was from Casselton.

She said, "Shirley, what is wrong?" I answered, "It is Chuck, he's turning blue." She said, "Hang on, I will call Dispatch." I said, "Don't leave me, don't leave me," and she answered, "I will be right back, Shirley, I will be right back." So, she skipped out to make the connection and then I really panicked because there was nobody on the phone and I was holding Chuck. I totally lost it. Chuck was turning blue and I had no idea how to help him.

Just then, as I was on the phone calling in, our neighbor who was an ambulance driver and lived right behind us was listening to the radio at the time and he overheard me talking to her, so he jumped over the fence and ran and came to the front door and came in. He told me to get out of the bathroom and he would take care of Chuck. I did that and was crying hysterically. He took Chuck and did CPR until the ambulance got there to assist. He saved Chuck's life. They did use the paddles on Chuck after they got there to shock his heart and keep it going and then they took him in the ambulance. The neighbor took me to the hospital behind the ambulance. Chuck had to have a pacemaker put in at the hospital. This was a very frightening incident and I was so grateful for the help that we received in saving his life.

We were at church meetings a few weeks after that and a young lady was going to play Chuck's violin that his Grandfather Torkelson had carved from a tree stump. She was playing it in our sacrament (worship) meeting. Just before the meeting, she told me that the violin was not too good so she planned to use her own violin if that was okay. I told her that would be fine.

Just as she was going to play the violin, Chuck's heart began to race rapidly and I saw it coming and I softly said, "Help." Brother David Cobia, who was the Stake Patriarch, came over and touched Chuck and just his gentle touch brought

Chuck's heart back to normal. Chuck didn't even know something had happened. He just listened to the violin music and was calm and smiling. You could see the pride that Chuck had for his Grandfather's violin. He believed it was his violin that he was hearing and none of us were about to tell him anything different. I will never forget that moment because Chuck's heart began to race and he started to fall back in his chair, but then when the hand of the Patriarch touched him it was gone. The touch of the Master's servant brought peace to his heart.

Upheaval and Troubles in Casselton

After we had lived in Casselton for a number of years, other things besides the health difficulties began to make life even more challenging for us. One of the neighbors began to try and exercise control over Chuck and I, and I was getting a little afraid of him. I was not sure what I should do about it as I didn't want to cause any trouble, and yet I didn't like the way he was helping himself to things out of our garage.

I also began to have trouble with my hip and the medical doctors that we consulted with wanted to do surgery on it. I went to our Bishop and explained to him all that was going on with the neighbor, my hip, and Chuck's health. He sat there and listened about our situation, then told me that we needed to get Chuck back into Fargo. So, we put our home up for sale and moved back to Fargo.

I had hip surgery right after that and Rick continued to take care of Chuck. I honestly don't know what we would have done without Rick at this time. He helped us to move and set up the new apartment in south Fargo so that it would work for us. The apartment was near my Mom and Dad. So, Mom took care of me while I was recuperating from my total right hip replacement surgery and Rick took care of Chuck.

I had to be very careful while I was healing from surgery for six weeks. I went to the doctor for my six-week check-up and he told me I could start putting weight on my leg again. So, I went into the bathroom and pulled myself up on my legs by holding on to the transfer pole alongside of the toilet. It felt so good and I was so excited about being able to stand on it again. I had surgery on my hip in 1997 and I had been told to stop standing on it in 1984, so it had been a long time since I had been able to stand on it. So, you can imagine how grateful I was.

Soon another little challenge came up in this time period. Mom had come over and asked if we wanted to go to Walmart, so Rick loaded all of us up in our van and we made the trip. We were right by the Walmart store in Fargo and a man ran the stoplight and hit us on the right side of the van. The impact caused both Charles' and my wheelchairs to twist and the collision damaged his chair very badly. My chair was all right but the twisting motion caused my hip surgery location to give me a lot of pain. The new hip twisted in my leg and broke through on the side of the bone. So, I had to go through another six weeks of not bending and hoping that it would heal the bone back into place, which didn't happen.

My hip difficulties caused me a lot of pain and I had to have reconstructive surgery on it a year later. So, I had to start all over again. I was very frustrated at this time and the healing process was very slow. Not being able to walk at all after this caused the weight to pile on and I had a lot of pain from the hip injury.

As an addendum to this part of my health story, later in 2008 I went to a different surgeon and he X-rayed the leg and hip again. He told me that the reason I was in so much pain was that the hip was trying to push its way through my back. So, that meant another total reconstructive hip surgery. This time I got a blood clot in my leg. But, finally the pain slowly went away and my leg got stronger, but I have not been able to stand on my legs again.

As much as I loved our home in Casselton, I didn't feel any regrets about moving, mainly because I was afraid of my neighbor who was trying to take control of us. Also, it was time for us to transition to a new phase of our lives. We had loved our sojourn together in our own home in Casselton but we now entered a new season of our lives together.

Chapter 24
Change and Loss

Making Changes and Losing Loved Ones

The time that we had together in Casselton and the support we received from so many relatives and friends was a highlight of our lives together. However, things eventually change and the health problems and other challenges we endured made it so that we needed to make some adjustments in our living circumstances. Also, we had other family members with their own health concerns also and during this next time period we experienced the passing of loved ones who were close to us.

Finding a Canine Companion for Chuck

Living back in Fargo, things with Charles began to get much more complicated as his health situation had ups and downs. The continuing health concerns were so tiring for him and also frustrated him. I knew that my Sweetheart was beginning to give up. My pet name for him was "Chucky" and I loved him so greatly and it was hard to see him struggle. He was so dear to my heart and I just didn't want him to give up.

After we had moved back to Fargo, one day I talked with Charles' niece, Jill, and she suggested that we should perhaps find a dog for Charles. Dogs are often wonderful companions for individuals with health concerns and provide a loving presence, as well as a reason for the person to engage each day.

Jill took me to the dog pound after we searched the newspaper and went to West Acres looking for the perfect dog. There were only little tiny dogs at the places we went to and one dachshund that just didn't feel right. However, they had twin dogs at the dog pound that were up for adoption, which were a male and female cockapoo dogs. They were about three years old and were black and were in bad need of hair cuts. The female weighed about fifteen pounds.

I held her for a while and she looked up into my eyes with her big, beautiful brown eyes and my heart melted! We adopted her and took her home. We named her Kandi.

Charles was laying down and we took Kandi in to him and laid her on the bed next to him. She crawled under Charles' arm and looked into his eyes and won his heart also. Charles lived for five more years with the companionship of this precious little dog. We would take turns taking her out for walks and she was indeed part of our family.

I taught myself to groom her hair and toenails. People liked her grooming so much that I became the neighborhood dog groomer. My mom cut women's hair and I cut dogs' hair. Kandi was a happy dog. When I came into the room, she would jump on my wheelchair foot pedals and then up to my lap. She was also strong and protective. Charles was able to enjoy her for five years. After his death, I was able to have her for another five years and then my niece had her for another six years, so we had her in our family for a long time.

New Live-in Aides for Chuck

Rick, who had spent several years as an aide for us, was going to be leaving soon and so I began looking for another attendant to help me out with helping Charles. One weekend I was at church services on Sunday, and there I met a young couple, Matt and Cindy, and told them about Charles' need for a live-in attendant.

To my surprise, the two of them were students at North Dakota State University and needed an extra income. So, they explored the idea and then agreed to move in and began taking care of Charles. This was an answer to our prayers.

Charles and Matt became very good friends and had a good time together. I am not sure how long they were with us but it was at least two years and maybe longer.

Matt liked roller blading (which is a type of skating) and would take Charles for walks driving his wheelchair and roller blading behind him. They were quite a pair. One time when they were out, I guess they got going quite a high speed and

Charles' manual wheelchair hit a rock and came to a screeching halt! Matt went flying over the top of Charles, and since he was holding on to Charles' handle bars, his chair went over also. Neither of them got hurt very bad but I guess it was quite comical.

Another time Matt and Cindy took us to see Matt's parents. Matt took Charles outside and then brought out one of these vehicles that have huge wheels on it and strapped Charles to him and they both went for a ride on it. It was so much fun to see Charles enjoying that ride with Matt as they would go into the woods. Charles was sitting behind Matt as he drove the recreational vehicle. Matt was wonderful with Charles and they loved each other a great deal. Matt and Cindy were a tremendous support to us during that time and made a meaningful difference in our lives.

Continuing Enjoyment of Church

One of the things that Chuck and I shared was our membership and devotion to our church. It had aided in bringing us together and we both felt blessed by our active involvement in church worship and activities. In addition, our lives were immensely blessed by our many friends that we knew through our church activities.

When I would get discouraged about something, or if I didn't know how to do something, he would say, "Let's pray about it." We would have prayer together and then the solutions would come to us. He helped me to depend more on the Savior than I did on my own prior to our relationship. Chuck was the most spiritual person that I have ever known. He was sensitive to me and to the Spirit. He just knew how to make me a better person.

I doubt that there were many days that Charles and I missed attending our church meetings. We enjoyed going so much.

One time when we had a large regional meeting known as Stake Conference, I was sitting in the back of the chapel and it was the end of the meeting. Then President Andrews, who was a member of the Stake Presidency, asked if I, Sister Robideau, would come up to the front and give the closing prayer.

So, I was wheeling my chair down the aisle and someone tapped me on the shoulder and kiddingly said to me, "That will teach you to hug them guys!" I have a habit of hugging the people I love, and President Andrews was so special to me, and whenever he saw me he would hug me. I was so tickled by what was said to me as I went down the aisle that I broke out laughing. By the time I got up to President Andrews it was a little difficult to get control of myself, but I did it and gave the closing prayer.

On a different occasion, President Andrews was scheduled to speak in Jamestown when I was living there. He went to Jamestown on the same Sunday that I was in Fargo for the weekend. When President Andrews saw that I was not there, when it was his turn to give a talk, he said, "Shirley told me once that she really enjoyed my talks. Well, since she isn't here, I am not going to give a talk!" He then sat down and did not give a talk! When I returned to Jamestown, everyone gave me a ribbing about that! So funny!

The Passing of My Father

Despite the positive elements of our lives with having the dog Kandi come to live with us, the support of Matt and Cindy as live-in aides, and our enjoyment of church activities and friends, this was also a season when we experienced loss and disappointment. One of the most impactful losses of my life came with the passing of my father.

In December of 1998, my Dad and Mom came to visit us at New Horizons Manor (the apartments where we lived). After they were there for a while, we were walking down to the front of New Horizons and I noticed my Dad was having so much trouble walking. I could tell he was in a lot of pain but he never would let us know when he was hurting.

I remember one day when we lived in Casselton and we were visiting with some people that had stopped by to see Mom and Dad. I was sitting by Dad and had my arm around him, and after the people left Dad asked me to slowly take my arm off of his neck. He was in extreme pain from a case of shingles and I didn't even know that I was hurting him. He didn't want to let his visitors know he was hurting so he just let me have my arm around him. I felt so bad. That was my Dad—he always was concerned about how others felt and sacrificed his comfort to keep from hurting or embarrassing another.

The next day after he was there visiting us, I called Mom in the morning to see how things were going. Mom then told me that Dad had died during the night.

She told me that he had gone to bed and was cold so she got an extra blanket for him. During the night she heard a noise and got up to check on Dad. Dad was in the bathroom by the sink and Mom asked him if he was all right. Dad then turned towards her and said, "Rosie!" He then fell face down on to the floor right by Mom's feet.

Sister Jessie Stockford with their father, Clair Stockford, prior to his passing.

I felt so bad for Mom and did all I could to help her during this time. I went to stay with her for a while and helped with funeral arrangements along with my brother and sister. I helped with the notification letters to people that Dad owed money to and also assisted with any other business that Mom needed help doing. I never felt that I could do enough to help her.

We were at the funeral home with Mom and my brother John put his arm around me, and then said that I needed to let Mom do this as she was picking out the coffin. My heart broke. I didn't want Mom to hurt and I knew I had to let her go through this experience. My sweet brother knew what I was feeling and he comforted me. He never knew how much that meant to me.

Dad had his viewing at the funeral home and I remember how scared I was of going down and seeing him in the coffin. My sweet Mother then came up beside me and said, "I will walk down with you, Shirley." I honestly knew that I couldn't do that walk alone and I was so grateful to Mom for being there for me.

Shortly after that, my niece Christina, John's oldest daughter, came in and she was afraid to make that walk. So, I offered to go with her, following what Mom had done for me. I felt so good that I could help Christina like Mom did for me.

That was a hard day for us. I stayed at the funeral home until the viewing time was over so I stayed beside Dad the whole time. I remember it was so cold in there but I didn't want to leave him. My Dad was such a powerful and meaningful presence in my life and I am so grateful for his many loving and supportive acts to me across my lifetime.

The next day they had the funeral and it was held at our Fargo chapel for The Church of Jesus Christ of Latter-day Saints. Since it was wintertime, it was too cold to break the ground to bury Dad, so in the springtime they called us to meet at the cemetery in Wheatland to have a dedication of the grave and to bury Dad. That was equally hard to go through. The grandchildren had beautiful roses to put on his coffin as they lowered him into the grave. I was so sure that poor Mom was going to collapse as she went through this again. Bishop Bryan Brown gave a beautiful prayer at his graveside and dedicated the grave for my father.

The Passing of Charles' Mother

The passing of my father was followed soon after by another family loss. Not long after Dad died, Charles got sick and was in the hospital again.

The next day, just down the hall, his mother Cora Robideau was also placed in a room at the hospital and she was very ill. I spent time going back and forth between the two rooms. Finally, Charles was able to get up in his chair so that he could go down and visit his Mom. She was not doing well at all and they were talking about sending her to a nursing home.

Just as she was about to be transferred to the nursing home, she took a turn for the worse. So, they didn't send her to a different facility, and Charles and I and his niece Jill were alone in the room with Cora.

Jill took Cora out of her bed and sat her on Charles' lap, and then Charles held her close to him as he bid her good-bye for now. It was such a tender moment to me. He talked with her and told her how much he loved her.

Shortly after this special moment, all of the family members and I were gathered around her bed and she died. She was the first person I had ever seen actually die so it was a little hard for me.

These changes in our lives and the losses that we experienced brought both happiness and heartache into our lives. But these experiences are part of life and we accepted them as best we could.

Chapter 25
A Long Good-Bye

My Final Years with Charles and Saying Farewell

My life changed in a beautiful way when I met Charles Robideau and we became husband and wife. He brought light and goodness into my life. He was a caring companion who shared humor, support and wisdom with me. We were able to form a very supportive companionship and had many wonderful years together. Even though we faced physical challenges and other difficulties, my years with Charles were such a blessing in my life.

Due to his health condition, Charles continued to need support and experienced a variety of physical challenges which took a toll on him and his overall well-being. This section recounts the story of our final years together and his eventual passing. Saying farewell to him was another challenge but it was attended by support from many others and our Heavenly Father.

A Move to Arthur, North Dakota

Our live-in aides Matt and Cindy eventually needed to move back to the college apartments, so I began the process of looking for a new aide for Charles. This did not develop very quickly. After Matt and Cindy left, Charles' health became significantly worse. He was getting weaker and just not feeling well. He had chronic diarrhea and the work of taking care of him began to totally take a drain on my health as well.

When talking to our social worker about the situation we were not able to find someone to help out as an aide, so she then suggested that Chuck go into a nursing home for his continued care. A part of me died that day. It was so hard for me. When we told Charles of the decision, he looked at me and said, "Shirley, you gave up!" That comment haunted me ever since he said it, but we could find no other options.

They were not able to find a nursing home spot available in Fargo and so they sent him to Arthur, North Dakota. Arthur is located about thirty miles northwest of Fargo. I went to visit him the next day and the nursing home staff there told me of apartments they had right there by the home, so I moved the following week to be close to Charles.

I had a nice little apartment almost connected to the nursing home and during the day he would come and be with me. This worked out well but I had no way to get groceries except to take the medical transportation to Fargo for appointments and then get myself to a grocery store and then back home. This approach was quite costly and not very practical.

It was nice that during the day they would bring Charles over to my apartment and we spent the day together. Kandi was there with me so Charles would play with her when he was there.

One day the lady that lived in the apartment next to mine came over and brought some leather bone strips over for Kandi. She really liked to chew on them but this particular day a piece broke off in her throat. I looked over at her and she was sitting with her head up towards the ceiling and I could tell something was wrong. Well, the bone piece was stuck in her throat and she was holding her head up so she could breathe. I went and got the lady next door and she took Kandi over to the vet and he got the piece out. She was all right but totally exhausted from fighting for her life.

I think we were in Arthur for about a year and missed being able to go to our church services. Charles finally applied to find a nursing home spot in Fargo where he could be relocated. He got an opening at Villa Maria and we then moved back to Fargo.

Medical Troubles for Chuck

At this time as we moved back to Fargo, I had to come ahead of Chuck and his move to look for a place that I could live. I had to use the medical transportation to look for an apartment and found one just three blocks from Villa Maria nursing care. I moved about three days before he was transferred to Villa Maria. He was so upset that I had to go ahead of him. He didn't ever want to be apart from me. It was heart-breaking for him.

Not long after Chuck was relocated to Villa Maria he got sick again and was admitted to the hospital. He had a nurse that was from another country that couldn't speak English very well, and I had so much trouble understanding her. I thought she was telling me that Charles was going to die. I was really broken up trying to handle everything and keep a smile on my face for him.

The Doctor was talking to me later and through an interpreter she communicated to me that he was doing well and was not yet going to die. I will never forget the relief I felt at this time. However, when he was ready to be released from the hospital his room at Villa Maria was gone, so they transferred him to Elim Nursing Home.

Chuck did not like it there at Elim Nursing Home at all, and so before I even knew what was going on, I got a call from Villa Maria that he was transferred back to Villa Maria as they had an opening for him. This was a challenging time with his medical troubles but we appreciated the care available to him.

A Final Trip to the Bismarck Temple

By this time in our lives, there had been an LDS temple established in Bismarck, North Dakota. It made the temple much closer and more accessible to us. Chuck had long wanted to complete some temple work for his family and so that was one of our objectives.

One of the single adults from Church that we knew volunteered to drive us to the Bismarck Temple so that Chuck could take care of having his parents sealed in marriage for Time and All Eternity. This is a special religious ordinance performed in the temple by those with priesthood authority to do this ordinance. Also, Charles wanted to also seal his deceased sister, Sandy, and himself to their parents, which is a similar religious ordinance.

Jeremy Williams drove us out to Bismarck with Charles reclined in his manual wheelchair in the back of our van. I was sitting next to him to help him as needed. It was kind of comical because as we drove on the highway Charles would vibrate and slide down on his chair. Jeremy had to stop about every fifty miles to help Charles to be pulled back up into his chair.

We finally made it to the Bismarck Temple safely and had the temple endowments performed for Charles' Mom and Dad, and his sister, Sandy. We went in to do the Sealing Ordinances, and when it came time for Charles to be sealed to his family, they said we were done. I asked if we were going to seal Charles to his parents and they asked if we had the paperwork done. My head dropped in realizing that I had forgotten to submit this necessary paperwork. In my mind, I was thinking that Charles would not be able to come back and do that, but the Temple worker said, "Let's go in the back room and do it now!"

Charles and Shirley Robideau, sweethearts to the end.

I was so thrilled that the Spirit of the Lord whispered to him that we needed to do it now. It was such a wonderful miracle because it was long after the Temple workers were to go home and yet they stayed to help us with these important sealing ordinances in the temple.

We went into the computer room and Charles answered all of the necessary questions, and then we returned to the sealing room and were able to have Charles sealed to his parents and his sister. It was such a sacred experience that I spent a good share of the time crying. I was so grateful to the Temple Sealer for his devotion to us and helping us to fulfill that last temple blessing for my sweet Charles.

The Last Days

There were both some challenging and incredibly sweet experiences that Charles and I had together in the final weeks of his life. There were supportive caregivers, family and friends who were helpful to us.

Charles called his favorite doctor this one day and asked her if she would come and see him. Dr. Garness was an exceptional person and a wonderful doctor.

She did come and visit him and spent a couple of hours talking to him. She suggested that he go on Hospice, which would help provide supportive care in the last period of his life. He also talked to her about some of his last wishes, which were to have his brain, spinal cord and heart donated to the Friedreich's Ataxia Foundation for research to help other children and adults with this horrible disease.

Charles' friend, John K., who was his friend at New Horizons Manor, had passed away just a year or two earlier than Charles and that weighed heavily on him. Dr. Garness set up Hospice care for Charles and assured him that she would see to it that his organs were donated. This kind lady took care of the charges and everything and saved me from having to go through all of that.

Charles asked me on December 14, 2001, if I would spend the night at the nursing home with him since it was our sixteenth Anniversary. I did do that and it was beautiful. My Sweetheart had a room for us and had it made up special and had a vase with two beautiful Lavender Roses. I knew he was saying good-bye to me and I really had to control my emotions. The Spirit of the Lord was with me and I was able to help make that a special night for him.

I began talking with the Hospice volunteers and they helped me to follow what was happening. Then one day, I was talking with Charles and we were playing Yahtzee together and the Spirit told me that if I didn't do something about my health, then I was soon going to be in a nursing home. My weight at that time was up to almost 300 pounds. I never did know what my top weight was but I knew it was past 285 pounds because that was the last amount I had weighed at the last physical where they were able to weigh me and that was about two years earlier.

I heeded the promptings from the Lord and began searching the Internet for diets that followed the Word of Wisdom. The Word of Wisdom is a health code described in the *Doctrine and Covenants* of The Church of Jesus Christ of Latter-day Saints, which we consider to be modern scripture. One day when I was studying the Scriptures, I felt the Spirit of the Lord tell me that the Word of Wisdom "is" a diet!

I was so surprised. I couldn't believe that I didn't realize that concept before. I began studying everything I could find related to the Word of Wisdom and put together a diet with lots of fruits and vegetables, small amounts of meat, and then stayed away from sugar and anything like sugar and began to lose weight. I lost 35 pounds in a short period of time. Charles wanted to have our picture taken one more time and so we did that on Christmas week.

For Valentine's Day that year, Charles had the staff members come to his room while I was there, and they sang "Let Me Call You Sweetheart" to me. What a sweet thing for him to do for me. It was also on that day that I received a prompting from the Spirit of the Lord that Charles only had two more weeks left, so I should call his family to come and visit him while he was able to visit with them. I did call his brother Joe and told him it would be a wise thing to have his family come and visit Charles, but I didn't tell them what the Spirit told me. It was wonderful, as all of his nieces and nephews, brother and sisters and their families, everyone came that weekend to see him. He was so happy to see them and was able to visit and enjoyed himself a great deal.

"Be Still, My Soul"

I would like to explain a bit more about our support system of loving church members and Charles' final Sunday at church. We had the most wonderful support system among our fellow members in The Church of Jesus Christ of Latter-day Saints. We had the most wonderful Home Teachers (visiting ministers) anyone could have. So many friends and so much love. For example, Charles Walen and his son Adam were our Home Teachers, and they would come every Sunday to the nursing home to pick us up so that we could go to church together.

One of our friends, Mark Gustafson, had taken Charles to a Fargo-Moorhead Red Hawks baseball game during the summer. On this Sunday, he was sitting in the foyer and I could tell something was wrong and I went to say hello to him. Mark very sadly said to me, "Charles doesn't look good." I told him, "No, this is his last Sunday at Church." He looked at me then and tears were in his eyes.

I love the members of the Fargo Wards that were there to help me at this time and I knew that they loved us. My Dad had passed away in December of 1999, so it was just Mom and my brother John that were here in Fargo to support us. So, it was wonderful that the church members adopted us and let us know we were loved.

In these final weeks with Charles, I spent as much time at Villa Maria as I could and we would read the scriptures together, pray together, and play Yahtzee, which Charles loved that game. We were playing Yahtzee near the end of February 2002 and after finishing the game, he looked at me and said, "I don't feel so good, Shirley."

I told him to lay back in his chair and I would call the nurse to help him lay down. He did lay back and seemed to be asleep instantly. They were having shift changes so it was a while before they could help him lay down. I was sitting beside him as he had his arm around me and I had my face on his chest. I just didn't want to let go but knew it was almost time.

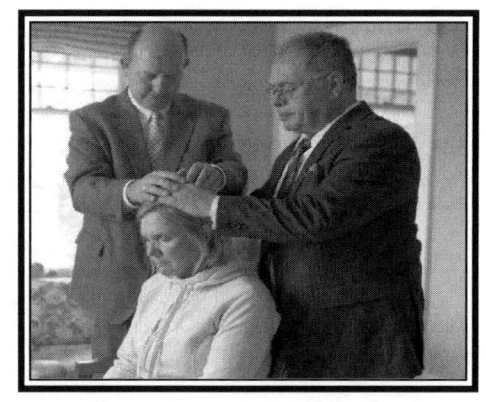

An example of a priesthood blessing to receive comfort from God.

I was crying and then in walked my Home Teachers, Charles Walen and Lee Allen, both of them fellow church members. I asked them to give Charles a blessing. They did give him a blessing and then gave me a blessing.

The Hospice nurse came in and said that his kidneys were shutting down and that it was time to move him to a private room so that the family could be there with him. I called his brother, Joe, and told him that they were moving him into another room. Joe came over and was watching as they were moving him. He went over to a corner and sat down and I could tell he was having a tough time with what was happening. He said to me, "Is Charles dying?" I told him, "Yes, Joe, he is."

The staff at Villa Maria were so kind and gave me a room there so I could be by Charles, and when they moved him into this room, they allowed me to sleep in his room. Martha Olsen came to see me the first night and she came to my room where we were alone. I broke down and cried in her arms and asked her, "Martha, would you sing a song to me?" She did. She sang a hymn, "Be Still, My Soul," while I cried.

Then the nurse knocked on my door and said that Charles wanted to see me. So Martha and I went to be with Charles for a while. He wanted so much to get up and visit with Martha and me but was so weak. He went into a coma-like state that night. Charles Walen came and told me that he would stay with me at the nursing home until it was over. That wonderful man stayed by my side for three days.

Several people came over and visited, both friends and family, and also Bishop Todd Hendrickson came by to visit and gave Charles a blessing. After a while, the visitors who were not members of the Church began sitting in the corner and making so much laughter and noise that I was getting upset. So, not wanting to make a problem, I asked Charles Walen's wife, Joy, if she would go with me to the restroom. Joy could tell I was upset and asked me what was wrong. I told her that they were making so much noise that it was taking the reverence out of the room. She asked me if I wanted her to tell them to leave. I said, "No, I will know what to do at the right time."

We went back into the room and they were still there laughing and giggling. I looked around the room and looked at Joy. She was standing in front of the window and as I looked at her, I felt the warmth of the Spirit and saw the Spirit of the Lord shining on her. I looked at her and said, "Joy, will you read to me?" She said that she would and asked me what I wanted her to read. I asked her to read 3 Nephi 17, a section of scripture from the *Book of Mormon*. She smiled at me and said, "Sure, I will." As she read this beautiful chapter of the *Book of Mormon* about the Savior blessing the little children, the Spirit grew stronger and stronger and the people that were making so much noise left the room. Peace was restored.

Too soon, the final few minutes came and I felt it as I had laid down to try and get a little sleep. I sat straight up alongside of him and told him good-bye for now, and to tell our little girl, Judith Ann, that I love her. I kissed him and said good-bye to him. I then watched him leave his body and knew it was over for him, and I took the oxygen mask off of his face and said, "You don't need that anymore, Charles." Then I held him until they came to take him away.

I asked them not to zip up the bag they had him in just yet. When I was able to handle it, then I let them do that. That was so hard for me. I thought in my mind that I wished I could take the defibrillator pacemaker out of his chest for him. I know that sounds strange but it was my feelings at the time. Chuck Walen called Dr. Garness and told her that Charles was gone and she sent the undertaker to take him to the hospital to take care of his last wishes.

Several months later, I received a letter from Dr. Garness telling me that she received a letter from the doctor in England that was over all the research for Friedreich's Ataxia, and that he thanked us for Charles' donation and was amazed that he lived as long as he did with the heart that he had. Dr. Garness told him that she credited Charles' long life to his faith and to his wife. I felt so good about what she had said about Charles. She is a good friend.

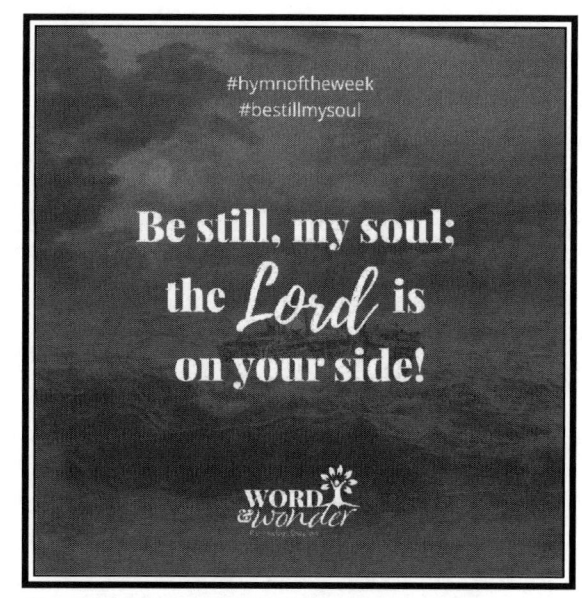

"Be Still, My Soul," the words of the hymn that comforted Shirley when Charles died.

The next few days were so hard as we got ready for his funeral. My friend Martha Olsen sent her beautician over to my apartment to do my hair for me and I went to the funeral at the chapel. I wish I would have been thinking of my sweet Mother at the time because she told me later how hard that was because Dad had been in the same spot with his coffin just two short years prior. Everyone was so supportive of me and slowly time began to heal my loneliness. I doubt that all of the loneliness will ever go away until I am standing beside him again.

In the months that followed, there was sadness at his passing but also gratitude for his great companionship in my life. I wrote in a brief journal entry three months after his death:

> Chuck died three and a half months ago. It has taken me this long to be able to write it. I don't know how far I will be able to write tonight but I got the hardest sentence written now. I am happy he isn't hurting any more but I sure miss him.
>
> The last three days with Chuck were so wonderful yet very hard watching him pass through the veil. Wonderful because of the Spirit of the Lord was so very strong. There was a feeling of excitement in the air as Chuck

departed. Family and friends waited for him to pass through to their side. But sadness for those who were watching him go. The room radiated to me so much I couldn't feel sad.

 Later the grief began setting in hard. I am trying to keep my spirits alive by reading and trying to learn. Hopefully, one day at a time it won't hurt so much. (Shirley Robideau Journal Entry, June 2002)

I felt his loss deeply and just tried to get through each day as best I could, knowing that my life had changed once again.

I am so grateful for our Temple Sealing which seals Charles and I together for all of Eternity. My heart goes out to the people whose beliefs teach them that there is no life after death. I remember a dear person that was terrified when she knew she was dying because this was what she was taught. I sure hope I said something that helped to ease her fears. For myself, I know that I will see Charles again, be together with him, and enjoy the blessings of being united in love and companionship beyond this life.

Section 5
Sensory Losses and Moving Forward

Following the death of her husband Charles in 2002, Shirley now faced life in her later years with a new set of challenges. She had concerns about her physical health and undertook a steady diet that helped her to improve her health condition. She also took steps to attend college and further her education for a period of time.

After several years as a widow, Shirley met another man who she married and he became her fifth husband. She also went through the loss of a second parent, her mother, and adjusted to life without both of her parents. Her second husband Dave also had some physical challenges due to Multiple Sclerosis, and together they underwent a health journey that resulted in some significant health blessings in their lives. Shirley credits her adherence to a careful diet and living the principles of her faith's health code, the Word of Wisdom, for much of her positive health experience in these years. Life had continuing difficulties, however, and after five years together Shirley and her last husband Dave divorced.

Shirley moved forward with a year-long move to St. George, Utah, which took her to a warm climate with fellow church members close by. Health concerns brought her back to live in Fargo again, and she began to experience greater changes in her loss of vision and loss of hearing. Much of the next few years in her life was spent in learning to adapt to these sensory losses, and she benefitted from the aid of Community Living Services and other programs to assist those with such challenges. The onset of blindness took her to a training program in Minnesota to adjust to this new reality, and she has made her home there in the Minneapolis area since 2018.

Chapter 26
New Chapters

Transitional Experiences

When my husband Charles Robideau passed away in early 2002, a series of life transitions occurred in my life beyond his passing. Of course, being widowed as a result of his death was the most significant transition that came into my life at this time. However, in the couple of years that followed, there were additional meaningful changes that I experienced. These transitional experiences related to my health, my living circumstances, and my education.

Health, Diet and the Word of Wisdom

I have already related some of the health-related concerns that were affecting me in the final years of Charles' life. I was taking a variety of medications related to my health concerns and had also gained weight due to my limited mobility. The Spirit had warned me that nursing care was ahead for me unless there were some changes to my health. Again, I was inspired to implement guidelines from the Word of Wisdom, a health code in our Latter-day Saint faith, and these efforts began to guide my health in a more positive direction.

I continued working on my diet according to the promptings of the Spirit and the things I was learning as I studied about foods and nutrition. I was on several medications at this time and wanted to get off of them. So, I made an appointment with my Internal Medicine Doctor and then told her when we met that I wanted to go off of my medications. She was upset with me and told me that I could not do that and asked me why I wanted to do that anyway.

I told her that I was trying to lose weight and I felt that the medications hindered my progress. She then told me that I would not be able to lose weight because I was in a wheelchair and physically inactive. I told her I was going to try anyway. She reluctantly helped me to gradually wean off of some medications and to drop those that could be discontinued as I continued on with my diet program.

I had already lost 35 pounds by the time Charles passed away and I was determined to follow the Lord's warning from the Spirit that had been given to me. After a year, my doctor asked me to come back in for a medical check-up. When she saw me at this time, at first she was very concerned and ordered several blood tests and found that I was quite healthy but minus sixty pounds by this time. When the blood test results didn't give her what she was looking for, she then told me to go to the Nutritionist so that I could make sure I was eating correctly. I smiled and said that I would do that.

I copied down the format for my diet that I had created from study and the guidance of the Spirit and took it with me to this appointment. When I met with the Nutritionist and gave her my diet format, well, she was astonished! She wrote in her report to the doctor that my diet was the best that she had ever seen! I was so happy!

I remember that I went to a Relief Society meeting that night. They asked each person to write down something about ourselves that no one else knows and not to put our names on them. Everyone was supposed to guess who it was that had recorded each item. I wrote down that I had lost sixty pounds! They didn't guess that it was me!! So fun!

I gradually lost weight using that approach since I was in a wheelchair and I was not able to do a lot of exercising. However, the miracle though to me is that it took me about ten years of obeying my diet and I did not fluctuate. My weight stood still for a while for many weeks but never went up at any time. Instead, there was a steady downward loss. I reached 135 pounds and have stayed there. I had lost 165 pounds very slowly and kept my health well in the process. How grateful I am for the Scriptures and the Holy Spirit as a guide for our health.

A Home for John, Mom and Me

Mom and I were still living at the apartment on 32nd Avenue in Fargo near the Villa Maria nursing home following Charles' passing. After a while, my brother John wanted all of us to live together and so he asked us to look for a house that we could all live in. He asked us to look around to see what we could find within a budget he gave us. The houses were so expensive and it was difficult to find anything of any worth in the budget range. Mom and I looked at twenty or thirty houses, hoping to find one that would work in the budget that John gave us as he didn't want to go higher than a certain amount, but we had not found anything that was really a good fit. So, we searched and saw many but nothing appealed to us.

I was with Mom whenever we went to look at houses and we saw houses that really were bad! I had never had the opportunity to look at houses as a prospective buyer before. We were all looking for something within a certain price range. Some of the houses we saw were so filthy that I was literally afraid to go into them.

One day we went to see this old house that was one hundred years old. While looking at it I felt nothing. It was a nice house with two bedrooms and an attic and basement. The dining room had a full wall that was a mirror which made the area seem much larger. Mom and the realtor went downstairs to look at the basement, leaving me alone on the main floor near the dining room. As I sat thinking about the house, I noticed an area of the wall that seemed to be moving. While they were down looking at the basement, I was in the living room area and suddenly I saw the room seem like it was dissolving in the middle of the room. Then, I felt the Spirit and saw the face of my deceased husband Charles push through this opening as it separated.

He looked at me and it was the first time I had seen him as a non-handicapped person. I kind of gasped but felt very calm as I looked at him. I kept looking at him and he looked at me. No words or thoughts were exchanged, just a communion to let me know he was well. He didn't say a word, but it was enough for me to know that there is indeed another side of life and a spirit world where we continue to live after we have passed beyond this life. He disappeared when Mom and the realtor were coming back upstairs.

Mom and the realtor came back up and we went outside. I was kind of in a trance at the miracle I just saw as we were leaving the house. I felt a very strong spiritual impression and so out of the blue I said to the realtor, "You need to put Mom's name on this house as soon as you can." Mom said, "Shirley!"

Mom then looked at me I could tell she was upset with what I had said. I repeated what I said and the realtor looked at me and said, "I will do that as soon as

I get to the office." The realtor went back to the office and put Mom's name on the house. She called me later that evening and told me that right after she placed Mom's name on the list, six more names popped up afterwards, meaning if she had not done that then she would have lost the house. I asked her, "What do you suggest?" She suggested that we should put an extra $5,000 on the requested price as an offer. So, we did that and the house was ours.

It was just a few months later that Mom was diagnosed with Alzheimer's Disease and would not have been able to help us get any house. So, we moved in shortly after that and had a ramp made and some doors widened so I could use the bathroom and one bedroom. In this instance, I was most grateful that my sweetheart Charles guided me, as it seemed he wanted us to choose that house. That decision was aided because Charles came from the other side and made himself known to me and he wanted me to know what to do. Mostly, I am grateful that he let me know that there truly are people on the other side that care about us and help us if we are open to them.

A Season of Illness

I was able to live with them in the house for about six months. On December 25, 2002, the same year that Charles died, I got a very high fever. Mom called the ambulance and sent me to the hospital and I was diagnosed with meningitis. I was in the hospital for about two weeks with that illness and then came back home. I then made the decision that I was going to move into New Horizons again, and I did that on the first anniversary of Chuck's passing in 2003.

A Return to School

College where Shirley Robideau attended in 2004.

In the season after Charles' passing, I also decided to go back to school to try and begin my life alone again. I applied and then went to Minnesota State Community and Technical College in Moorhead, Minnesota, taking classes on Medical Technology. There was a little bit of a journey in getting to this point, which I recorded in a long journal entry in September 2004:

I have been desperately trying to lift my spirits since Chuck died and it has been a real struggle for me. It was nice to go to bed last night with a smile on my face and actually feel joy in my heart. So what is it that I am doing to bring my spirits up and gain confidence in my choices and accomplishments?

To begin with about six months ago, I really felt low, unloved, and useless. I had enough of my faculties about me, however, that I knew things were getting out of hand and wanted to climb out of my depressing state. Donna, manager of New Horizons, put a notice up on the board that a student from NDSU would be coming to give free counseling sessions to all who are interested. I saw the flyer but didn't do anything about it. A few days later Donna approached several of the residents individually, including me, and tried to drum up business for this young lady. I told her no, but it kept nagging me to the point that when I saw Michelle near the mailboxes I approached her.

As I approached I saw that she had a Seeing Eye dog. Wow, did I ever take notice to that since I was feeling sorry for myself because my vision was taking a dive. I set up an appointment and then began sessions with Michelle, Cindy and Jackie; about two or three months with each one. Michelle gave me a little confidence that maybe there is something that I can do to feel more of worth. That has been important to me. To feel that I, Shirley Robideau, can contribute to the world I live in and thus display the blessings the Lord had given me. My Talents: What are they? What is it the Lord gave me to give to others? I wanted to know.

Then came Cindy; what a delightful young lady. She was almost my age, with a family and going to NDSU full time. That fascinated me and I told her so. So these counseling sessions began to spark my desire to get out, do something instead of sitting in front of my computer playing games. She taught me how to write a resume, to look for jobs and/or volunteer work, and I started to feel like I can do these things. I went at it as though my life depended upon my getting a job. Each step I had taken, however, was shot down by my eyes, hearing or disability. I didn't give up though; I kept on trying to go a step higher. Then one day I found myself at NDSU in front of the admissions desk. I honestly can't tell you how I ended up there but I was there registering to take classes. It didn't feel right so I kept searching for what I should do. To shorten this, I will just say I am now at Minnesota State Community and Technical College in Moorhead.

It was difficult for me just to begin because I was so nervous about stepping out onto unfamiliar grounds. Low lights, many people walking around, the thought of studying, pressure of taking tests, the list goes on and on. I was mortified but determined to change the course of my life. So here I am today, a student, and beginning to feel better about whom I am with confidence that I am going somewhere positive.

My first day at MSCTC, I wanted to run, fast and hard to escape the feelings of fear and uncertainty. The Lord knew my thoughts and prompted me to take just one day at a time. The second day wasn't much better. I was so near tears that I didn't think I would make it out the door before they fell. The feelings were real and overwhelming, but the Spirit of the Lord would edge me on just for one more day, until I look at my watch and the day is gone, then a week, and now a month. (Shirley Robideau Journal Entry, September 2004)

The important thing about this episode in my life is not the classes I took, but instead the confidence I gained and the reassuring sense that my life could go forward despite the emotional difficulties and physical challenges I had encountered.

I had a fantastic note taker who assisted me that I became very close to during this period. She and I are still friends. Thanks to her, my GPA was 3.90 when I finished classes there. I really enjoyed my classes and did well in them. I got to the last semester of classes and was told that I would not be able to finish the degree because my vision would prevent me from accomplishing what was required. My eyesight did not allow me to process 85 records an hour, which was required, and so I was unable to complete my degree. So, that ended my classes at MSCTC, but I enjoyed the learning experience.

Chapter 27
A New Marriage, A Mother's Loss

Gains and Losses

So, within a couple of years after my husband's death, my life had gone through a variety of transitions and I was trying to manage my loneliness and move forward with my life. There were good days and there were challenging days.

I was actively involved in church activity and felt supported by friends in the Church and also my family members. I had the chance to live with Mom and then transition into independent living back at New Horizons. I improved in my health and pursued education for the next season of my life. So, some positive things were happening and some gains came into my life, but I also experienced loneliness and questions about what the chapters of my life would be like. The several years that followed became a season of gains and losses.

Meeting Dave and Marrying Again

It had been four years since Charles died when I was finishing up my educational experience at Minnesota State Community and Technical College. It was 2006 and I was living at New Horizons. At that time, there was talk of a new man that had come from Enderlin, North Dakota and was moving in down the hall. I was talking in a kidding way to the manager and asked her, "Well, is he cute?" I was told that he indeed was and I laughed.

I had just invited my niece Kati to come and spend a month with me at this time. So, we were running around and doing things around New Horizons where I lived and we went for walks in the park and in back of New Horizons. On one of these walks with Kati, a man on a scooter passed by us and said hello to us. Kati said to me that he was cute! I laughed with her and then it was not long and she was going to go home soon.

One day we went out to the garden with my friend June Stine, who was helping me with my garden that year. June was using a tiller to pull up the weeds and the ground was so solid that the blades would not go into the ground. The guy that we had seen on the scooter came over and introduced himself to us. His name was Dave. He told June that the reason that her tiller wasn't cutting into the dirt was because the blades were on backwards! After we all laughed, Dave volunteered to turn them around for her. After he had done that the tiller worked much better!

We picked a large cabbage and put it into a bag and hung it on Dave's door as a "thank you" for helping us out. Later that day, I had a bag placed on my door with corned beef hash in it (which was something I would never eat since I had been faithful to my diet for all these years since Charles died). I had lost about 100 pounds by this time. Anyway, our friendship began after that. I invited him for dinner and he brought me a bouquet of flowers. He was very kind to me.

Mom was having trouble at this time and I began going to medical appointments with her. She had taken some tests at the clinic and they suspected that she had Alzheimer's Disease. I do not really believe that she did have that diagnosis because the testing they did on her was focused on things that she had never seen in her life and were totally unfamiliar to her. She only had a third grade education so I just don't believe she had Alzheimer's Disease. I did know, however, that she was hurting but I didn't know why. She took a lot of Tylenol.

John took some time off of work to be with her for a while, and when he couldn't take off any more time, Mom came and stayed with me for a time. It was difficult for me to know what to do because she wasn't sleeping at night and would wake me up being very nervous. One night she woke me and I was absolutely at a loss in knowing what to do, so she told me to call the ambulance. She was shaking so bad and was very afraid. When the ambulance crew came, she sat on the bed and didn't respond as they were asking her questions. It was like she was there physically but wasn't there otherwise. They took her to the hospital and her blood work was off the charts. So, they helped to balance her and then she came back to my brother's home.

After this occurrence, John stayed home with her until there was a nursing home spot available for her. She went to live at Rosewood on Broadway, which was about ten blocks from New Horizons Manor, so I would wheel down to see her as much as I could.

In the meantime, Dave and I became very close and eventually we decided on marriage. We were married two months before Mom died. We were married on April 28, 2006. So, I went through a gain in my personal life while looking ahead to a potential loss.

Getting to Know Dave

So, that is the short story of how I met and married Dave Jackson five years after Chuck died. He worked on the railroad for many years prior to getting Multiple Sclerosis, which was one of the reasons why he moved into New Horizons. We enjoyed each other and got to know each other better with each passing day.

Dave was a cowboy in every sense, both in the way he dressed and in his behavior. He had acted in several movies as an extra during the 1990s—*Dances with Wolves*, *The Last of the Dogmen*, and many others. My favorite movie that he acted in was *Miracle in the Wilderness*, a 1991 TV movie. This movie was about a couple that were taken captive by a tribe of Indians who wanted their baby. The woman was a Christian and taught the tribe about the birth of our Lord and Savior, Jesus Christ, and they finally turned them loose as they saw many miracles in the wilderness to confirm what she taught them. Kris Kristofferson was the star of this movie. Dave was one of the soldiers that went out in search for the missing couple. It is a good, clean movie and so enjoyable.

As noted, Dave had Multiple Sclerosis and pretty much was confined to a scooter for his mobility. He would fall a lot and so we had the office install several hand bars for him to help him to balance when he needed to walk.

Mother and Nursing Care

I went often to the nursing home where Mom was residing during this time. I tried to be present and help Mom as much as I could. One day she told me about a lady that lived down the hall from her, and this lady requested that Mom help her to get into bed. Knowing my sweet Mother, she did help her to bed.

Rosie Stockford, Mother of Shirley Robideau.

I told Mom that doing that might not be a good idea because the people at the nursing home may not realize that she used to take care of people like that. As near as I know she didn't do it again, but I could understand her because she never liked to see anyone in need and not help. She was such a loving person.

One day I went to the nursing home to find this wonderful mother of mine sitting in a chair in the community area. I knew that her time was near because Mom could not walk at all now. Her physical abilities were in decline and I worried about her often. I sat beside her and held her hand, and then my dear friend Joy Walen came walking in and stayed with us for a while. Joy had been there for me during many major events in my life and I so much appreciated her support.

The Loss of My Mother

After Dave and I married, Mom continued to go downhill and my sister, Jessie, came from Bisbee and stayed with John for a while. So, we were all together for a brief season to take care of things.

The night that Mom died, I wanted to stay with her all night. The nursing home didn't have anywhere for me to sleep so I intended to sleep in my chair right beside her. Dave came up to check on me and I had to go to the restroom, and while I was gone, he talked with Mom and told her that he would take care of me so she didn't have to worry about me. I came out of the restroom and the entire room just glowed with a warm and peaceful feeling.

The nurse came in and told me that it would be all right for me to go home and that Mom would be all right during the night. I hesitated but Dave encouraged me to come home and he would bring me back in the morning.

I gave in and went home with Dave that evening. Then, about half an hour after we got into bed, the nursing home called me and said that Mom was changing and not doing well. We rushed down to the garage, and while I was loading on the van, they called back that she was gone.

My heart just sunk! I wanted to be there with Mom. I cried and cried! It still bothers me that I was not there with her, but I think perhaps Mom was waiting for me to go home before she let go because she knew it would be hard on me.

Mom's funeral was also held at my Church. It was hard for me to lose both of my parents who were there for me all of my life. Mom, especially, had been my support and champion for all the years of my life, and her loss was painful and brought me a season of grief.

Moving Forward

As noted, this was a season of gains and losses in my life. So, sometimes I was feeling good due to my recent marriage, and then at other times I was struggling due to my mother's illness and passing.

About two weeks before Mom died I got a training job under the Experience Works Program which was really fun for me, and that also gave us an extra four hundred dollars a month. I was working at the courthouse and worked there for three years. I learned how the Legal Assistance Staff work. Based on this experience, if I had known about this type of job in my earlier years I would have gone for it.

I worked for Social Security in helping to gather information to assist people in getting their Social Security or retirement pensions. Working there helped me to understand why it is such a slow process. There are so few people trying to gather all of this information for so many people. Most of these people were Baby Boomers just like I was, born right after World War Two.

I learned how to use several different types of office machines that I had never operated before. I loved the scanner that would scan several hundred pages into the computer from paper copies. I actually enjoyed doing all the work I did there and was very sad when I had to leave when the program stopped for me.

I did appreciate the positive work experience I had there and the support I received from the office staff. A couple of the staff members wrote letters of recommendation for me when it was time to be done working there. For example, Gail Lorenzen was the Administrative Assistant and wrote in her letter in May 2008:

> To Whom It May Concern - Shirley Robideau has worked with the Office of Disability Adjudication and Review since July 2006 through the Experience Works program. Her responsibilities have included photocopying case files, typing exhibit lists, running labels, scanning exhibits into electronic folders, sending case files to representatives, and any other tasks she is asked to do. During her time here, Shirley has had a positive impact on the work flow process in the office. She is able to multi-task and deals with changes to our different work tasks readily. She has a very good turnaround time with the tasks she is given to do and is organized. Shirley is reliable, punctual and gets along well with all the office employees. She has done an excellent job for us and I would highly recommend her for the position. . . . (Letter of Recommendation for Shirley Robideau, May 2008).

I was very appreciative of the positive recommendation that I received. The office supervisor also wrote, "During this time, I have found Shirley to be pleasant, tackling all assignments with dedication and a smile," and that I was a "hard worker" and "team player" who would "make a great asset to any organization." So, this was a positive experience but then it had to come to an end.

It was a somewhat strange season of my life with everything happening at the same time. Gains and losses. I had just gotten married to a wonderful man, started working at a job I really needed, and my sweet Mother died. I had a very tough time losing Mom but tried to remember the happy times with her.

Memories of Mom and Dad and John

I did a lot of thinking during this time about both of my parents and other family members. Losing each parent made me want to draw closer to other family members, such as my sister Jessie and my brother John, and my nieces and nephews.

Ever since I can remember, my Mom loved rummage sales! She never could resist one. She would always come home with a car load of things that she felt were a good deal. She would have rummage sales to sell the things she got at rummage sales! A vicious cycle! But, she usually came out ahead no matter what.

I remember one special time I had with Mom. Mom was always hurting and whenever I would ask her how she was feeling, she would tell me how bad she was hurting. So, I just expected her to tell me that she didn't feel good whenever I asked her. One time when I had asked her how she was feeling, she said, "I feel good!" My mouth dropped in surprise! She looked at me and saw the look on my face and broke out laughing and we had a good laugh about that.

There were not many days that Mom showed that she was happy. She was such a hard worker all of her life and didn't know that it was all right to be happy once in a while. I know that she and Dad are happy now. I miss them both, more than I know how to say. Dad's wide open smile is so hard to describe. He was never one to talk a lot, but when he did, then he would say what he felt and was never critical of anyone. Mom would be the first one in line whenever someone needed any help.

John Stockford, Shirley's favorite brother!

As noted, I also thought a lot about my other family members at this time and grew in appreciation for them. For example, I thought quite a bit about my brother John and his special influence in my life.

Having served in the Marines, John was a handsome guy. In some periods of life, John liked his hair long and had it just below his shoulders. He and his first wife were married and they had three children: Christina, Amber and Jonathan. Later on, he married a second time and they had a son, Matthew. I used to babysit for these nieces and nephews. I grew to love each of them so much. It is hard to believe that they are all grown and have families of their own.

Now, John is married to a wonderful lady, and I enjoy getting cards with pictures from them. When I had better vision, it was fun to see John in his 6-foot 4-inch frame and his wife standing beside him (who is a little above five feet tall).

John enlisted in the Marines when he turned 18 and was there for four years. He spent part of his enlistment in Okinawa. I was so happy when he came home and remember it well. It was hard on Mom and Dad to not have their son home with them. Every chance they had, they would go to see him in California on the base. My brother grew up a great deal when he went overseas.

John had three of his former classmates that spent a lot of time with him. Randy B. was one of them. When I was in El Paso, Texas, Randy was stationed there for a time before they sent him to Germany for his remaining time in the Army. While in El Paso, he learned about The Church of Jesus Christ of Latter-day Saints and went to church services with me. It was such a beautiful experience for me to help with his discussions about the Savior. He was baptized before he left El Paso. It was hard when he left for Germany. I really enjoyed these young men that John went to school with and they were good friends.

After Chuck died, John came to the apartments that Mom and I were living in and talked to us about buying a house with him. John was working as a truck driver for many years and was gone all the time. This was a new experience for me to go and look at houses, but we did find a house and bought it. John is still living in that house after all these years. He has been such a supportive brother to me.

Shirley Robideau in her later years as she lived in an accessible apartment for those with disabilities.

Chapter 28
From Health to Hardship

Moving Ahead

Life seems to have a way of slowing us down and it is often our challenge to move forward despite life's difficulties. I had tried hard to move forward in my life following Charles' death. I spent time with my Mother and other family members, went back to school, and met a good man who I was able to marry in 2006. The current of life kept moving along and I moved with it.

During this next period of time from 2006 to 2012 I stayed busily engaged with my church congregation, worked to build a positive relationship in our marriage, and continued on my health journey. My health journey also became intertwined with Dave's health concerns and so we shared much of that together. This chapter tells much of the miracle of that season in Dave's health but how it evolved from health to hardship.

A Multiple Sclerosis Treatment in Mexico

Multiple Sclerosis is quite a challenging disease. It is an autoimmune disease that affects a person's nervous system, making it more challenging to move with ease and triggering symptoms such as fatigue, numbness, muscle weakness and spasms, and difficulty with balance and coordination. Its exact cause is unknown, but the symptoms can be managed and even improved with treatment and support, while a person's health with MS may range from mildly to severely impaired.

After we had been married for a period of time (I think it was in late 2008), my husband Dave decided that he wished to go to Mexico and receive stem cell treatments for Multiple Sclerosis. His desire and decision to seek such treatment in Mexico came after he had been on a phone call with a friend of his that gave him hope that his health could be better. At that time, as it was Dave couldn't walk very well from the hallway to the bathroom without falling. We had received assistance from the office staff at New Horizons to install hand rails all over the apartment to help him with his mobility.

Well, the decision for Dave to pursue treatment in Mexico seemed promising but it was also somewhat costly. I made a few hundred packages of treats to sell in order to help raise the money for his trip. In addition, Dave's father assisted him financially with the funds that we were not able to raise ourselves for his trip. Dave's sister, Shauna, went with him on this trip to Mexico. They were in Mexico for a period of time and I could not call him, so I had to wait until he returned to the home of the people they were staying with before we could visit and I was able to find out what was happening. Dave had three days of treatments and then the day came that he was supposed to have the animal stem cell injections. I will describe to the best of my ability what Dave told me happened to him.

The attending doctor had him lay on a table and gave him several injections in his back along the spine. Then, the doctor had him turn over and he gave Dave several injections from his neck down to his navel. He told Dave to sit up on the table. The doctor next walked several feet away from Dave and then told Dave to take in several deep breaths. After he had done that, with his sister watching all that was happening, the doctor then told Dave to stand up and walk to him. Dave hesitated but did as he said. And he walked! With tears flowing from him and his sister, he walked. After giving him a lot of instructions, they walked out of the office with Dave pushing his own wheelchair in front of him. When all of the people who were in the office area saw him (along with those in a long line waiting to get in) walking out, they all shouted with joy and applauded!

It was pretty strange for me when this man, my husband Dave, came walking into New Horizons Manor the next day! I hardly recognized him. I saw him walk long distances! It was so amazing.

This was a season of health for Dave and this transition seemed like a miracle. When Dave's friend called me to see if Dave was doing all right, I told him that Dave was now walking. He didn't believe me and came right over and just cried as he held Dave in his arms. It was indeed a beautiful thing to see. We had a welcome home party for Dave that night and I began to realize that this was my Dave! I honestly didn't know him as a walking person so it was a little strange for me.

Three or four months later, the ability to walk that Dave had gained began to disappear. He began losing the ability to go long distances again and began to fall again. It was so sad to watch it happening. However, the positive effects of Dave's stem cell treatment in Mexico also had an influence on my own health.

My Own Vision Treatment in Mexico

In April of 2009, Dave had me also go to Mexico to have stem cell treatments for my vision. Dave's deterioration in health was not as apparent yet, so we had hope that I would be able to save my vision which had degenerated somewhat.

A friend from my job at Experience Works was willing to travel with me and so we went down to Mexico so that I could receive pretty much the same treatment program that Dave had received. I obtained a Priesthood Blessing prior to going to Mexico, which promised me protection from any uncleanliness that was in Mexico and could affect my health. It actually surprised me when I got to the clinic in Mexico and there were flies everywhere and it was a pretty dirty health clinic. However, I remembered the priesthood blessing that had been given to protect me and had faith in the Lord.

It turned out that my friend who traveled with me also saw the conditions, and so she did some checking and found other places for me to take most of the pre-stem cell treatments. So, my blood work was done in a very nice clinic. I felt the protection of the Lord the whole time I was there. When I got called into the health clinic office for my turn to receive treatment, the floor was slanted a great deal into the doctor's office. I could not see this drop because of my limited vision. I turned to go to his office in my wheelchair, but then my friend grabbed my chair just in time before I would have lost control and gone down the steep ramp and would have slammed into a brick wall. I was so grateful that she was watching out for me.

Upon being admitted into his office, the doctor there talked with me and wanted to try an experiment. He gave me an injection into my neck with a long needle and then told me to let him know if I saw any changes. We were sitting there waiting and suddenly, my vision cleared and I could see my friend. It was such a breath-taking sight for me that I gasped. I looked at my friend and said, "I can see you!" It was pretty humbling for me.

So, the doctor there told us to return the next morning after receiving treatments at the other clinic. We did so and he then gave me animal stem cell treatment injections in my navel. It was quite surprising because then I was able to see somewhat better almost right away. I was so humbled and grateful that I was not very talkative all the way to the airport as we drove to meet our plane to fly back to Fargo.

As we drove to the airport, I was looking at road signs again and the plants on the desert. I was in tears most of the way. I was speechless. I just didn't know how to express what I was feeling. I sent up a sincere prayer of gratitude for the protection and blessings I had received with my health.

Just as with Dave's stem cell treatment, three or four months later the positive effects of the treatment began to fade away. However, I was grateful for the experience and decided I would go on taking care of myself the best I could by eating right. This led us to some additional positive health experiences.

A Multiple Sclerosis Improvement for Dave

During our subsequent Christmas together, Dave got a book for a gift from his aunt. The Book was *Healing Multiple Sclerosis* by Ann Boroch, a certified nutritionist. He was fascinated by the book. I was looking at him reading the book and thought to myself, "I have never seen him so engrossed in a book before." Then the Spirit of the Lord told me that the book was good, so I was at peace.

Not much later Dave was reading the book and I looked over at him and I saw a light shining on him and I knew something special was happening. Pretty soon after he had been reading, he closed the book and came up to me and knelt down in front of me and said, "Shirley, this book has a diet in it. Would you help me to do it?"

He asked if I would be willing to prepare meals for him according to this book. The book offered a diet guide and recipes to help those dealing with MS. Since the Lord's Spirit had told me the book was good, I told him without any hesitation that I would assist him. So, then he gave me the book to read. I began to read the book and I was so amazed at the claims this lady stated in the book about the body's ability to heal itself by eating clean foods and taking supplements. Oh, my, it was very instructive and followed the way I cook anyway with a few adjustments and lots of supplements.

Ann Boroch had experienced Multiple Sclerosis when she was in her twenties and went to these doctors that told her to follow this plan. First, she had to go to the dentist and have them remove all the silver mercury from her teeth. Well, Dave didn't have any teeth since he had plates, so he was good there. Also, he would have to follow this diet protocol for the rest of his life since it is food that was used to treat the symptoms of this autoimmune disease. I set out on an adventure in helping Dave with this diet. It was amazing.

The book, Healing Multiple Sclerosis, that Shirley and husband Dave followed.

We set out on a three-year course and focused on changing everything that we were eating to the foods and dietary supplements that were in this book. The supplements were extremely costly but Dave told me to find a way to do it. Purchasing organic foods was a new concept to me so I had a lot to learn. Also, I was working part-time and had to have meals ready for Dave when I was gone and bring food with me for lunch. At first it was very overwhelming, but I promised Dave I would be there for him and I was determined to keep my word.

We had to begin by getting rid of all the foods that had sugar, preservatives, salt, dairy, and so on. When we looked at our foods in the pantry after we had eliminated the certain foods suggested for removal, the cupboards were bare! So, we had to go grocery shopping! We were fortunate that Cashwise Grocers had a wonderful selection and a knowledgeable clerk to help us with our efforts. All of these things were so different to me. I was used to healthy eating, or so I thought! But I had to totally change the way I looked at things and focus on healthy nutrition in a different way.

Dave's health improvement began immediately and soon he began to feel changes. Two weeks later after beginning the diet plan, he had to go to his MS

Doctor because he felt numbness in his legs and was told that he was getting too much Baclofen medication for his leg spasms. So, the doctor chose to cut down on the medication for his leg spasms. At the time, Dave had a Baclofen pump located in his stomach area that automatically controlled the amount of medication that was fed into his body. He had to start going in every two weeks for a medical visit to have the amount for his medication decreased. Then, the day came that they told him they could not go any lower or the pump would shut down. So, they decided to put water in the pump to see how Dave did without taking any medication at all. Dave did great and the doctor mentioned possibly removing the pump, and Dave had such faith in this diet that he told them to take the pump out. So, they did!

When he went in for the removal surgery, the surgeon told him that he had put hundreds of these pumps in or had replaced pumps so that extra medication could be administered—but never had he taken one out. What a miracle! Dave continued with the diet and the supplements as Ann told him to do in her book. It was a huge blessing for him and also a miracle for me to observe what was happening with his health as he continued to improve.

As time moved forward and this diet effort continued, Dave's health continued to improve and his symptoms lessened. He began walking without hanging on to the railing in the apartment, and soon he was walking and rarely using the scooter. He was able to button his shirt easier and his legs continued to get stronger. His chest began to fill out and his facial features began to become even healthier. His hands, legs, and chest began to show muscles again and he had a Cat scan and was told that the lesions were almost gone. He finally had reflexes in his legs again.

He faithfully followed this diet for two years and was almost totally relieved of the symptoms of MS. It was so beautiful to watch him as he would exercise on the treadmill and stand up straight and tall.

We applied to move into a new building that was going up behind New Horizons Manor. We went out in the summer before they were tearing up the ground and Dave would tell me where each of our rooms were going to be, and after it was built then it was almost exactly where he said they would be. We moved into Sunrise North apartments in 2009. We continued following the program to reverse his MS and he was doing so well. I was in amazement as I watched him getting stronger and stronger.

Then, something changed and I observed that suddenly Dave began to lose progress rapidly. I noticed him falling again and other things like before. He began to drink alcohol secretly and went back to eating things on the side that he was warned against in the book.

Hardship and Divorce

Although we had generally had a good relationship and this health journey was a great blessing, unfortunately these blessings did not last. As noted, Dave's health took a turn for the worse and his symptoms resumed when he did not follow the diet plan any longer.

The day before Thanksgiving Day in 2010, I was going to go over to Hornbacher's Grocery Store to get some food and I went to get my jacket out of the closet. I paused, thinking something was wrong, but I didn't feel anything certain or couldn't find what it could be so I set out for the store. It was a beautiful morning and the sun was shining after a gentle rain and I was thinking how of bright the colors were outside. I was improving with my vision because of the diet I had been on and was realizing how bright everything was around me.

I got near New Horizons and looked over at the cars parked in the parking lot to my right and looked to see if anyone was moving any cars. Seeing that everything looked clear, I started to cross over to the sidewalk when I felt an excruciating pain in my legs. My head flew forward and my face hit the back of a car. The driver of the car did an illegal back-up and had actually backed out of the parking lot to go out the wrong exit. In doing so, he backed into me and my wheelchair.

I don't know if I was unconscious or not, but I did have a vision during that time before the man touched me telling me that this would be a blessing. The people there helped me back off of the car and my wheelchair was damaged pretty badly and I had a huge bruise on my face and both of my legs hurt. The ambulance came and took me to the hospital to have X-rays, and to my surprise there were no broken bones but I was bruised from my knees down to my toes. Lots of pain but it slowly healed.

In this period of time, things began to happen soon between Dave and I that were negative and I wondered if we would be parting soon. Our marriage began to be very difficult and he began to treat me differently. One day he told me that he wanted out of our marriage or he would blow his head off. I told him that he didn't have to do that and I would go. Thus ended our marriage. Dave requested that I move out and we were divorced on July 15, 2011.

I was uncertain at the time as to why things had turned in such a direction. But, as it turned out, there was a bit more to the story. I found out later that Dave's father had told him that he was going to mess up his retirement if he continued to get better. Dave did not want to go back to working again and feared financial hardship if this were to happen. Also, it plunged him toward depression, and he turned back to alcohol and other negative coping mechanisms. So, he went back to dealing with the MS rather than face this situation differently. How sad.

Of course, going through a divorce experience again was not easy and it was hard for me to be alone at times. I wrote to a friend several months after the divorce:

> I have been feeling happier and find myself laughing again. It is one thing to smile but quite another to hear yourself laugh. I have been able to make it with maybe one cry per day now instead of several. I cried a while last night but I could feel the Lord near me and was comforted. (Shirley Robideau email, August 2011)

I was grateful to have friends, family and fellow church members to extend support to me during this time.

It was one of the greatest learning experiences of my life to see how the Lord has provided the foods and supplements to heal a body that was so deep into this autoimmune disease. We were married five years.

It was this marriage that helped me to look back and see the many blessings I had from each of my former husbands. This perspective helped me to grow in my acceptance of the Gospel of Jesus Christ and my ability to see His divine hand in our lives.

Chapter 29
A Season in St. George

Life Transitions

At 64 years of age in 2011, I had experienced so many of life's ups and downs that I wondered if things would ever calm down in my mortal journey. Soon, however, I was going to enter a season of life far from the winter weather of Fargo in far-off Utah. But, first I had to face the loneliness I felt and continue to deal with some of my own health concerns. This chapter describes a new season of my life following the divorce from Dave and a move to lovely St. George, Utah.

Multiple Crossroads in My Life

Following this painful divorce in July 2011, I was alone again and really struggled with emotions of that time period. I was having so much trouble affording the supplements that I had been taking and had to stop them because I was getting sick on them. It turned out that some of them were toxic. The writer of the book was not prescribing the supplements correctly, and with our little knowledge of them, we had no way of knowing what was not safe. So, I totally stopped taking those supplements at the time.

I needed a place to live since Dave had asked me to move out, and so I moved to Crossroads Apartments on July 12, 2011. I was the first one to move into this new building that was located directly across the street from my church building in Fargo. My own apartment was spacious on the main floor and was designed in a way that allowed me to function well with my wheelchair. I liked the apartment being across from the church building.

I wanted to continue attending church services in the Fargo 1st Ward because I knew everyone there. Also, even though I now lived in a different geographic boundary and should be attending church in a different ward (although each Fargo

LDS congregation met in the same building at different times), I was nervous about going to the Fargo 2nd Ward because I didn't know too many people there. The accident also caused my vision to begin to rapidly decline so I couldn't see faces very well and it was hard for me to recognize anyone.

During the first week I was there at the apartment, I headed over across the street to go to church services in the Fargo 1st Ward. As noted, since the new apartment was in the Fargo 2nd Ward geographic area then I was supposed to go to services in the Fargo 2nd Ward. While I was wheeling across the street to attend the Fargo 1st Ward, I heard the Spirit of the Lord telling me that I was to go and talk to Bishop Sean Brotherson of the Fargo 2nd Ward. I began getting really nervous and the Spirit told me that everything would be all right. I told the Spirit I would obey but hesitated, and the Spirit said to me again "Talk to Bishop Brotherson."

I went in the door of the bishop's office and asked if Bishop Brotherson was there. I couldn't see anyone so I had to ask. Just then, Bishop Brotherson spoke and asked me if I was here, meaning whether I was moved in across the street, and I told him that I was moved in. Bishop Brotherson came and put his hand on my shoulder so that I knew where he was, and then said, "I am here, Shirley, what do you need?" He told me to go to church services and he would talk to me after I finished in Fargo 1st Ward.

When I was done with classes that day, I went to Bishop Brotherson's office and told him that the Spirit of the Lord told me that I was to go to Fargo 2nd Ward. Bishop Brotherson was so kind to me and I found that he was very easy to talk to and we became friends. I was feeling lost and and rejected at that time after my divorce and the move, and so I was hurting pretty bad, but that was all wiped away with a priesthood blessing and the love and kindness he showed. Also, he introduced me to Sister Linda Boatman, the Relief Society President, who welcomed me and equally gave me feelings of worth with her kindness. I so appreciate all that each one of them did for me. Eventually, Bishop Brotherson became the person that helped me to write my life story.

As time went forward, I began to make myself busy trying to pull myself out of the slump I was in. I was feeling pretty hopeless since the divorce and didn't know how else I was supposed to feel. I went to Sacrament Meetings at church and kept as busy as I could and also attended Institute Classes at the church once a week. On this one day at Institute Class, my friend Diane Peterson was there and she offered to walk me home after class. Talking with her about the supplements I was then taking that were not agreeing with me, she told me instead about USANA Supplements, which are nutritional supplements sold by USANA Health Sciences company. I met Diane's friend, Carol Howland, the next day. I knew from what I had seen with Dave that good nutritional supplements could help me keep up my health, but I didn't know how to find safe ones to take.

Promotional flyer for USANA Health Sciences, with Shirley Robideau as featured speaker, Fall 2014.

Carol soon helped me to understand what had happened and I began taking USANA supplements that same day. I threw away all the supplements I had gotten from the other lady. Basically, I figured that if I was starting over, then I was going to totally start over. My biggest concern was my vision at the time but I also knew that I had other problems physically that I needed to address. Since USANA is a multi-level marketing company and I could receive help with purchasing supplements if I shared them with others, I had two people sign up under me right away and that brought me in 100 dollars per month right away. So, I was able to continue taking them because I could now afford them easier. My first big health change was that I was able to stop taking allergy shots which I had been taking every week for about ten years.

During the months that followed I became quite involved as a distributor for USANA Health Sciences. I liked the products and was even featured as a speaker by USANA in some promotional seminars, such as one held in Fargo during October 2011. On October 15, 2011, USANA held a "Health and Freedom" seminar at the Holiday Inn in Fargo, and supported me as a USANA Associate and "featured speaker," with the opportunity to tell my story and also my "why" for supporting the company and getting involved. I was able to participate in such events occasionally and enjoyed the opportunity. I wrote in a letter to a friend in November 2011:

> I am an activist with healthy lifestyles. I am constantly coaching my friends and family as to the necessity of cleaning up their diets, balancing with quality supplements and exercising to build up our muscles and strength. I have been working with Carol Howland as a speaker to help people to know and understand that even though there are bad foods available, it is easy to change our habits to convert to healthier choices. I have been enjoying giving these workshops in our area. . . . I feel good that I am doing things to help my income and assist people to lead healthier and wealthier lives. (Shirley Robideau Letter, November 2011)

In November 2014, I did another "Health and Freedom" seminar for USANA in Fargo, sharing my experience as one of the speakers and encouraging others to live healthy lifestyles.

A Spiritual Prompting to Move to St. George, Utah

I lived at Crossroads Apartment complex for six months and then I felt prompted to move to Utah. I began to do some Internet searching and found a potential apartment in St. George, Utah, which interested me because of its warm climate and nearby temple. I had many blessings that made the move possible for me. When there were items that I could not do for myself, local church members such as Linda Boatman, Bishop Brotherson, Brad Leeser, Marji Meyer and others helped me so that I would be able to go.

I flew into St. George, Utah on January 16, 2012 and went to my new apartment. A couple of months earlier I had met a member of the Church online through my friend Kilene M., who was the daughter of my friend Marza Cardon. Dale B. was a member of the Single Adult group in the Church down in St. George, and he agreed to be helpful with my move there. When I arrived at my apartment in St. George I found it completely furnished, all ready for me. Dale and the other members of the Single Adult group had done that wonderful thing for me. I was so grateful and I just cried. A few minutes later, Dale walked in carrying a bed for me to use! It was quite a day. Also, not to mention but the weather in St. George was sixty degrees at the time and I had just left Fargo where it was -20—20 degrees below zero!

That first night in St. George was a little hard for me because I had some of my things unpacked and something fell over in the bedroom and I thought it was outside my patio door. I was petrified! I went out into the hall because I didn't want to stay in the apartment if someone was on my patio! I met a sweet elderly lady out in the hall that was exercising with her walker. She was my very first friend I met in the building. She helped me to feel more calm and I went back into my apartment and then someone came to visit me. It was Sister Laura Cooper. How I loved Sister Cooper! She and I became friends when she was a missionary in Fargo, ND. She helped me to find out what happened and checked the patio door and everything was fine. She found the clothes that had fallen and then I knew what the noise was I had heard. After Laura left I was fine. I was jittery about being 1700 miles away from Fargo but it was a good experience for me.

On my first Sunday in St. George I went to church services at the Senior Branch. It was a Branch because in the summertime all the "snowbirds" went back home and there were not enough members to be a Ward. In the summer months there were not many people there and I was more comfortable, but in the late fall there were so many people there that it was hard to move around. It was strange to me that the Sacrament was passed by Seniors instead of the Aaronic Priesthood boys. I really missed that while I was in the St. George Utah Senior Branch.

When I first joined The Church of Jesus Christ of Latter-day Saints that was one thing that impressed me so very much. The young Aaronic Priesthood boys were so reverent and so grown up as they passed the Sacrament to the congregation. It was such a joy to watch them. From the time I first joined the Church in 1973, I would pay attention and watch these young boys as they grew from Primary age (school-age) to become young men holding the Aaronic Priesthood. Then, I would raise my hand in support for each one of them as they progressed in the offices and responsibilities of the Priesthood. It was a special part of my life. Thinking back, I wonder how many young boys I watched grow in the Church in this manner?

My Branch President was a wonderful man, as was the Relief Society President, and my Home Teachers were so awesome. I met a couple of the people that I became friends with that lived in my building. One of these friends was interested in my way of eating. She had to eat in a special way too so she would share recipes with me as I did with her.

Dale B. would also come by and bring me food from his yard often. He had a mango tree in his yard and also had a wonderful garden that he shared with me. The fresh fruits and vegetables there were so good. In St. George, I found my first store that only sold organic foods. It was so fun to see new things and meet new people, and I very much enjoyed my experience as I was living there.

Settling Down in St. George

Though the move to St. George had brought with it a bit of anxiety, soon I was becoming more familiar with things there and feeling more comfortable. I also met a variety of people who blessed my life. Things began to settle down for me.

After I had moved to St. George, I soon met a chiropractor that lived close to me that was a member of the Church. He was so good to me. One time I was feeling just as down as I could be and asked him for a priesthood blessing. He and his associates did give me a priesthood blessing and I felt much better. I really grew to appreciate this good man.

My medical doctor there was also a member of the Church. He asked me on my first visit what I thought of St. George, and I told him that I loved it and I had even seen my first lizard! He laughed and told me that I would see thousands of lizards on the walls of the buildings and everywhere. He then said that I might also see a snake under the sink when I opened the cupboard door! I told him, "Why would you tell me that? Now when I open my cupboard I will be scared!" He was so funny and I enjoyed him so much. He was also serving in the Stake Presidency of the stake where my Branch was located so I saw him from time to time outside of the medical clinic.

I soon signed up with a program in St. George that took me shopping and I was fortunate to get this very kind gentleman that was 72 years old assigned to assist me. He would pick me up in a Cadillac and along with taking me to get groceries he would also take me on tours of the area.

He took me to Snow Canyon and I saw the beautiful cliffs and bluffs with volcanic ash and rich colors all through the cliffs. It was such an awesome sight and I was so grateful to the Lord that I was able to see well that day so I could see the beauty of His hands. I saw the hills and cliffs in a pink color in the early evenings too. So, it was fun. He also took me to the old airport in St. George so that I could see how the planes used to land and take off. At the end of the runway was a cliff drop-off, so if they didn't take off of the runway on time they would drop into a canyon! So breath-taking!

St. George Utah LDS Temple, where Shirley attended the temple in 2012 while living there.

I was able to attend ordinance sessions at the LDS Temple in St. George several times while living there. I had a friend named Levi and he would meet me there and we went through temple sessions together. I really loved the Temple. I would go on their Handicapped Transportation bus and it only cost me five dollars for a round trip. These experiences in attending the temple, making friends, seeing the local sights, and feeling support made my experience in St. George a positive one.

An Unexpected Prompting and Move

While I had many positive experiences living in St. George, I was also challenged by the continuing difficulties with my loss of vision and hearing. These problems continued to be a daily challenge for me and affected my confidence, my social interactions and my ability to understand others. It was lonely at times.

At one point early in my experience there in Utah, I wrote to a friend and recounted:

> I am content with being here, believe that or not, I really am. My vision is my biggest fear that I know I need to overcome. This is such a difficult trial for me. I have talked to Heavenly Father about how difficult it is for me and he has comforted me many times over it. The fact is, I am really, really having a tough time with it and that isn't like me. I can usually find ways to do things I need to do, except this. That isn't an excuse, it is in fact what I am dealing with—loss of sight. I am afraid I am not going to be able to "endure to the end" with this trial. My body, because I am taking care of it, is still ready and willing, but my sight limits what I am able to do and I don"t know how to handle it. (Shirley Robideau Email, February 2012)

I was beginning to learn the reality that dealing with loss of sight and hearing would be challenges that would remain with me and be a struggle for years to come.

In about September or October of 2012, I had a feeling come to me that I should check on apartments back in Fargo. I soon discovered that available apartments were scarce because of the oil boom occurring in western North Dakota at the time, because workers coming to the region were taking all of the apartments available nearly all the way to the Twin Cities in Minnesota.

I simply could not find an apartment. I put my name into many places to live and was willing to go to Minnesota or Fargo. However, when I didn't hear anything and knew that my name was on a waiting list of at least eighty-some people that were before me, I felt that perhaps the Lord wanted me to stay right where I was.

I decided to try and get more actively involved with the people in the building where I was living. In December 2012, one day I went down to the community room in my building to help out for the Christmas Dinner. I was working in the kitchen when my phone rang. I went out of the area for some privacy and answered it. It was the manager of New Horizons Manor back in Fargo, North Dakota. I asked her why she was calling me because I was so surprised that it was her. She told me that she had three apartments available and I could have one if I wanted it. I said, "It is cold outside back home." She laughed at me and said, "Yes, it is." I asked her how much time I would have available to move home and she told me less than two weeks. I had to be there by the 1st of January. I told her, "No, I don't think so."

I hung up the phone after my response and I felt a very dark, heavy feeling come over me, and I knew it was guidance from the Spirit of the Lord. I looked upward to the ceiling and said, "But I thought you wanted me to stay here?!" Then I heard Him tell me, "It is time for you to go home!"

I called the apartment manager back and asked her to let me have the weekend to consider it. Then, I would call her on Monday Morning to let her know for sure if I would be taking the apartment and she did that for me. I talked to my Branch President and made plans to come back to Fargo. Things moved quickly and I was home by January 3, 2013. My sweet brother John paid for my flight home and I moved into Apartment Number 306 at New Horizons Manor on January 3, 2013.

Shirley Robideau in her apartment in Fargo, circa 2014-16.

Shirley Robideau at home in her apartment in Fargo, North Dakota, circa 2014-16.

Chapter 30
Lessons in Learning to Adapt

A Life of Adaptations

Moving back to Fargo in 2013 was a bit unexpected for me after I had made the effort to shift to a new and warmer climate in St. George, Utah. I had appreciated my time in St. George where there were many fellow members of my faith in a retirement community with a warm climate. Yet, I knew and trusted the Lord and the inspiration that had come for me to return to Fargo in this next chapter of my life. It was an adjustment but I would find out that the next several years would bring me continuing lessons that I needed to learn in adapting to the unique challenges and circumstances of my own health and life. This chapter explains the things that unfolded next in my life and my journey in learning to make adaptations to enhance my health and living environment.

Adjustments and Sensory Challenges

I lived again at New Horizons Manor in Fargo for the next two years. While I appreciated the familiarity of that residence and being back in Fargo, I also found that I was really having a difficult time emotionally in trying to change my feelings about Dave. I would see him occasionally because we lived close to each other. I kept wanting him to tell me that he still loved me and wanted to marry me again. After a while, I knew that I had to make a complete break because it was hurting more than I was able to handle that he no longer cared for me. So, I began to look for another apartment that I could relocate to where he was not living outside my back door.

This season of life brought new challenges and adjustments. Life began to change for me from this time on. My faith in the Lord Jesus Christ changed to be stronger then ever before. I was determined to be the best person I could be so that my Heavenly Father and Jesus Christ would be proud of me.

Since I was living inside the geographic boundaries of the Fargo 1st Ward, then I quickly found that I was back in my old Ward again for church services. The first day attending church was exciting for me because I was able to see everyone again after being gone for a year. The Bishop ordered a Hearing Loop so that I could hear the speakers using the microphone during Sacrament Meeting. That was a wonderful device and it helped me for about a year.

However, as my vision went down and began to decline, so did my ability to understand the sounds I was hearing. These sensory changes continued and over time it was getting so difficult for me that I was feeling like I was in a little box unable to see or to hear. I knew there were people all around but there seemed to be no way to really communicate with anyone. I kept my hopes as high as I could but I found myself coming home from church services feeling starved. I wanted to hear the words being taught to me and I didn't know how to do it. When I had left the area a year earlier I was able to hear and see somewhat, so now no one seemed to be able to understand that I couldn't see or hear them very well. So, I found myself becoming so lonely. I found that when I was at home and only one person was visiting me, then I was able to understand a little more. However, I also recognized that my vision and hearing had deteriorated quite a bit in one short year. For this reason, I believe, I began to understand why the Lord told me that it was time to go home and receive greater assistance.

Assistance from Community Living Services

The sensory changes that I was experiencing during this time in my vision and hearing certainly made it more challenging to communicate and function. In addition, I also began to experience a variety of health effects related to Post Polio Syndrome. Post Polio Syndrome is a health condition linked to a previous bout of polio that occurs many years later and includes symptoms such as muscle weakness, joint pain and stiffness, fatigue, difficulty speaking and other features as well.

From 2013 forward, Post Polio Syndrome began to become a problem in my life also, so my strength had diminished enough to make things a bit more complicated for me. I soon found that I needed help during the evening hours because that was when I was most tired. So, I talked to a company in Fargo called Tami's Angels, which provides personal, non-medical care for individuals with disabilities in their homes, to see if I could get some help from them. My social worker was wonderful about helping me to get things in order. I also had a wonderful young lady from Community Living Services (CLS) named Rachel assigned to assist me who was so in tune with accessibility needs concerning vision and hearing. She was with me for three years and I valued her friendship and the services she helped to provide through CLS. I soon transferred most of my support and care needs to Community Living Services (CLS) and they were the company that I continued to receive all of my services from at this time.

Logo for Community Living Services, the organization that provided Shirley with much assistance.

I began to receive several hours of assistance per week through Community Living Services. They helped me extensively so I would like to share some of the things that they have assisted me with or done for me, so that if anyone ever needs in home care then they may have some idea of what these wonderful programs can provide. The purpose of Community Living Services (CLS) is to allow people to remain in their homes as long as possible and not have to move into a nursing care facility if they choose not to do so.

As one example, shopping is something I absolutely used to love to do. Not being able to see prices anymore or even being able to see what is on the aisles anymore really put a damper on my shopping time and experiences. However, with my aides from CLS, I am able to go with them and they tell me what is down the aisles. Since I have done it for myself so many times previously, I am familiar with what I want and they check dates for me to make sure I can have the freshest products possible. At the time of this writing, my CLS aide Rachel had been with me for three years, so she was familiar with everything that I buy and which made it a lot easier. We also checked ingredients on some products to see if I can have them. Rachel also knew what I will and will not eat, so she could look at the ingredients quickly and if she found something that she thought I might like, she would then ask me if I wanted that item.

Rachel also helped me with the purchase of clothing. Again, not being able to see sizes, colors, and things like that makes buying clothing very difficult without help. She has grown familiar with the styles I would or would not typically wear, and she is always looking for things of bright colors that work together. She knew I liked to look good and she was absolutely wonderful to make sure that I would feel confident in what I was wearing.

I have also received some help with paperwork as well as paying bills. Most of my bills are now paid online and Rachel makes sure that I do not get an over-draft in my accounts.

As another source of help, Cristina is an aide who has come once a week to help me prepare some meals in advance so I can make what I want during the week. We work together, as all my aides let me do what I can do for myself. I usually have things ready and started by the time she comes to help me. Cristina likes to help me make hummus, which I absolutely love! I have grown to use a lot more garlic than most people do and she is the same way so we get along very well. Both Cristina and Rachel helped me to keep things organized and in place where I am able to reach them and find them.

Both of these aides from Community Living Services also helped me with laundry and cleaning chores. Some tips for people with limited vision that Rachel helped me with included that we took some little 4 x 5 index cards and she cut some of them in the shape of a pair of pants. We then punched a hole in them to put a rubber band through the hole. The rubber band is then hung on the hanger with a pair of my pants with the color written on the 4 x 5 card in big black letters. While I was able to see, I then knew which color the pair of pants I had was, and she did the same thing for my shirts or blouses and it made it easy for me to match them. After my vision got worse, she actually put together outfits for me. I never hesitated to take out a set and pull it on because I know she put them together for me so that I could look nice. We have an area in the closet for the casuals and also space for my Sunday clothes.

In the mornings I get up to shower with an aide here to make sure I don't fall when showering and transferring. They help me to get ready for the day and with a few things to make it easier for me during the day. I very much appreciate the assistance I have received from my Community Living Services aides, as they have helped me to maintain my independence and be able to stay in my own home.

A Move to a New Apartment

In this period of time, I was having so much trouble with allergies and emotions while living in New Horizons Manor that I decided to try and move to an apartment that had its own washer and dryer in the apartment. I knew this was going to take a long time to find because to my knowledge there weren't any new apartments being built at that time.

In February of 2015, I was called to come to the Housing Authority to fill out the finishing papers for Section 8 so that I could go looking for an apartment. I was kind of discouraged because when you are approved for Section 8 housing you only have a few months to get an apartment or your name goes back down on the list and you have to start all over again with the paperwork. I got into the Housing Authority Office and Rachel and I were waiting for my appointment, and I was thinking in my mind that I was going to tell her forget it. Just then, I heard a voice say to me, "Hi Shirley, it's Jill!" Jill is the wonderful lady I used to babysit for. I heard her comment but at first it didn't register with me. Then, all of a sudden I felt like the Spirit of the Lord was giving me a strong nudge, and I realized that I was supposed to ask her if I could talk to her. So, I asked her if we could talk with her.

She took us back to her office and I told her the problems I was having at New Horizons. Then she said, "Oh, I can't believe I didn't think of you before, we have a vacant accessible apartment!" My heart jumped and I knew this was of the Lord! Then she said that she had to check with the manager of the apartment building to see if it was still vacant. My heart sunk! With the luck I had been having, I was thinking to myself that it would be rented.

My mind went back to about three months earlier when I first heard about these new apartments, a brand-new building and they were just opening in November of 2014. I kept calling the manager of these apartments as soon as I heard about them and no one would call me back, so I figured there were no apartments available. With only two accessible apartments available per building, I was sure that someone else got them. I remember talking with Rachel and telling her that if I got an apartment in this new building, then it would be a miracle.

Jill got a voice messaging answer that said the manager was on vacation. Then my heart really sunk! She said that I could go to my appointment and she would email the manager and see what happens. We were just finishing up with the Section 8 paperwork when Jill came walking in and said, "You got it!" I didn't catch what she had said, and Rachel then said again, "Shirley, you got it!" I still didn't get it! It slowly sunk in that they were telling me the apartment was mine! Tears began flowing and I was so excited. I felt that the Lord came through to help me again.

My aides, Cristina and Rachel, helped me to pack and clean my apartment, and the missionaries of the LDS Church helped me with packing pictures and last items as well as other things. I moved into my new apartment on March 1, 2015.

Learning to Adapt to Challenges

I feel that in my life I have always been able to find ways to do things that I couldn't normally do. I give credit for that to my Mother and also to the education I received from Physical and Occupational Therapy while in high school.

I eventually adopted a motto for myself that there is nothing that I could not do. Or if there is—then figure out a way to do it!

I remember when I was about 24 years old that I was living in my Mom and Dad's apartment and the bathroom really needed painting. I had no trouble with doing the walls but when it came to the ceiling that was another problem! With the effects of Polio in my arms, I could not hold my arms up over my head. I really got mad at myself when I realized that I could not hold my arms up there! So, I went into the kitchen and got the kitchen table and brought it into the bathroom and climbed on top of it and tried again. Still, I could not hold my arms up there. I was so upset with myself and made myself calm down and think about it. Pretty soon I thought of the idea of using a longer handle on the paint brush. I found a stick and got some tape and taped it to the brush—and guess what? I painted that bathroom ceiling!

So, I have spent much time in my life learning to adapt to limitations or dealing with challenges. This determination to figure out solutions has been of great help to me. In addition, there are many creative people and much "assistive technology" that has helped me to overcome or manage some of these limitations. And, finally, I have been helped by an army of people throughout my life, whether family or friends or fellow church members, that have helped me as well. In this section, I want to briefly highlight some examples of learning to adapt to challenges with daily living and physical limitations.

Showers and Transfers from a Wheelchair

When you live much of your life in a wheelchair, then it is a common issue to need to "transfer" from that chair to other spots such as a bed, a toilet or a shower. This can be quite challenging.

I found a way to transfer myself from a wheelchair as safely as I possibly could when I take a shower. When I lived in St. George, they did not have a roll-in shower like they had at my apartment in New Horizons. So, at first I had a tough time with that because I had to transfer on a sliding board across a bathtub and then onto the shower bench in the tub. It was very dangerous and I never want to do it again.

Shirley Robideau illustrating the process of transferring from wheelchair to bed.

Now, I have my shower bench turned with its back against the side wall. I then drive my power wheelchair up to the shower bench and put my legs on top of the bench. I then drive the chair up to the bench and turn off my power chair and transfer on to the bench, then I turn on the power of my chair and move it back out of the shower and turn off the power until I finish showering. When getting out, I just do it in reverse the same way.

I also had a shorter transfer board made for transferring on or off the bed and from manual chair to power chair. The shorter board is made out of a hard wood with a slight slant on both ends and it is highly varnished to make it easy for me to slide on it. I then put my chair next to the bed and use the board to slide over on to or off of the bed.

Also, I have two transfer poles that I use as needed, with one of them in my bedroom by the bed while the other is by the toilet. Transfer poles are a floor to ceiling pole that is securely tightened to keep it in place. An organization called IPAT (Interagency Program for Assistive Technology) in Fargo, North Dakota, helped me to get these poles. The transfer poles help me to have something to grab on to, so that then I can pull myself from my wheelchair to/from bed or toilet. These poles have saved me from falls hundreds of times and I am so grateful for them.

Adaptations in the Kitchen

Another area of my living situation where I spend a significant amount of time is the kitchen. My kitchen area also has some adaptations. The main accessibility feature in the kitchen is that it is open under the counter by the sink, so that I can quite easily wheel my chair under the sink so I can reach to wash dishes. They also put a Lazy Susan near the sink to use for those of us that cannot reach the upper cupboards. One additional feature I really appreciate is the counter that goes from the sink to the stove because my arms aren't strong enough to carry hot foods very far. So, I slide the pots from the stove to the sink, and then I put the pot in the sink to be able to dish it up on a plate for myself.

My aides help me with chopping celery, onions, carrots and other vegetables, and I put them into a two-cup container that is BPA free. I have them placed in my refrigerator so that I have chopped veggies ready for when I am making something. I just use what I want for whatever I am fixing. This is a helpful strategy.

I am still watching my diet since I lost all the weight over a period of years, 165 pounds in all, so I do a lot of fresh fruits and vegetables and small amounts of meat. I use whole grains for whatever I make in the kitchen. I do not use refined flour so cooking is pretty simple. When I make extra amounts, I put them into containers and freeze them for future meals.

In my forty-three years as a member of The Church of Jesus Christ of Latter-day Saints, I have learned so many things through the Women's organization, which is known as the Relief Society. The Relief Society is the oldest and largest women's organization in the world. We meet every week on Sunday and also once a month in the evening for Enrichment lessons and activities. In the evening meetings I have participated in over the years, I have learned to cook, sew, and do just about any other household task that you can imagine! I even have had a lesson on plumbing! We were taught how to take care of the toilet if something breaks inside the tank. Anyway, my point is that I have learned so much through this wonderful program. As I developed my ability to cook from the many lessons I have been taught, I would expand on them and grow my abilities. For example, I had my sweet mother-in-law tell me that she would look into my cupboards and see very little food and would not know what to prepare, and then I would go to the same cupboard and make a fantastic meal. She was always complimenting me like that.

Shirley Robideau preparing meal ingredients in the kitchen.

I have been truly blessed by the Lord with wonderful examples to help me learn to grow gardens, cook, can and freeze foods, dehydrate foods, and repair home appliances and fixtures. I have even taken a hammer and crowbar and taken out a wall in my home! I have painted, built, fixed and preserved all of my life, and for this I am so grateful to the Lord for giving me a rich life.

Managing Laundry

My laundry room is located in my bathroom and the appliances are each a front-load style washer and dryer. I took pictures of those I had but since then have gotten a new washer and dryer, and the new ones are even in height with my sitting position which is so nice for handling laundry. My sink countertop in the bathroom is also open underneath so that I can wheel under the sink and have an easy reach to the sink.

Adaptability Equipment for Hearing

Though I have experienced mobility challenges for much of my life, it was in my later years that things became much more challenging with my sensory abilities like hearing and vision. Some time after I returned to living in Fargo and my hearing abilities were diminished, I went to see Ardell Olson at the Sanford Clinic and told him how much trouble I was having with hearing on my phone. Ardell then told me about a gadget called an iCom, which is a wireless device that uses Bluetooth technology and connects hearing aids to other devices such as phones or computers. The iCom works for the phone, and so we got it set up and pretty soon it was taking the sounds of the phone and connecting them to my hearing aids. I was absolutely amazed at what this little iCom device did for my ability to hear on the phone.

I went in to see Ardell again some time after that experience and he told me about another type of technology called a ComPilot, which is basically similar to the iCom but the battery power lasts much longer and it was capable of working with my computer and cell phone. Both of these devices bring the sound from a phone or TV, for example, directly to your hearing aids. If you have two hearing aids, as I did, it is even better because the sound is so evenly distributed. So, we proceeded forward and I was then able to get a ComPilot, and in this case it was also IPAT (Interagency Program for Assistive Technology) which helped me to get that. IPAT also gave me a TV link so that I was able hear sound on both the television and the computer with my ComPilot device.

Even though the ability to use the ComPilot helped me so much, I still was having increasing difficulties with understanding people on the phone. Things in this period were getting so frustrating for me, as my vision was declining rapidly and I was no longer able to hear the sounds from the microphone at church meetings. I guess that instead of using the word "hear" perhaps instead I should say "understand"—I was no longer able to understand much of the sounds I was hearing.

Without being able to read lips, there was simply no way for me to figure out what people were saying to me. So, I couldn't hear the people talking to me at church nor could I hear in the meetings, and so it was like being there and yet not being there. I would come home and cry every Sunday. I was still able to talk one on one with individuals, but sometimes they had to repeat their words several times and people would get frustrated with me and just say, "Never mind!" Such incidents would leave me feeling so bunched up inside that I couldn't release the feelings. I was afraid that I was going to eventually be at home 24/7 with no one to talk to at all, instead feeling like I am inside a little box while knowing there are people around me but yet being unable to see or hear them.

During this period of time, I became so unhappy and began to feel like I was starving inside. My love for the scriptures and the Gospel wasn't feeding my spirit sufficiently and I felt like I was literally starving! I just didn't know how to handle this trial the Lord gave to me so I prayed to Heavenly Father to help me.

Receiving a Cochlear Implant for My Hearing

In May 2015, I had finished a hearing test with Ardell Olson and he was sitting beside me and said, "Shirley, I want you to meet Dr. Miller." I then asked him who Dr. Miller was. It turned out that Dr. Miller did surgeries for hearing difficulties including cochlear implants. This made me anxious and I started to say "No!"—but I paused. I heard the Spirit of the Lord whisper to my mind in a quiet impression, "This is good." So, I calmed down and said that I would meet him.

I saw Dr. Miller a while after that and was told that I happened to be a good candidate for a cochlear implant. A cochlear implant is an electronic device which is designed to provide a sense of hearing to individuals with significant hearing loss or challenges. When I saw Dr. Miller, I had an interpreter there with me from the School for the Deaf, and between the both of them I was able to understand that when I did this operation then I would be totally deaf in my right ear. It would require three weeks of healing before I would get the actual hearing application for the outside of my ear.

The surgery took place on June 22, 2015, which was my Dad's birthday, and I felt that it was the right thing to do and I trusted the Spirit of the Lord that told me that this is good. My friend and Visiting Teacher from church, Sue Brayton, came to take me to the hospital that morning, and she stayed with me for the two hours or more prior to the surgery. When I woke up from the medical procedure, she was there with me. She was like an angel in my sight. Sue followed me as I went home

Shirley Robideau showing her use of assistive technology for hearing.

on Ready-Wheels Transportation. The procedure went very well but I was pretty nervous about not being able to hear anything except what little I could hear in my left ear. The Sisters in the Relief Society got together and had someone to stay with me for the first twenty-four hours, and then they had someone come and be with me an hour or two twice a day for three weeks so that I would not be afraid of not being able to hear. These ladies were all angels to me!

I went to the medical clinic on the third week and received the implant hearing device, and to my surprise, I could not understand one word. I felt like I had Donald Duck quacking in my ear! They adjusted the sounds so that I had both high pitch and low pitches coming through the implant. I have to admit that it was not a thrilling first few months, as I did not understand that it takes time for the brain to learn to hear since I was so deaf in that ear. Once I understood that process and the need for some time, then things seemed to go smoother for me and I adjusted better.

The cochlear implant doesn't sound like a human's voice so it is still difficult to tell who it is that is talking to me. I don't know if that will ever change because it is a bit different for everyone. As I am understanding more now than I did when I had two hearing aids, I can't tell you how blessed I now feel. I still have trouble understanding things sometimes but it is getting better as time goes on. I have a tough time adjusting to the high pitch sounds as they cause me to be very nervous since I am not accustomed to them. So, at this time we are going slower with adding the high pitched sounds. At first, I wondered why I needed to have the high pitched sounds, but as we go along with the process I am understanding why I need them. Without the high pitched sounds, I won't be able to hear everything. So, gradually, we go up on the sounds and take a month or two in between new settings. I remember the week that I was first able to hear the sparrows tweeting while I was sitting outside and listening. I didn't know what the sound was so I asked someone and was pleasantly surprised to find out it was the tiny little birds.

This process of gradual adjustment and improvement with my hearing due to the cochlear implant continued over weeks and months. In January 2016, I wrote this brief note:

> I understand things so differently than even a week ago. Like, I feel as if I am just now beginning to grow and yet every step of the way I have grown. Since June 18, 2015, when I received my cochlear implant, it seems like a whole new world is opening. I am hearing more, talking more plainly, and yet still have a long way to go, but I am in awe at this new life I feel growing within my heart. I pray that with this blessing that I can serve the Lord in a more productive manner and be able to show my love and gratitude to him.
> (Shirley Robideau Journal, January 2016)

It was my hope that improved hearing would not only help me to learn more but also that it would let me help others.

By the spring of 2016, it had been almost ten months since I had the surgery and I came to know for a fact that I can hear better now than I could prior to the implant surgery. Now, I get so thrilled when I hear someone say something behind me and understand that someone is talking to me and I am hearing it. I began picking up more and more sounds so that going to Sunday School each week is an absolute pleasure. I felt the pleasure of learning again by hearing others share. I also started listening to broadcasts from my Latter-day Saint church on the computer and hearing music like I have never heard it before. I love to listen to it over and over all day long. I find it hard to take the implant off at night. I just love to hear the sounds!

The hardest part of adjusting to the hearing situation over time with the implant became when two or more people are talking to me. It takes the implant a few seconds to pick up a new voice and sometimes I get totally confused, but it has gotten better as time goes on.

After more than a year had passed since I had the cochlear implant installed, I have experienced an increased understanding as each month goes by. I began to understand voices and recognize who they are. I was able to go into Sunday School and Relief Society classes and understand most of what was being said. I still had some trouble with understanding speakers at the microphone during Sacrament Meetings, but one wonderful member of the Bishopric got the idea that I would understand better if I had a headphone connected to the microphone adaptive equipment I had used in the past. That adjustment allowed me to better hear the speakers, the music when people sing, congregational singing, the organ or piano, and the Sacramental prayers and speakers. It has been so enlightening and encouraging to know how the Lord and modern medicine is helping me every step of the way. I love how God answers prayers—it brings such a good feeling to my heart.

Chapter 31
Blindness Ahead and a Future in Minnesota

A New Chapter in Minneapolis, Minnesota

Having lived in the upper Midwest for most of my life, moving back to Fargo from Utah brought me "home" in a way that was comfortable and familiar to me. This move happened in 2013 and it was needful for me because it allowed me to receive support from individuals and organizations that had been part of my life, since my health conditions became more complicated in the time period following my return to Fargo. I am so grateful for all the assistance that I received upon my return to North Dakota and the health journey that I struggled with due to hearing loss and other issues.

One of the unique blessings that I had living in Utah was the opportunity to live close to and participate in religious ceremonies at the LDS Temple in St. George, Utah. I had never lived so close to a Temple and it is a beautiful, peaceful place. I love the Temple. I hoped that perhaps I could find the opportunity to be closer again to a Temple. I have also lived a good portion of my life in Minnesota and have many family members and friends who live there as well. So, when the time eventually came that there was a possibility for me to move to Minneapolis, Minnesota, then a new chapter opened for me and I have been on that new journey for the past several years.

Continuing Sensory Challenges and a Move to Moorhead

The health issues that I have faced in the later chapters of my life have required me to make many adjustments and learn new things. Both hearing loss and vision loss have altered my life and required me to adapt in significant ways. Once I returned to Fargo, then I lived again at New Horizons Manor for the next two years from 2013 to 2015. Then, I moved to the new accessible apartment in 2015 that allowed me to receive much assistance from Community Living Services. While I appreciated the familiarity of being back in Fargo, I also found that my health demands were challenging and that perhaps I needed a change in my life.

I stayed in the Fargo area until the fall of 2017, and then I moved to Moorhead, Minnesota to help me qualify for an eventual move to Minneapolis. This shift became necessary in my life due to my loss of vision. I needed assistance. As noted, Community Living Services was most helpful to me, and I wrote in a brief journal entry in summer 2017:

> I have been using CLS (Community Living Services) to help me in my daily needs and I have grown to love each of the ladies that comes and helps me. One of my ladies, Kara, won't be helping me anymore, which has really left a sad feeling in my heart. She is a young girl, about 23 years of age, and I had grown very fond of her. The Lord had truly blessed me to have known her. Hopefully, I will be able to see her again once in a while. (Shirley Robideau Journal, July 8, 2017)

My aides from Community Living Services were instrumental in helping to make the eventual move to Moorhead in 2017. I wrote an account of what prompted this move and my feeling that the Lord wished me to move in the summer of 2017.

When I returned to Fargo from St. George, Utah in January of 2012, I wanted then to live in Moorhead because I had heard the benefits for the deaf/blind were much better than in Fargo. However, I found that the transportation was very poor for the disabled and that there was no transportation at all on Sundays to Fargo from Moorhead. On top of that, the apartment situation for accessibility was very poor, so I changed my mind and tried to let the idea go.

By 2017, my vision loss was getting to the point that I knew I needed more training to be able to prepare myself for the future. At 70 years of age, I just was not ready to give up on my independence. I could not get any more help in North Dakota to help me adjust to the onset of blindness. I had received my first cochlear implant for hearing loss in 2013, which was a great aid to my hearing, but other resources were limited. In March 2017, they had a meeting in Moorhead accepting MAT

ParaTransit to take care of all the transportation in Moorhead, including Sundays. My hopes then began to rise that maybe now was the time to make that move. I tried to get help to find accessible apartments in Moorhead and had absolutely no luck and no one seemed to know what was available in Moorhead. I prayed about the situation and put it into the Lord's hands.

    I took the matter to the Lord in prayer and asked the Lord if this was not what he wanted for me. I told him that if he wanted me to stay there at North Sky Apartments, I would do as he asked of me. I had all but let the idea of a move to Moorhead go when Carolyn (my aide) and I had gone to an appointment, and I was waiting in the car for her to load my wheelchair into the trunk. I was very quiet when she returned to the car and she asked me if I wanted to go and get groceries. I told her, "No." So, she asked me where I wanted to go, and I told her, "Moorhead." She then said, "Where do you want to go in Moorhead?" I looked at her and said, "I don't know. I only know I am supposed to go to Moorhead."

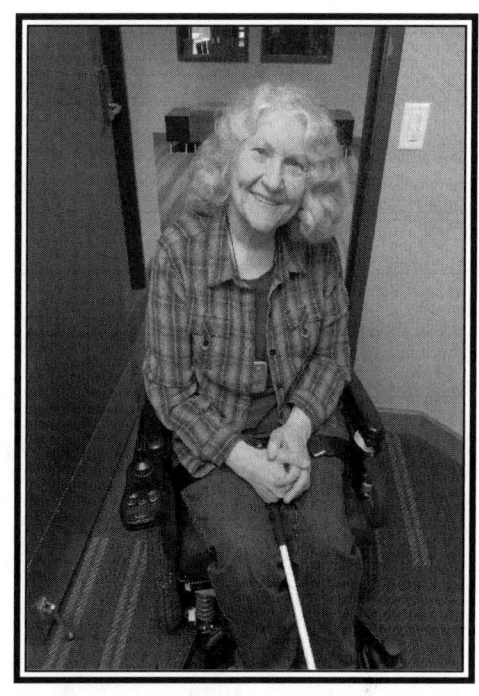

Shirley Robideau in her wheelchair, 2019.

    She looked at me kind of strangely and just began driving towards Moorhead. We got to the Moorhead bridge and I felt prompted to call the Moorhead Housing Authority. Even though I didn't have any luck with them before, I didn't question the prompting and dialed them again. This time there was a different person that answered the phone, and I asked her where I might go to find an apartment for the disabled in Moorhead. The lady that answered told me, "I usually refer people to 'the other housing Authority'." I was stunned and said, "The OTHER housing authority?" She told me there were two housing authorities in Moorhead, so I called this other number and was told to come on over and talk with them about an apartment.

    I called the number just as we were crossing the bridge to go into Moorhead. I was surprised when I was invited to come to the apartment building and asked her where it was. She told me to make a left when we crossed the bridge. So, I told my driver to do that at exactly the right time. And there it was! We went in to receive a tour. I asked for the paperwork for an apartment. There were none empty so I could not look at the apartment in advance, so my driver told me that I didn't even know if I could get into the bathrooms! I told her that the Spirit of the Lord was directing me and that it would be okay.

So, we went there and as I listened to her talking, I could see a checklist in the back of my mind where I checked off the things that I had been looking for that she said they had. While my thoughts were on this checklist, I heard the still, small voice of the Spirit say to me, "This is where you need to be." Tears welled up in my eyes as I absorbed the answer that the Spirit gave to me. The Lord's Spirit confirmed that I was supposed to be in Moorhead and that this was the place I needed to be. I asked the lady if she would help me to fill out an application, and then was told that because I was disabled and a senior that I would go at the top of the list.

That was such a a wonderful feeling, knowing that my Heavenly Father knew my feelings and approved of what I was thinking. The Spirit's still, small voice was so quiet, yet so touching, that I knew without a doubt that he was guiding me to where I needed to go. Now I just needed to wait upon the Lord, and trust that He would open the apartment for me at His time. God knows the whys and what ifs about everything, so I trust the Lord. I was so grateful to have that knowledge that the Lord is mindful of me and my needs.

A Time of Transition

I moved into the apartment in Moorhead on Thanksgiving weekend in 2017. Then, by mid-April of 2018, I was living in Minneapolis, Minnesota and going to school at BLIND Inc. I knew that this experience illustrated the Lord leading me and I believe in the power of prayer.

This move to Moorhead, Minnesota was not a long-term situation but it was a needful transition to help me with my health circumstances. In December 2017, I recorded in a brief journal:

> I moved into Park View Terrace two weeks ago yesterday, and it feels good to have much of my things organized. . . . I am feeling much stronger

today than I have in several months. The stress I went through in the other apartment really was hard on me. . . .

I have never had so many problems with hitting things with my power chair as I have in the last two years, as my vision has dropped quite drastically. My friend, Lee Allen, is trying to help me so that I can have plenty of preventive options here, such as bumper guards. Also, Lee Allen helped me to do the repairs at the other apartment as much as possible. I will be forever grateful to him for the many times he has helped me.

My aide from CLS (Community Living Services) was a true friend also. She saw to it that I had plenty of food and supplies to make things easier for me. She worked so hard to get my apartment in order before she was done working for me. I need to let go of her now and go forward with faith that the Lord will help me to do the things I need . . . although I don't think there will ever be another like her. She will be my friend forever.

When I consider all those who made it possible for me to make this move, I am awestruck. The Elders Quorum from the church moved me two Saturdays in a row. It was not an easy thing for them to do. The Missionaries also were a wonderful help. Cindy and Tiffany from Freedom Resource Center, Kim from Moorhead Financial Social Services, Jeanie from Services for the deaf/blind, and countless others have helped me in getting this far. I am so grateful to the Lord for putting people in my path that will help me along the way. I love them so very much.

The Lord is my light, I depend upon Him so much. With my vision dropping almost to not even being able to recognize light, I see His heavenly light protecting me and guiding me to help me not be afraid. I don't even know how to pray to Him the words that I feel. I have so much gratitude and words can't describe what I feel. I am told that I will have the help I need here to teach me how to get around more confidently in Minnesota, and that is my hope and prayer. Three months ago I was led here and told by the Spirit of the Lord that this was where I needed to be. (Shirley Robideau Journal, December 10, 2017)

Just two days later I made another entry that highlighted more aspects of this transition to living in Moorhead:

> Living in Moorhead is sure different. The people are so kind and helpful. The people in Park View Terrace are so helpful to me. They seem to want to assist me in getting around. I wish I could see their faces so that I know who they are and that way I could remember who they are.
>
> Lee Allen is coming tonight to work on more accessibility needs for my apartment. Each kind thing that he does for me makes me feel that I can do this. Teri Zollinger was here yesterday also and she put up my pictures. Each thing that gets put away just makes it feel more like home. What I need now is to have a Priesthood Blessing on my home. Oh, the gifts our Heavenly Father gives to us! My heart is so full. (Shirley Robideau Journal, December 12, 2017)

Truly, I was so grateful to the many "angels" around me that assisted me during this period of vision loss. Though I had anxieties, my fears were diminished by the loving effort and support of my fellow church members, community professionals, and others who took the time to uplift and assist me in so many ways.

The Lord provided all the means for me to attend BLIND, Inc. in Minneapolis, which would allow me to learn more skills to adapt to being blind.

To explain, in the 1980's a nonprofit organization known as BLIND, Inc. (Blindness: Learning in New Dimensions, Incorporated), was established in Minnesota by the hard work of many individuals and advocates who supported services for the blind. BLIND Inc. is an adjustment-to-blindness training center that is located in Minneapolis, Minnesota. This training center helps students of all ages who have experienced vision loss to develop the knowledge, skills and confidence to live in their homes and communities despite the challenge of blindness. With my declining vision, I was in need of such services and also would benefit from being near to the resources that this organization and others offered.

As already explained, I had received my first cochlear implant to assist with hearing loss and was doing very well with hearing, but the vision was really causing me more difficulty. So, I moved to Minneapolis, Minnesota on my 71st birthday in 2018.

I was soon enrolled in learning through BLIND, Inc. and rapidly learned a variety of skills to help me adjust to the loss of vision that I had experienced. I completed my training and decided to stay in the area and reside in Minnesota. This move allowed me to be just eight minutes from my Ward (local congregation) of The Church of Jesus Christ of Latter-day Saints and just fifteen minutes from the Minneapolis Minnesota LDS Temple. Oh, how I love the Temple! I have now lived in this area since 2018 until 2025, a period of nearly seven years, and it has been a great blessing to my life.

The Lord's Timing and My Time in Minneapolis

I didn't realize at the time I made these transitional moves how closely the Lord was timing all of these blessings. He not only made it possible for me to receive needed assistance for my physical challenges, but many other blessings also.

My sister, Jessie, became ill and her son Mark and daughter Michelle went to Bisbee, North Dakota and picked her up to take her to the doctor in the Twin Cities. She had cancer. She died on June 20, 2018, and because of the Lord's perfect timing, I was able to be with her almost every day and was holding her hand when she went to the other side of the veil. It was a special gift the Lord gave to me, which allowed me to be in Minneapolis at that particular time and to be with her in the weeks before her death.

I completed my training related to blindness seven months later and had to find a place to live or I would have needed to return to Moorhead. I turned to the Lord again, not really wanting to return to Moorhead, and went out looking at apartments. I was shocked at how small the spaces were that these places had. I had just about given up when I got a call from my Supervisor. She said, "Shirley, I found you an apartment!"

I was pretty sure that it would be another disappointment and told her that I didn't have my manual wheelchair there to go look at an apartment. She said that she had it in her trunk and was on her way to take me there. I still wasn't too convinced but said all right. We went to check it out and the rent was about the right price, and then we went in to see the apartment and to my surprise it was a very nice, large apartment. The Lord was in the details for me again! I was able to move in there in early 2019 and remain in Minneapolis.

Continuing Blessings in Minnesota

The worldwide COVID-19 Pandemic happened a year later in the spring of 2020. I was well protected from all of the violence that was occurring all around me in Minneapolis. There was one time I was really nervous and that was when George Floyd was killed. Mark and Penny, my sister's oldest son and his wife, took me to their home for a few days and then I was all right to come back home.

In 2022, I began receiving a spiritual prompting that I needed to look for another place to live. I talked with the manager of my apartment building as she and I had become good friends by this time. She was leaving and I was getting nervous about that. She told me about a new place being built in New Brighton, MN, and I thought, "Oh, maybe I am supposed to be closer to JoAnn?" I began the paperwork for this place. Then in March 2022 I went to fill out the application for it, paid the rent, and before I got home I knew I was not supposed to go there. I followed the prompting and canceled my contract.

Shirley Robideau with two police friends in Minnesota, circa 2020.

Several months earlier, I was talking to my friend Jamie and she helped me to fill out several applications for other apartments. I never heard from any of them, so I concluded that I was supposed to stay where I was at the time. A week later, I got a call from Rae Ann, manager of Concordia Arms. I had already consigned myself to the fact that I was to stay there and told her I was not going to move. I hung up the phone and the Spirit said to call her back! My aide was sitting in the dining area and watched as I had a conversation with the Spirit and said, "No, Shirley, you said you would stay here!"

I said to the Spirit, "I thought you wanted me to stay here?" The Spirit repeated to me, "Call her back now!" So, I did and made an appointment to go and see it with JoAnn. While we were driving to see the apartment, the Spirit whispered to me, "Don't look at it that it is too small, look at it thinking how can I make it work?" So, I knew I was going to take it. Miracle after miracle happened as things took place that enabled me to make the move.

The other apartment wanted me to pay about $12,000 for damages that my power wheelchair had done to the apartment. I was given a copy of a law that protected me from them trying to do that.

Everything fit nicely in my new apartment. Rae Ann had them take out the carpeting and put in beautiful flooring for me. A year later, my friend from Church, Jim Vannelli, moved in and so a person with the Priesthood to bless me is close by if needed. One thing after another has happened to let me know I am here because it is where the Lord wants me to be.

I am a part of a talking Deaf-Blind Group that talks by phone each month to support each other. I am a Companion by phone to an elderly lady in California and both of these have been for about a year and a half. I am a letter writer to several ladies in my Ward as their Ministering Sister. I find these opportunities meaningful and fulfilling.

There is a park along the side of my apartment building that I like to go in and spend time during the summer months. My church building is just five miles away and the St. Paul Temple is just eight miles away. I try to go to the Temple every week and I don't know how to express the feelings of gratitude to my Lord for bringing me to this location at this time in my life. I will be 78 years old in April of

2025. I still live independently in my own apartment and feel so much love from my ward members and temple workers when I visit. I am blessed. I am blessed.

Shirley Robideau in the gardens in front of the Minneapolis Minnesota LDS Temple, circa 2022-23.

Chapter 32
A Stunning Family Surprise

Finding Unexpected Family Ties

Since I have been raised in a supportive family and also come to have strong spiritual beliefs about the importance of family ties, I have developed a significant interest in my family ancestry and relationships. We are encouraged to learn more about our family ancestry in the Latter-day Saint faith, and so this has been a learning experience for me over a number of years. However, this learning journey took an unexpected turn for me one day after moving to Minnesota, and it has become a beautiful story of surprise and family connection.

DNA Research and Family Ancestry

During the first part of the 21st century, new technology has developed that allows a person's DNA to be examined and analyzed so that their family ancestry can be identified. For Christmas in 2017, a dear couple in Fargo gave me the gift of a DNA Sample kit. They worked in the Family History area and liked doing the work to help people learn about their ancestors.

I moved away shortly after receiving this test. However, I did follow through and was able to receive my DNA ancestry results. I found out that my lineage is mostly Scottish and some English, though I had believed much of it was Irish. The official summary of my DNA results was given to me by a professional genealogist in Minnesota, and it states:

> Your DNA ethnicity estimate is 45% Scottish, 38% English and Northern European, 10% Irish, 3% Welsh, 2% Swedish and Danish, 1% Finnish, and 1% from the Aegean Islands. More specifically, in Scotland, you

have ancestors from Argyll and Bute in northeast Scotland, just off the northern coast of northern Ireland. Since you heard that you had more Irish in your family than your DNA says you do, it's likely that many of your Irish ancestors were Scots-Irish, or Scottish people who settled in Ireland in the 1600s and 1700s and then later immigrated to America. (DNA Report for Shirley Robideau)

There was also some very interesting information about one of our family's ancestors, Mary Sophia Stockford, who did an apprenticeship in the fur business. She went on to make fur wraps for Queen Victoria and also a fur wrap in 1903 for Queen Mary, the wife of King George V of England.

So, learning about our extensive Scottish ancestry and the presence of ancestors such as Mary Stockford, furrier to the British royal family, brought me a few surprises. However, these surprises were nothing in comparison to the information that was soon to arrive at my doorstep.

An Email Out of the Blue

My parents' lives together began during the height of World War II, and they had little time together before my father Clair Stockford was deployed overseas to Europe. Their lives were in upheaval due to the war and not a day passed in which they didn't wonder if he would come home alive. My father was sent to the front lines in Germany soon after reaching Europe and the German military surrendered only a short time later, but he spent many months there as part of an American occupying force.

Many years later, when I was in my twenties, I had a conversation with my mother and she happened to tell me that I had a brother living overseas. I expressed an interest in finding him some day but this seemed to upset her, and I could see it was a tender subject, and so I left it alone.

Just before I left Fargo and moved to Minnesota, I received an email out of the blue from someone named Susan Funk. It came through the FamilySearch website but I could not read it without help, so I was unable to respond at that time. Then, in 2022 near the end of the year, my brother John contacted me and asked me if I knew anyone whose last name was "Breezee." I told him that I didn't know someone by that name, and then he indicated that someone had contacted him on Facebook and wanted to see if our families were related. He explained that she'd had DNA testing done and it seemed to suggest that our families were strongly related. John was not familiar with DNA testing and so he did not want to answer.

I encouraged him to send me the email and told him that I would contact her. At first, he did not want to give it to me because he thought it could be a scam. Finally, he gave me Susan Funk's phone number and I called her. I felt good about the things she told me and sent the information to the Family History Library in New Brighton, Minnesota and also to Sean Brotherson, a professor at North Dakota State University (Sean has been helping me with my book). The information shared by Susan Funk suggested that we were connected as family relatives. Specifically, she wondered if my father or one of his siblings or cousins could be her mother's father, and her mother was originally from Germany.

Sean Brotherson studied the DNA documents that were shared with me and also did some careful research on my father's travel history in Germany during World War II. He determined that my father was in this particular area where her mother was born at this particular time when she would have been conceived. So, those details fit with that part of the story.

Then, at the Family History Library, the DNA expert studied out that possibility along with other things that he researched, and told me he was 97 percent certain that Susan's mother was indeed my father's daughter. Wow! A bolt out of the blue! The son that my mother had told me about was not a son after all—but a daughter. Her name—Anita Marie Bauer Breezee.

So it was that I learned by surprise of the existence of another relative of mine, a half-sister, born in Germany in 1946. When talking to Susan Funk, her daughter and my niece, she told me she had sent me an email in 2020 that I had not answered, so I now knew about her efforts in trying to find me for several years. We met Susan Funk and her husband in the Spring of 2023 and were delighted with knowing of our other family that lives on the East Coast of the United States.

Unfolding the Family Mystery

Of course, it took a bit of time to figure things out and unfold this family mystery that had come to me as a surprise. Susan Funk and I began to exchange emails and gradually the information we shared began to illuminate the family relationship that existed. There are multiple descendants on that side of the family and so I will keep their information largely private, but the history of this family connection and how it unfolded for us is quite an interesting story.

In one of my first email exchanges with Susan in January 2023, I wrote to her and said:

> Wow! My mind is running with so many questions. What was your mother's name? Where in Germany was she born? Just so many things are going through my mind. I am thrilled to hear from you. . . . I do have people here who can help me to be able to tell you more, but need more information to help fill in the blanks.
>
> What you said about my Dad fits when he was there in Germany. I do not know where in Germany he was, but had a document of when he was released and need someone to open it for me on the computer since I am blind. Your mother's age fits perfectly in the range that my Dad was there. I am assuming that your mother was born after Dad came home from Germany. Do you have a birth certificate that tells anything about James Stockford? His age, where he was from, parents and so on . . . . I think you and I can solve this mystery. So many possibilities. (Shirley Robideau Email, January 2023)

Soon, I received an email back from Susan and it provided a bit more information about her mother (my likely half-sister at that point) and the circumstances of her life. Susan noted:

> Unfortunately, my grandmother was not forthcoming with any information at all to my mother about her father. I remember my mom telling me that she asked him to send her a picture of himself, and he did. However, her stepfather threw it in the fire before she could see it. . . . My mom had green eyes. The biggest question she always had in regard to her dad was

whether or not she had siblings through him. I really wish I knew more. (Susan Funk Email, January 2023)

So, both of us had a little bit of information but this was a story that was still unfolding. However, answers began to come quite quickly.

Without providing an extensive family history, let's just say that my father had multiple siblings and other family members and the name "James" was common in that family. So, we really needed to do a little more detective work to confirm that the "James Stockford" identified by Susan as her mother's father was the same one as my father. We passed information back and forth comparing pictures of her mother and my family members, exploring whether there were any samples of my dad's handwriting in her family, and sharing what details of the situation had been shared in each of our families. Susan shared with me about her mother:

> I am so grateful that you were willing to take some time to speak with me. Unfortunately, I don't know a whole lot. I'm hoping between the two of us we can figure out who my grandfather is. You and I seem to be very closely related (by DNA information). . . .
>
> Here is what I know. My mother was born June 26, 1946 in Germany. Her father was in the military. He went by James Stockford. She remembered seeing him last on her seventh birthday. She said that he sent a car for her and they brought her to the military base there. . . . My mother is deceased and has been since May of 2006. I am really hoping to learn about her side of the family. (Susan Funk Email, January 2023)

This potential family connection would have made my father to be Susan's grandfather, and her mother as my sibling (sister) by a different mother there in Germany. The way that she learned more is not because my father was listed on her mother's birth certificate, but instead because her mother had hired a private investigator years earlier to learn more about her biological father.

The private investigator had given them the name of "James Stockford." Susan's German grandmother was Irma Bauer, and her mother's name was Anita Bauer. Anita was born in 1946 in Lampertheim, Germany, and there was a military base nearby in Stuttgart. Irma Bauer was not married when she met James Stockford

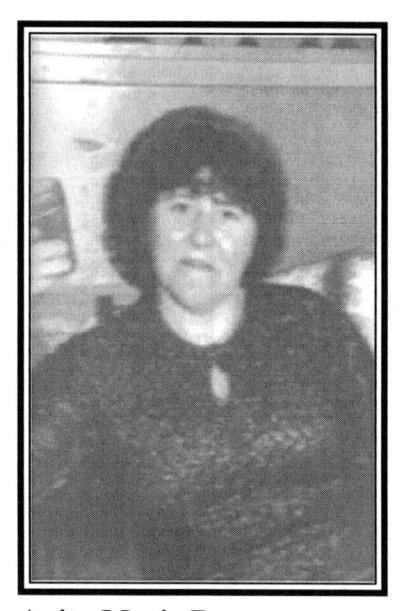

Anita Marie Bauer, German half-sister of Shirley Robideau

and had a child by him (Anita) who was born in 1946, but she did marry a couple of years later to a man named Stanley Zobrekis. These were the details that were shared with me by Susan.

Anita Bauer was raised in Germany and eventually she met a man named Earl Roulette and moved with him to the United States. They had a couple of children together, then Anita returned to Germany with these two children (in the mid-1960s). Anita met another man who became Susan's father, George Benjamin Breezee, and Anita then moved back to the United States to live in Illinois with him around 1968. So, Anita lived in that area and had her daughter Susan, as well as others, and these were the family members that reached out to establish a family connection. Anita herself passed away in 2006 due to the effects of cancer.

Although navigating the information and emotions that come from such a family discovery can be challenging for some, for me this was a meaningful opportunity to learn more and connect with others tied to our family. Susan wrote in an email about this desire for connection:

> Throughout my life, I remember, my mother always talking about how much she remembered her father loved her. My mother lived a very, very hard life. Her mother was very abusive to her, so I guess she really held those memories about her father. She used to always tell me that she wondered if she had siblings from him, she wanted to find him and meet him, and be wanted by him more than anything in the world. That is when my dad (George Breezee) hired a private investigator to find him. [The private investigator] sent the information to my dad. He gave it to my mom, but she could never bring herself to reach out to him, in fear that he would reject her. I feel not only for myself, but for my mom, that this can bring a lot of healing in bringing our families together. My mom had a beautiful heart. She loved her children. She died at the age of 59. (Susan Funk Email, January 2023)

In hearing and understanding this information, my heart went out to this sister of mine who I had not had the opportunity to know in this life. Children who were born out of wartime circumstances in Germany that were fathered by American or other military service members were often rejected in families and not treated well. This seemed to be the situation for Anita as well.

This was largely new information for our family, and so my brother and I talked and worked through how we felt about this circumstance. We were cautious and needed to get more certain information about this connection. I voiced some of these thoughts to Susan and wrote:

> How do you feel about this? Tell me your thoughts. Tell me about you. For me, this is like a seventy-year gap in my life, if you know what I mean. A secret part of my dad's life. I hope you understand. . . . Wow, my mind is just flooding with wanting to know so many things. (Shirley Robideau Email, January 2023)

As we continued to exchange information, for me there was a spiritual element in this family connection beginning to come together. I further wrote:

> I have been thinking that you are right, that we may not be able to prove (this family connection) one hundred percent, but I believe that this is the Lord's work to gather our family together, because that is the only thing we take with us to the other side. Our family and our personal knowledge.
>
> I believe when your Mom passed away it was about one month before my mother died. Coincidence? I don't think so. I believe our family on the other side knows each other just as well as on this side. I believe if this is to be, they will guide us to know within our hearts that we are indeed family. . . .
>
> Families are meant to be together forever. I believe that with all my heart. . . . So, my advice to you is, "Doubt not, but only believe." (Shirley Robideau Email, January 2023)

In response to this connection that I felt included a spiritual tie as well as a family tie, Susan wrote this heartfelt email that resonated so closely with my own feelings:

> This message brought tears to my eyes and filled my heart with joy. I have always wondered about my mom's side of the family. I would love more than anything to be part of your life.
>
> When I took my DNA test, my whole world changed. I didn't know anyone except my kids and my brother who showed only as a close family member. I found out that the man who raised me was not my biological father and both my parents knew and chose not to tell me. Not knowing my mom's side of the family, I just felt lost. I didn't know who I was or where I came from, but God is good and he led me to a wonderful man that is my biological father. I also have a couple of sisters still living, and one deceased, and I now have a wonderful relationship with the last step to healing. My heart is finding you guys, I know, by the DNA test and in my heart, that you are my aunt that he was my grandfather. I am so thankful to you for talking to me. And again, I would love to be part of your life. (Susan Funk Email, January 2023)

I could not have anticipated the beautiful connections that would unfold as part of this developing relationship, but I trusted the Lord and things seemed to come together and fall into place in a most remarkable way.

In addition to the information that we shared between us and sought to confirm, there was the additional confirmation of a family relationship that came as a result of the DNA research. I had my DNA test done in 2017. With assistance from a friend, our test results were shared with David Moberly, a professional genealogist and fellow Latter-day Saint, who runs a genealogy business called The Handwritten Past and is also a director of the Minnesota Genealogical Society. David analyzed the DNA test results for myself and Susan Funk, and then shared a report with us, which a few details are noted here:

> AncestryDNA shows that Shirley Robideau and Susan Funk share 826 centimorgans of DNA (cMs). This is an unusually high amount and indicates that there is a close family relationship. According to Ancestry's metric and a little process-of-elimination (Shirley is definitely not, for example, Susan's grandmother), there is a 97% chance that Shirley is Susan's half-aunt (i.e. Susan's mother is Shirley's half-sister). If Susan's grandfather is Clair James Stockford, we would expect the DNA results to show exactly what they do

show. Shirley and Susan both share DNA matches with other Stockford and McKay descendants, just as we would expect to see if Clair were the connection and not someone on Shirley's maternal side. . . . Conclusion: Clair James Stockford is Susan Funk's mother's father. (Report by David Moberly, January 2023)

Being able to confirm this family connection was a most satisfying result of having been brought together by family motivations that reached beyond us.

Steps Forward in a New Family Relationship

I did not expect to identify a German-born half-sister when I was in my seventies, nor did I expect to welcome a new family connection that included nieces and nephews and others. I would like to share the story of our first meeting in person as family members.

I met a good friend, Jim V., when I moved into my current church congregation in Minnesota. I arrived at church one Sunday morning and he came up and introduced himself to me. He helped me over time with some family records that I was working on and we became friends. He had a rough health experience with COVID and found that keeping up his house was a big challenge, so he eventually decided to move into the apartment building where I live. Each week, we meet for Family Home Evening and he is also helpful to me if I need a blessing or am ever in need. He is a good friend.

Well, after my niece Susan Funk and I met on the phone, then we planned to meet in person during the summer. This was in 2023. Susan and her husband Doug left their home in North Carolina and drove all night to Wisconsin and spent the day with her father. Doug drives a semi truck and so that is the vehicle they drove on this trip. After being in Wisconsin, then the next morning they were coming to be with me and other family members for a couple of days. My brother John, my sister's oldest son, Mark and his wife Penny, my niece Mary and one of her sons, and also my cousins, Don and Connie McKay and Don's sister Arla—all were coming to meet them the following day.

As Doug and Susan got closer to arriving in Minneapolis, I received a text from them that said, "We are one hour away!"

I smiled and was getting so excited. I called Jim V. and asked him to wait with me and so we went outside and waited. Then came the next text: "One half hour away!" Jim became my eyes and ears then, as I could not see them coming, but he relayed each text as it came to my phone. Fifteen minutes. Ten minutes.

To add to the excitement, Susan kept sending texts and she then began the countdown! Jim was telling me everything that was happening as it occurred. He reported: "Ten Minutes; Nine Minutes; Eight Minutes; Seven Minutes; Six Minutes; Five Minutes; Four Minutes; Three Minutes; Two minutes—One Minute!"

Tears were falling as Jim announced the large semi truck was pulling into the driveway and it stopped!

Jim said, "Susan is getting out of the truck at the end of the driveway. She is running all the way to you!"

Then we embraced, both crying uncontrollably, and I knew for myself that this was the beginning of another chapter with my new family, and I loved them as though I have always known them.

This connection has been a very meaningful development in my life, and I have gradually been able to forge a connection with Susan and other family members through phone contacts and other means of communication. It has been and will continue to be my desire to nurture these family connections and to offer the Lord's blessings to them.

I am grateful to know that I have another sister, Anita Marie Bauer, born in Germany on June 26, 1946. We never had the opportunity to meet in this life. She passed away in the United States in May 2006. And yet, I love her as I do my other family members. Also, how grateful I am that her daughter Susan reached out, bridging the gap of years and lack of knowledge, and thus opening a new and sweet chapter in the story of our family.

Section 6
Reflections and Testimony

Shirley Robideau made the move to Minneapolis, Minnesota in 2018, seeking to gain assistance with the onset of blindness and other sensory losses. There, she has settled in and continued to grow in patience, faith and gratitude for the variety of blessings from the Lord that she perceives in her life.

Family has been a cornerstone of her life. An important milestone in her life was the passing of her older sister, Jessie, and the opportunity to spend her sister's final season together in Minnesota. In the first chapter in this section, she shares a reflection on some of her Roberts relatives, this loved sister and her appreciation for Jessie, and also her gratitude for her brother John.

Perhaps the most consequential experience of Shirley's life has been her spiritual conversion to The Church of Jesus Christ of Latter-day Saints. This experience has led her to a long and serious exploration of faith and her appreciation for the Savior, Jesus Christ. In a second chapter, she shares a "Christmas testimony" reflecting on her love and appreciation for the Savior.

Finally, in conclusion, Shirley concludes this volume with her testimony of God, His plan for all of His children, and the variety of spiritual and temporal blessings that have come to her life. She shares some experiences but mostly her gratitude for family members and others who have been part of her unique life. She reflects on the spiritual aspects of her life and her fervent belief that God knows and loves each one of us, and that each one of us can also receive His blessings by faith in the Savior, Jesus Christ.

Chapter 33
A Tribute to My Family

Life and Memories with My Family

I would like to share some of my precious memories of my family members, including my siblings, Jessie Stockford Meyer and John Stockford, and how we felt about each other and how we supported each other. These reflections include some of our experiences growing up and memories from our adult years.

The Roberts Side of the Family

As I have noted, my mother Rosie was born in Kentucky and her family members primarily lived there. Because of the geographic distance between North Dakota and Kentucky, we had very limited interaction with my mother's side of the family. However, I would like to share a bit more about memories with those relatives.

My mother Rosie had seven siblings (four brothers and three sisters) and two or three more that died in childhood. Not all of them were living when we went to Kentucky to visit my Grandpa Johnson Roberts. Mom, Dad, my brother John and I went to see Mom's family in Kentucky in 1972. I was 25 and John was 19. There were so many cousins and it was so fun to meet them all.

When we met them, Mom's sisters Arina and Linda were so gracious to us, and I fell in love with them instantly. I remember both of them as dark-haired beauties like my mother. Aunt Linda had a reddish hue to her lovely locks.

Aunt Linda used to make quilts. She gave Mom one of her bowtie quilts as a gift and before my mom died she gave it to me. There is a picture of me holding that quilt which is included here.

Shirley Robideau with a bowtie quilt made by her Roberts relatives in Kentucky.

I was so glad to see my Kentucky grandfather, Johnson Roberts, for the first time in at least 20 years. When he was able, he and I wrote letters to each other while I was in school. He was tall with white bushy hair. He was a different kind of preacher. Mom told me when they were little, he would go outside and yell at God. When he did, Mom and her siblings hid under the bed in the house.

During our visit with our Roberts relatives, I especially remember their Kentucky accents and their different foods like squirrel. For one meal, Aunt Linda and Aunt Arina took out huge metal trays full of food for a feast in our honor. They had a long snack bar counter where they placed all these trays side by side full of food. It was so beautiful to see!! One tray had heaps of fried eggs. Another tray had bacon. Other trays held tomato slices from their garden, cucumbers, onion slices, biscuits, gravy, and more. Aunt Linda took the grease from the bacon and added flour and rich cream to make the best gravy ever. I felt much heavier after eating from all those trays.

One night while staying there, I was asleep in one of the bedrooms. Suddenly, I was awakened by my Aunt Linda coming in. She went to the head of the bed and with both hands grabbed a hold of the metal head frames—whoosh! She yanked it up and swung it over to the side. I was no longer asleep! She then proceeded to pull up some floor boards revealing some money and liquor. Quickly, she removed a whiskey bottle, stuck a roll of money in her bra, replaced the board and picked up the head of the bed and replaced it to its original position. I fondly remembered an episode I had seen on *The Andy Griffith Show* where they were trying to close out bootlegging activities in Mayberry! With a "Good night, Shirley!" she turned off the light and closed the door. Please keep in mind, this was a coal mining town with limited ways for women to make an honest living except for waiting on tables.

Also while we were there, a little girl who was one of my cousins (six or seven years old) came over to meet me. She was thin, wore a pretty dress, and had dark blond hair and blue eyes. Aunt Arina, who was near us, asked her, "Do you know the girl in the picture that you carry in your pocket?" The little girl nodded her head. Aunt Arina pointed at me and said, "This is that little girl in your picture."

My little cousin, grinning, was delighted to show me my picture that was taken in the hospital when I was being treated for polio. For some reason the baby picture tugged at her heart, and she had carried it around with her for a long time. It was worn out. Aunt Arina said my little cousin often asked about wanting to meet her cousin Shirley.

Memories of Jessie in the Growing Up Years

My memories of my sister Jessie in the years that we were growing up together are cherished by me. I used to sit and watch her stand at the mirror with scissors in her hand when she was setting her hair with rollers. She would part her hair for the roller and take the scissors and snip off the ends as she would do each roller. I thought it was smart to do it that way because she was cutting off the split ends and rolling up her hair for her dates.

Jessie usually didn't like her school pictures that would end up in the yearbooks each year. One year she came home with her package of pictures thinking and commenting that they were "so bad"! So, she went into the garage and climbed up on the ladder and hid them in the rafters of the garage hoping that no one would ever find them. But Dad did find them!

My parents and our Dad's brother, Grant, used to go to the lakes in Minnesota on the weekends in the summer. On one occasion, we were driving there and Jessie and I had to go to the bathroom, so Dad stopped at a gas station for us and filled up the car with gas. After my folks left and had driven several miles, Mom realized that it was too quiet in the car and looked in the back seat and said, "James, you forgot the girls!" Dad screeched the car to a halt and turned around and went back to the gas station, where he found us standing there and crying while the gas attendant tried to keep us calm, as he knew Dad would come back for us.

Jessie and I were together all the time until our family moved to Jamestown in 1959. She then went to a different school than I did and made new friends. One particular friend of hers was Paulette. I watched them many times in the front room as they would dance to the radio together or sing along with the songs on the radio.

Jessie liked religious music back then. She and I would listen to Tennessee Ernie Ford sing hymns and she would write down the words and we would memorize the songs together. I loved doing that with her.

Memories of Jessie During Adulthood

The two of us, Jessie and I, moved into young adulthood during the 1960's and remained supportive of each other. I observed and tried to learn what I could from her.

I particularly remember when Jessie had started dating Bill Meyer from Pingree, ND. One time when he was attending college out of town, she had a date with another young man. They were sitting on the couch and talking when the doorbell rang! It was Bill! Jessie quickly jumped up from the couch, leaving her date sitting there with me, and I went over and sat by her date as Jessie went out the door with Bill. The poor date didn't know what was happening, and Bill never suspected anything, but he did look a bit bewildered to see me on the couch with a "man" since I was only in the 10th grade at the time. Stockford sisters did some quick thinking in that situation! It was so funny to me.

Jessie got married shortly after her graduation to Bill Meyer. Her example of marrying quite young probably influenced me in that area of life as well. Jessie asked me if I would watch the Guest Book at her wedding. Jessie and Bill had five children together: Mark, Mary, Michelle, Paul, and Melissa. I love each of these nieces and nephews so much.

Jessie loved people. She was always excited to know someone was coming to visit her and would plan and clean and bake to make sure their visit would be a good one. In this way, she carried on the tradition of my mother's pattern of cooking a feast when guests were coming. She loved having company and entertaining them. There were many things that our Mom did that I also saw in Jessie. For example, Jessie would pick berries and apples that grew on their property. I always tried to do the things I saw my sister doing. She was very particular about keeping her place clean.

She also loved her two cats, Lady and Trouble. At one point a number of years ago, the mother cat brought the two kittens to Jessie's place when they were very tiny. Maybe somehow she knew that Jessie would take care of them. Jessie took pity on these kittens and nursed them and adopted them. The two cats took naps with her and when she was on the computer talking to me one of them was always on her lap and the other around her feet. She would tell me that at Christmas time the cats loved it when she brought out the Christmas tree, and during the season they would curl up under the tree.

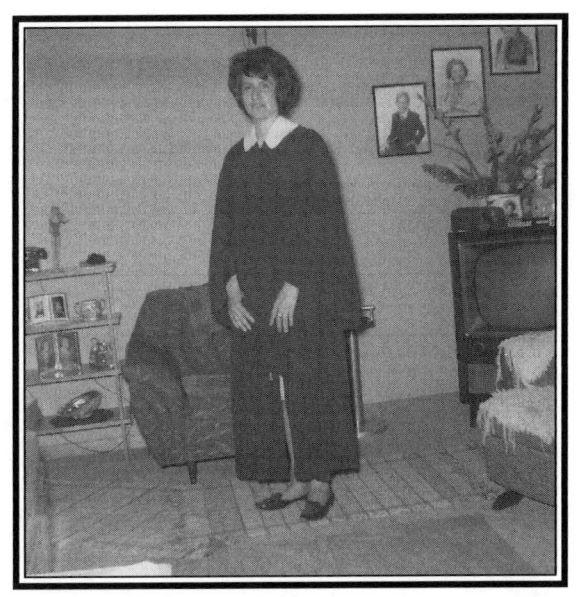

Jessie Stockford, Shirley's older sister, at graduation in 1964.

She also loved gardening and had several hummingbirds that would come into her yard regularly. I never saw the home that she had in Bisbee, ND, but she was very particular that everything be clean and in order when I viewed the places she lived in prior to Bisbee, so I picture it to be a beautiful place in my mind.

After she got married we were not together very much, but when the computers and then the Internet came into being she and I were in contact almost daily. The many miles of distance that we were apart kept us from seeing each other, so I was thrilled when her family gave her a computer one Christmas. Even though she was far away, she would send me emails of what she was doing that day.

Jessie loved talking to people online and had many friends online. She would write to me when one of them was ill and ask me to pray for them. She would also sometimes ask me questions about the Gospel of Jesus Christ and I would answer them the best I could. She told me she always saved them to a file so that she could re-read my answers. She was very interested in the Gospel and sometimes I could feel her hunger to learn more, so I believe that she loved the Savior very much.

She loved her five children, Mark, Mary, Michelle, Paul and Melissa. She would always report to me what each was doing and how proud she was of their accomplishments. She would email me when her children were coming to visit or other special people in her life. She would tell me that she had put a roast in the oven, baked apple pies, baked bread or whatever it was that she was preparing for her visitors. She would be so excited that they were coming.

Sisters to the End

Jessie and I had some experiences in common, and one of them was that we both struggled with vision loss in our later lives. When her vision began to deteriorate from the *Retinitis Pigmentosa* (Usher's Syndrome) that affected her, she would write to me of her fears of going blind and would ask me how I was doing with my vision loss. One time when she was working at the nursing home, she bent down to pick something up and hit her head on a table that she didn't see. She would share things like that to let me know what was happening to her and we would talk about it together online.

However, she also kept some things private and that hampered some of our communication. At one point a couple of years before her passing, she stopped using the computer and so all our communication stopped because she couldn't hear me on the phone. I felt like I had lost a friend because I missed her emails and that was hard on me. Rather than telling me what was happening, she would say, "Oh, I am bored with the computer"—when in fact, she couldn't see well enough to really use it any longer.

Jessie moved to Fargo for a few months while she had surgery on her knee and recovered, and I was so glad to have her close by. She moved into the apartment building I was living in at that time. I would wheel down the hall and visit with her every day. We would sit outside together during those summer months by her patio door. I absolutely enjoyed that time we were together. When she was well and her knee had healed, she then moved back to Bisbee.

Jessie believed in angels and would often sign her emails with this phrase: "Angels be on your pillow." I wondered if she knew there were angels watching over her all of her life.

It was nothing short of a miracle to me that she and I were in Minneapolis at this time of her passing from this life in June 2018. So, she and I were together as sisters to the end, and she and I held hands as she took her last breath and departed to the other side of the veil into the arms of Mom and Dad and the rest of our family who were waiting for her.

A Tribute to Jessie

After Jessie's death in 2018, I had some time to ponder my affection and appreciation for her as my sister. I wrote this brief tribute for her.

Tribute to My Sister

Jessie Mae Stockford Meyer

(October 24,1945 - June 20, 2018)

When did you become my Sister?

After birth?

Or was it long before?

Yes, We have always been Sisters.

And always will be, forever.

All other things fade as one you love departs from this life and you remain with your precious memories.

The plan of our Heavenly Father has always been for us to be an Eternal family and I know that is the way it will be.

Jessie, your love of animals, whether it be cats, dogs or whatever, you are free to do that now. Remember, Jessie, when you were young how much you wanted your own horse? I remember that very well. You asked Dad over and over to buy you a horse. My Heart smiles as I remember that.

Your compassion for others was shown in the way that you cared for the people who lived in Mom's Home for the Aged. You got married and carried that

The Stockford siblings, left to right, Jessie, John, and Shirley, in their later adult years.

with you. You helped at nursing homes, you cared for your husband's uncle until he died, and you even came back to Jamestown and continued working with elderly people in your home for a time. I always admired how you loved people.

I observed when you took care of your five children and did the best you could in everything you did. You lost a home and all you had in a fire but you kept on going through the trials you had. You dealt with vision and hearing issues but kept moving forward.

Your love for flowers, gardens, birds, trees—the list goes on and on. All you are is everywhere in the lives of others in the community where you lived and served, and the lives of your children and grandchildren.

You leave a legacy behind that will grow for generations. I love you so very much and miss you, but now you have a new work to do on the other side there in Heaven. Give Mom and Dad a hug from me—and Grandpa and Grandma too. A new legacy you will carry on now as you wait until all of us are together again, embraced in the arms of love. With love from your Sister, Shirley.

I want any readers to know that I believe in life after death and that I will have a reunion with Jessie. And because our Savior was resurrected, we too shall be resurrected and the day will come when we take a walk together. I look forward to that day. We are forever sisters.

A Tribute to John

My younger brother, John, was also a large part of my life while growing up and also in adulthood. He was several years younger than me but I have many positive memories of growing up together in Jamestown, North Dakota. I have related many of the experiences with him throughout this book as I recall them.

John's period of service in the Marines took him away from home to California and even overseas. Our family missed him during those years although we were able to see him at times. I was proud of him and his military service. It brightened up our lives when he was back living in the Fargo area again.

I have appreciated John's willingness to support our family in different endeavors over the years. He assisted our parents as they moved forward into their later years and moved to different locations or had particular personal needs or challenges. I have especially appreciated the nieces and nephews that came into my life through John and his family. They have been good to me and uplifted my life in so many ways.

In the later years of my life, John has been a person that I relied on multiple times. He made it possible for myself, himself, and our Mom to live together after my husband Charles passed away. He helped me after I had moved to Utah and health circumstances made it so that I needed to move quickly back to North Dakota. He counseled together with me when we had the unexpected surprise of learning about another sibling. I am so grateful that we have shared so much of our lives together as siblings and love and appreciate him a great deal.

Chapter 34
My Christmas Testimony

My Love for Christmas

As I move toward the conclusion of my life story, one thing I'd like to share briefly is my belief in and love for the Savior, Jesus Christ. In 2013, I wrote a Christmas letter and I think it captures much of my sentiment about the Savior.

Christmas is my most favorite time of the year. The Spirit of our Lord and Savior, Jesus Christ, is so very strong and love seems more apparent at this time during the holiday season. I have two stories from the Scriptures that I enjoy reading at this time of the year. These stories follow below with a couple of my thoughts.

"He Shall Be Called the Son of the Highest"

The first story that I enjoy reading from the Scriptures each year at Christmas time comes from the New Testament. The story is recorded in the Book of Luke, Chapter 1 (verses 26 through 38) and goes as follows:

>1:26 - And in the sixth month the angel Gabriel was sent from God unto a city of Galilee, named Nazareth,
>
>1:27 - To a virgin espoused to a man whose name was Joseph, of the house of David; and the virgin's name was Mary.
>
>1:28 - And the angel came in unto her, and said, Hail, thou that art highly favoured, the Lord is with thee: Blessed art thou among women.
>
>1:29 - And when she saw him, she was troubled at his saying, and cast in her mind what manner of salutation this should be.
>
>1:30 - And the angel said unto her, Fear not, Mary: for thou hast found favour with God.

1:31 - And, behold, thou shalt conceive in thy womb, and bring forth a son, and shalt call his name JESUS.

1:32 - He shall be great, and shall be called the Son of the Highest: and the Lord God shall give unto him the throne of his father David:

1:33 - And he shall reign over the house of Jacob for ever; and of his kingdom there shall be no end.

1: 34 - Then said Mary unto the angel, How shall this be, seeing I know not a man?

1:35 - And the angel answered and said unto her, The Holy Ghost shall come upon thee, and the power of the Highest shall overshadow thee: therefore also that holy thing which shall be born of thee shall be called the Son of God.

1:36 - And, behold, thy cousin Elisabeth, she hath also conceived a son in her old age: and this is the sixth month with her, who was called barren.

1:37 - For with God nothing shall be impossible.

1:38 - And Mary said, Behold the handmaid of the Lord; be it unto me according to thy word. And the angel departed from her.

This story sets up the account of the Savior's birth in Bethlehem, which is well known, and also always a joy to read especially at this time of the year. I am so grateful for the Savior's birth and His role as our Redeemer.

Another Testament of Jesus Christ

While many are familiar with the account of the Savior's birth in the Holy Land, the story of what was happening on the American Continent at this time is not as well known. This next account, which I also like to read during the holidays, comes from another testament of Jesus Christ, *The Book of Mormon*.

There were prophets on the American continent also who looked for the coming of Jesus. One of these prophets was Samuel the Lamanite. His account of the Savior's coming birth is included below from the Book of Helaman, Chapter 14 (verses 2 and 3):

14:2 - And behold, he said unto them: Behold, I give unto you a sign; for five years more cometh, and behold, then cometh the son of God to redeem all those who shall believe on his name.

14:3 - And behold, this will I give unto you for a sign at the time of his coming; for behold, there shall be great lights in heaven, insomuch that in the night before he cometh there shall be no darkness, insomuch that it shall appear unto man as if it was day.

Then, when the time was near for the Savior's birth as Samuel had taught, there were evil men in that society who planned to kill all those who believed what Samuel said if the sign didn't come to pass by a certain date. Another prophet named Nephi prayed mightily to the Lord in behalf of his people. While in prayer, this is what happened and is recorded about the Savior's coming, written in the Book of 3rd Nephi, Chapter 1 (verses 10 through 13):

1:10 - Now it came to pass that when Nephi, the son of Nephi, saw this wickedness of his people, his heart was exceedingly sorrowful.

1:11 - And it came to pass that he went out and bowed himself down upon the earth, and cried mightily to his God in behalf of his people, yea, those who were about to be destroyed because of their faith in the tradition of their fathers.

1:12 - And it came to pass that he cried mightily unto the Lord all that day; and behold, the voice of the Lord came unto him, saying:

> 1:13 - Lift up your head and be of good cheer; for behold, the time is at hand, and on this night shall the sign be given, and on the morrow come I into the world, to show unto the world that I will fulfil all that which I have caused to be spoken by the mouth of my holy prophets.

As had happened in the Holy Land, God sent messages to those who loved Him to share the event of his coming birth with those who would believe. Mary, Samuel the Prophet, and the prophet Nephi were such messengers. I have come to know in my lifetime that each of us can receive our own witness of the truth of Jesus Christ.

My Witness of the Savior

As noted, I love the Christmas season and the many uplifting things that happen during that time of year. I enjoy the music, the gifts, and the friendship that flows at this time of year. But, there is something even more important.

I know that the Savior was born just as the prophets have foretold since the days of Adam. I know it happened as was described in the Scriptures. I love the Lord, Jesus Christ, with all my heart. I do hope you enjoyed reading these wonderful words about the birth of our Savior and have a wonderful Christmas each year as we celebrate the birth of Jesus Christ. Merry Christmas, Everyone!

Chapter 35
In Conclusion

Writing My Story

I have thought much about this process of writing my story. One time a friend asked me if I had yet written down the things I have learned from my life that I wanted my family and friends to know. She then told me that in the account of the *Book of Mormon*, a prophet named Nephi had two sets of records which he used to write down the history of his people. In one set of records he wrote the history of the governments, wars, and contentions of his people. However, in a smaller record he wrote of the spiritual things or dealings with God which he wanted his family and future generations to have for their knowledge and growth. My friend, Sister Smith, suggested that I forget about the wars and contentions of my life, and instead focus on the spiritual things that I have learned and experienced.

This approach is what I have tried to do with this record of my life. This record does not recount the great wars and challenges of the world in my time, but instead focuses on my own life experiences and the spiritual elements of my life. I have written it and what I write is true to my knowledge, and if my words are not perfect that is all right, I have written it to the best of my ability at this time in my life.

To understand who I am, you need to know the things I believe, my values, my love for the Savior and for His Church, and for each of the members of my faith family as well as my immediate and extended family.

A Reminder of Our Decision to Come into Mortality

Before we were born on this Earth, we lived with our Heavenly Father. Heavenly Father called us all together in a great conference to announce His Plan for us. His Plan has been called the "Great Plan of Happiness." We were all his spiritual children and we loved Him very much, so much that we wanted to be like Him. Father told us that He would prepare an Earth for us to live on and we would be tested and given free agency to choose for ourselves whether or not we would follow Him.

Lucifer, who was one of God's children, wanted to be like Heavenly Father also. However, he wanted to be higher than Heavenly Father and take His glory and honor. Our Elder Brother, Jesus Christ, said, "Father, the glory be Thine forever." Lucifer wanted the Father's glory and to take away our free agency and force us to do things contrary to the Father's will. Many children of God agreed with Lucifer, and a third of the host of Heaven agreed with him and were cast out for rebellion. These spirits were cast out and were allowed a presence here on Earth to tempt us to follow them and Lucifer.

The Father then asked who should be sent to provide an atonement for the sins of mankind and also provide a way for His children to return home to the Divine presence once again. The Savior, Jesus Christ, asked the Father to send him and we rejoiced in Heaven. All of us wanted to become like our Father in Heaven, and the only way we could do that was to receive a body and prove ourselves to the Father, that we would choose to follow Him instead of Lucifer (or Satan as he was called after being thrown out of Heaven).

The Atonement of Jesus Christ

When the Savior, Jesus Christ, was chosen to come to Earth, He came as the Son of God and the son of Mary, a mortal woman. Being born of Mary, he was subject to hunger, thirst, and pain, just as we are. Being the Son of God, he was able to give up his life and take it again. It is so beautiful the way it was explained to me.

When I was baptized into the Methodist Church in Jamestown, North Dakota at the age of about 15, I wondered after my baptism what was missing. Reverend McDonald explained about the death of Christ and many things prior to baptism but it was so confusing to me. Many things didn't make sense to me, such as why they crucified him when he had done so many good things to help the Jewish people, or the miracles he performed among all the people—so why did they crucify him?

Now, I know that it had to be done in order for the Savior to atone for the sins of the world. The eternal sacrifice for our sins had to be done by one who was perfect in every way. His thoughts, words and actions all had to be perfect in the Father's plan and in perfect harmony with the laws of the Father. He suffered in the Garden of Gethsemane for each one of us as he performed the burden of the Atonement. If Christ had not finished what the Father sent him to do, all mankind would have been lost with no way to return to the Father's presence.

My Path to the Restored Gospel

I was taught these truths and so much more in the weeks before my baptism into The Church of Jesus Christ of Latter-day Saints. However, these are a few of the things that touched my heart. I decided that if I was going to get baptized, then I had better do as James directed in the Bible and ask God, the Eternal Father, in the name of Jesus Christ, if the things that the Latter-day Saint Missionaries were teaching me were true (see James 1:5).

As I have related in this account, one night I went to my bedroom and got down on my knees and prayed with all my heart to know if The Church of Jesus Christ of Latter-day Saints was true. I wanted to know if this church was God's true church upon the earth and if it was true that the Savior is indeed the head of it. I also wanted to know if the Prophet who was living and guiding the church was indeed the Lord's Prophet. My room glowed with such a warm, peaceful light as I finished my prayer and went to bed. I had barely laid down on the bed when I went into a "dream" or "vision." In this beautiful vision, I saw Heavenly Father and Jesus Christ conversing with the young man Joseph Smith—and I knew. I knew with all my heart that the Savior Jesus Christ is the head of His Church. I knew that Joseph Smith was a Prophet of God and the Prophets that live today are indeed Prophets of God. I knew that I would be baptized on April 28, 1973. And I was.

My heart is so full of love for my Savior—Jesus Christ. In writing my stories, I remember many special times I have had with my husband, Charles David Robideau, and also very difficult times that I have passed through in my life. I do not know where I would be today if I didn't have the Gospel of Jesus Christ in my life.

I see the Lord's hand in every phase of my life. I perceive it in periods of difficulty to help me come out of the pain and anguish I was feeling. Only the Lord could do that.

The Blessing of Peacemakers

The challenging times in which we live have been prophesied in the Scriptures. Our day has been foreseen as one with "fires, and tempests, and vapors of smoke in foreign lands; . . . wars, rumors of wars, and earthquakes in diverse places . . . great pollutions upon the face of the earth; . . . and all manner of abominations" (Mormon 8:29-31). Can we find peace in these latter days?

Jesus Christ was a perfect example of a Peacemaker. He has given us tools to show us how to be peacemakers so that we can be called children of God. He has given us the Scriptures. The *Holy Bible* and the *Book of Mormon* are both full of evidences of war and peacemaking. He has given us spiritual leaders, such as Prophets and Apostles, to teach us to love one another. In our own homes; in our neighborhoods; in our communities; in our country.

I have been blessed by peacemakers in my lifetime. Here are some examples from my life, such as individuals who served in Home Teaching or Visiting Teaching assignments to me, which are ministering assignments in the Church. I have had a testimony of the blessings of Home Teaching and Visiting Teaching since I joined the Church so many years ago. I know that each person called to be my Home Teacher or Visiting Teacher was called to be there at that particular time as I needed them and were called by Jesus Christ. I want to share briefly about just one set of Home Teachers that I had, although I could tell similar stories about all of them.

In February 2002, it was close to the time for my sweet Eternal Companion, Charles David Robideau, to pass from this life and go to the other side of the veil. The Spirit told me when it was one or two weeks until he would go. I listened to the spiritual prompting and called his family members and told them they needed to all come and visit him. That day was a wonderful day for Chuck. His brother, sisters and many of his nieces and nephews came to visit and Chuck was thrilled. I did not tell anyone what the Spirit had told me.

Three days before his passing, we were playing Yahtzee and he laid back in his wheelchair and I knew it would be soon. I sat by him and held him and he put his arm around me and held me. I had tears falling and asked Heavenly Father to comfort me. Then, my Home Teachers walked in the door. The Spirit brought them to me. Charles Walen and Lee Allen walked in and gave Chuck a blessing, and then turned to me and gave me a blessing. Chuck went home to Heaven on March 3, 2002. Home Teachers are Peacemakers.

Visiting Teaching is also a calling for women to be Peacemakers. When I had surgery for a cochlear implant, I knew that I would be deaf after they went in to place it in my skull. I was a little scared but knew by the Spirit that this was going to be a good thing for me. I had just moved into the boundaries of the Fargo Second Ward and didn't know very many people in the ward. My new Relief Society Presidency organized the Sisters so that I would have someone with me for twenty-four hours on the first day following surgery and also someone checking on me twice a day for three weeks. The Relief Society Sisters are Peacemakers.

I had the blessing of an aide through Community Living Services that was named Rachel. She was a very wise 28-year old. She amazed me with how kind and understanding she was. She understood my deafness, blindness, and disability more than anyone else I have ever met. She knew how to talk to me so I heard and understood what she was telling me. I thoroughly enjoyed her when she came to help with my laundry, cleaning and some food preparation. One day she told me while visiting that she saw the presence of a spirit that was in a wheelchair. She asked me if I was aware that someone was there. I told her, yes, I knew that Chuck was there watching over me. What an interesting spiritual observation from someone who was not of my faith but yet was sensitive to the truths of Heaven.

We live our lives here on earth as a probation to prove to ourselves and God that we will either follow the Savior and fulfill Heavenly Father's Plan for us, or else we will follow Lucifer's plan and not follow God. Those who have already passed on to the next phase of their lives, or in other words, those who have died, then return to the Spirit World to await the Resurrection. Some of these spirits, or angels as we call them, come to earth to help or watch over their loved ones. It takes a special and righteous person to be able to see or sense these spirits. Rachel was a very special person and I appreciated her spiritual insight. Rachel was a Peacemaker.

We Can Be Together Forever

These last many years that my sweetheart Charles has been gone have been sad but growing times for me. He was so perfect in my eyes. I want so much to be as much like the Savior as I can, so that Charles and I can be together again forever. We are taught in The Church of Jesus Christ of Latter-day Saints that when we go to the Holy Temple of God, and are sealed together in marriage by one who has the priesthood authority to seal us together for "time and all eternity," that we are together after this life on earth if we are worthy. Charles is my Eternal Companion. I am excited to return to be with him and my Heavenly Father and Jesus Christ forever.

At times, my thoughts rest upon the Eternities. It fills my heart with joy as I continue to think about sacred things, such as the Holy Temples and being sealed together with my sweetheart, Charles David Robideau. It is such a miracle to me that with the many wrongs I have done in my life, that the Lord would bless me so greatly with a beautiful little girl and an Eternal Companion. When thinking of Charles, I find it so humbling that the Lord would have blessed me so greatly to bring such a special man into my life not so long ago. We read the Scriptures together almost every night of our married life. It brought us so close and oh, how I adore him.

Though he graduated to the next life much sooner than I did, my dear Charles left a spiritual message in his journal that has remained with me as a treasure. This is what he wrote about his spiritual life and beliefs:

> If you know nothing about me, Charles David Robideau, know this: I am happy and know that in the next life, my wife and I will walk together, forever. As I learned in that one evening at Bishop Brad Leeser's home about temple marriages, we can be together forever. We went to the House of the Lord, the Chicago Temple, where Shirley and I were sealed together for time and all eternity at the holy altar. What a sacred ceremony. I will treasure that moment forever. In the temple, I felt equal to all the others—not rich, not poor, and especially NOT HANDICAPPED.

> Some may feel that being handicapped is awful, I'm here today to tell you that being handicapped is a blessing. The things I have learned in being able to cope with my disabilities, some people will never learn in the course of their lives. Being handicapped forces me to depend upon other people and therefore learn a love for people that I would have been deprived of otherwise. I am not saying this is easy to cope with, I am saying I am learning to cope with it. I am grateful for my wife and for my life and for the guidance I receive through being a member of The Church of Jesus Christ of Latter-day Saints. (Charles Robideau Journal Entry)

We shared so much of our lives together, but I must say that sharing our spiritual lives brought us closer than anything else.

I Am Still Learning

Life today is different than any other part of my life. Being alone has been good for me in the way of learning to appreciate who I am and where I am going. I am finding more contentment in having freedom to make my own choices as to what direction to go. I have my days of loneliness but as I think about what it was like before when I struggled with emotions of feeling no self-worth, I realize the many blessings I have now in the Autumn of my life.

The peace that I feel and the love I receive from my family and friends has made such a difference in who I am becoming. I now realize just how important each of us, as sons and daughters of God, are to the Lord and how much He loves us. The more I realize the love He has for me, personally, the more I want to please him and do all I can to become a better person today than I was yesterday.

My growth living in my own apartment alone has brought me closer to my Savior Jesus Christ then I can ever remember before. I feel the Spirit of the Lord guide me more now since there is so much peace in my home.

When a person isn't actively out in the community working or doing many things, you have so much time that can be idled away and if I am not careful my mind wanders to not so good memories. So since I now have all the adaptive equipment to help me hear better, I entertain myself actively listening to good music or uplifting thoughts as I listen to the channel for my LDS faith on the Internet. I love hearing conference talks as they help me see what aspects of myself I want to work on to make better. I try very hard to not let myself think negative thoughts that make me feel down.

As for the loneliness, I am thinking about my Charles who is waiting for me on the other side of the veil. Charles had such an uplifting attitude about everything. If he was having a difficult time achieving a task, he would laugh about it and make jokes. Together he and I could accomplish anything. I think of his smile and laughter and I can't help but to smile and feel so wonderful. I love him more and more each day that goes by.

My favorite part of our days with each other was when we would lay down together and talk each night. The whole world disappeared because this was our time together. We read the *Book of Mormon* every night together. Since he was not able to see to read, he would listen to me read. Since I couldn't see well either, I was a slow reader. One time when we were reading together he repeated an important concept to me and I was so amazed! I asked him, did you get that from my clumsy reading ability? He told me that he understood my reading very well and I felt like I was on the top of the world.

Another time, he and I went to Lindenwood Park and had a picnic together, and we were listening to a cassette recording that friends had recorded for us as a piano/organ recording. It was of the children's Primary songs and reverent music and we were sitting side by side in our wheelchairs just looking in the beauty of the park. While we were listening, I saw a vision of Charles and I walking together in the trees with the sun shining through the trees. I look forward to the day he and I will walk together, hand in hand in the beauty of a pure and clean world.

In pondering marriage, I reflect upon the hurt, sorrow and pain in some of my relationships that I just wanted to put aside and pretend they never happened. However, the prompting has come from the Lord to write this part of my life with the hope that it may help someone not to make the mistakes I made in my youth or at other times. Although I have been married several times, with even those that didn't work out, I have learned so much. The Lord provided me blessings that have helped me become the person I am right now.

With Andy, I became a mother of a little angel that is waiting for me on the other side of the veil. With Levi, I joined The Church of Jesus Christ of Latter-day Saints, the greatest blessing of my life. With Joe, I learned a lot about working in the business world managing a motel and creating a licensed group home. With Dave, I learned about taking care of my health and being able to control my weight. With Charles, I found true happiness and celestial marriage on August 21, 1987, at the Chicago Illinois LDS Temple. In December 2022, Judith Ann was sealed to Charles and I at the Minneapolis Minnesota LDS Temple as a celestial family.

My Faith in the Gospel of Christ

I feel so honored to be one of those who lives in these days of history. There are so many elements that have blessed me while living with my disabilities. No other dispensation would have had power wheelchairs, hand controls for automobiles, accessible apartments, and other benefits to help those of us that are not able to make a living for ourselves. I have a warm apartment and running clean water—there are many in the world who do not have these luxuries. I am grateful for the blessings I have which the Lord has given to me. Though I cannot see very much any more, I still have the blessing of being able to read though the aid of talking books! My computer and phone read to me each day. I have also received many other blessings, thanks to the Lord bringing amazing technology to our world to help with mass communication and to speed up His work on earth.

The Gospel of Jesus Christ spreads forth all over the world in our time at a pace that is beyond my comprehension. So many people are also being brought to the knowledge of their family ties all over the world. DNA research is helping the work along and helps each of us to really know that we are all Brothers and Sisters of our Heavenly Parents.

Each week I go to church to hear the messages the Lord will have us hear, but mostly, I go to partake of the Holy Sacrament and renew my covenants with my Lord Jesus Christ. I love being there at church and being in the midst of all the Saints of God.

I had a sacred experience in which the Savior came to see me. I was living in south Fargo and loved to listen to a channel on my iPhone called the Mormon

Channel. I was listening to it one day and there was a lady talking about meditation. I had always wanted to learn how to meditate, so I really was listening to this podcast closely. She was teaching us to think about the Savior. She taught in her message to imagine that the Savior was walking down this road directly towards you, and as he got closer you could see his beautiful blue eyes and radiant smile.

As I listened to her, I felt something draw my attention to the side wall of my apartment. The wall opened up and I saw a man walking on a sandy road straight towards me getting closer and closer. As He got close to me, I could see his blue eyes and a smile as radiant as I have ever seen before. It made me smile as He got closer and closer. When He was almost beside me, He disappeared with a whooshing sound over my right shoulder. It happened so fast that I could feel the wind as it went by my shoulder. I have reflected upon this experience so many times, especially when I am feeling a little low, because I remember that smile and it will cheer me up immediately. Was it real? Was it a dream? You decide for yourself what you think it was. I know it was as real as life itself. My Savior came to visit on that sweet day!

With all my heart, I know that Joseph Smith was, and is, a prophet of God. The knowledge I have received because of this man is so powerful. Because of Joseph, I know that our Heavenly Father and Jesus Christ are two separate personages—one in purpose but still two separate beings. I know that when Joseph saw them in the Sacred Grove that they did speak to him and told him not to join any of the churches that were then on the Earth, for the Church of Jesus Christ was yet to be restored again. I know that through the Savior Jesus Christ the Church was restored to the earth, and the Priesthood of God is now restored because of Joseph's prayer and service to the Lord.

I know that the *Book of Mormon* is the word of God. I know that the people who were described in the *Book of Mormon* lived here in the Americas. I love the Scriptures—The *Holy Bible, Book of Mormon, Pearl of Great Price*, and *Doctrine and Covenants* are all Holy Scriptures. As I read the *Book of Mormon* daily, my eyes are opened to understanding the importance of knowing our Savior, Jesus Christ. Without Him, we would not have free agency to choose where we would like to be after this life. I make that statement because I choose every day, with every choice I make, whether I am following Jesus Christ or Satan. Each day, I try to make new commitments to follow closer to my Savior.

The love of the Gospel began growing in my heart and mind when I was baptized and I slowly began learning about the Savior and his mission on Earth. I learned that it was foreordained before we came to Earth that Jesus would come to the Earth as a little baby to grow and minister among the people in Jerusalem. He ministered and formed his church, which at that time was called the Church of Jesus Christ. He taught his people and had many followers, ordained 12 Apostles, suffered in Gethsemane, was betrayed by one of the Apostles, and was slain on the cross for all of us. His horrible suffering was part of the plan to provide us with a Savior to redeem us and give us freedom of choice as to who we would follow, Jesus or Satan.

The more I learn, the more I want to live my life to be like the example He gave to us. I know He lives. I know that The Church of Jesus Christ of Latter-day Saints is His Church and this is the Last Dispensation of the Fullness of Times. I know that His Church will never be taken from the Earth again. One day, our Savior Jesus Christ will come again and usher in His Kingdom and will rein forevermore. There will be no hatred, envying, or harm to one another ever again. He will reign as King of Kings and Lord of Lords! What an exciting time that will be.

If I were able, I would dance in praise to Heavenly Father and Jesus Christ, in gratitude for the many blessings I have. My heart is so full of the Spirit of the Lord that I almost feel that I could step over the veil today, but know that I must wait until the Lord is ready for me to do so. I have thoughts of being with Charles, Judith Ann, Mom and Dad, Chuck's family, and my family that have already gone to the other side, but mostly I desire to be able to kneel before my Lord and thank Him for helping me to choose to stay on course to the Tree of Life. I wish to thank him for helping me to Hold to the Iron Rod—the course that leads back to heaven. It is true, it is true, my heart sings with pure joy! The Gospel of Jesus Christ is true.

Shirley Ann Robideau, in the autumn years of life, circa 2015-2025.

Made in the USA
Columbia, SC
06 June 2025

bd0bf203-c61c-4b27-b7ef-ffe2bed9d272R01